Arithmetic
for
Teachers & Students

Arithmetic
for
Teachers & Students

Baalaraman Srinivasan

Published by
PRABHAT PRAKASHAN PVT. LTD.
4/19 Asaf Ali Road,
New Delhi-110 002 (INDIA)
e-mail: prabhatbooks@gmail.com

ISBN 978-93-90378-04-3
ARITHMETIC FOR TEACHERS & STUDENTS
by Shri Baalaraman Srinivasan

Edition
2026

Paperback Price
₹ 500.00 (Rupees Five Hundred only)

Printed at
Jai Laxmi Printing Press, Delhi

Introduction

It can be said categorically that the methods elaborated from Lessons on Subtraction, Division, Multiplication, etc. are ancient methods and regarding addition it is probably an intellectual modification of the current method. Most of the ancient methods are supported by Vedic Sootras and the Vedic Sootras are extracted from Atharva Veda. For example subtraction is supported by a Vedic Sootra (निखिलं नवतश्चरमं दशत:) So also division and multiplication. There are 16 one line Sootras (like the one quoted above) and 13 sub-sootras or corollaries based on which entire Mathematics is woven. All Hindus know that the origin and beginning of Vedas are not precisely known and hence we like to attribute the origin of Mathematics to ancient mathematicians who contributed to the field.

More than 1500 years ago Bhaskaracharya in his work 'Leelavathi' (named after his daughter) and Aryabhatta in 'Aryabhatta Sidhdhaanth' have covered every aspect of Mathematics known to modern mathematician.

It is known to all that Pythagoras was in the period of 500AD; whereas the Vedic Mathematics procedure Triple (for solving Trigonometry problems) was in existence much before Pythagoras was born. The main source for this book is Vedic Mathematics by HH Sri Bharati Krisna Thirthaji—pontiff of Puri Sankara Mutt (between 1864-1960).

This book has come about through the knowledge gleaned from many ancient texts on Mathematics and I acknowledge their contribution to the field and the making of this book.

—Baalaraman Srinivasan

Preface

Dreadfulness of Mathematics:

Before delving into ancient Mathematics, let us first see the current scenario of the subject Mathematics. Mathematics is the most dreaded subject. Why? Is it because the subject is really very difficult or is it because we don't have good teachers to impart this delicate, but wonderfully interesting subject? Neither of this is a fact. Nevertheless, it is observed that in any school (of any medium and standard—standard from the point of view of its performance and reputation that the school has built up in their area of existence), hardly 10% of students are really brilliant and good as for as Mathematics is concerned.

Consider any state level/CBSE standard school in any city (from an Indian Scenario). On an average five sections – A, B, C, D, and E – in each standard are seen; and about 40 students are admitted in each section. This works out to 200 students per standard. As per educational policy in vogue, students are not failed or detained almost up to SSC level (This policy has been recently changed, but I feel that for obvious reasons not fully implemented and the old policy continue to be in force). So 90% of the students get promoted year after year with very poor mathematical base or foundation. Before we see how and why 90% of the students are poor in Mathematics, let us see how 10% of the students are good or brilliant in Mathematics –

a. may be due to genetic background;
b. may be the parents work with their children and the parents might themselves might be good in Mathematics;

c. may be 10% students are invariably front benchers and mostly the class teacher tows along with these front benchers and with a mere facial expression or body language of the front benchers, the teacher moves on with the syllabus to be covered (which is unfortunately quite heavy and huge) as fast as he/she can almost neglecting the other students (other than front benchers) though not deliberately. This happens almost unintentionally with every teacher, in every school.

d. One more reason (in favour of the 90% students) may be that even the most diligent teacher does not know some techniques in teaching (particularly in Mathematics) which when taught boost morale and interest of the students. To quote a few examples –

   i. How many of the teachers have any knowledge of checking Arithmetic (be it addition, subtraction, multiplication, squaring or even division) by **digit sum** or **digital root** method?

   ii. How many of the teachers know that most efficient method for subtraction (which is taught as early from II standard) is from left-most digit to right instead of right-most digit to left?

e. In favour of the 90% students many reasons can be quoted, but the fact remains that no concerted efforts are made to increase the students' interest in Mathematics from a mere 10% to 20% or more.

I have read an article recently in the supplement of a leading news paper, published from Central India (written by Smt. Lata Thergaonkar, a retired Principal) about 'Why do children fear Maths?' Smt. Thergaonkar quotes the following reasons (the full text of Smt. Thergaonkar is reproduced in the ***next section***)

- Most mothers do not teach or help with Maths at home.
- Most teachers are not comfortable teaching maths.
- Maths question paper is the only one with unfamiliar matter.
- Portions of successive years are linked closely.
- Most Maths teachers are poor communicators.
- Enough practice is not given to students.

- Low scores in Maths even for good students.
- Maths requires continuous concentration.
- No command over the language in which Maths is studied.
- Dyscalculia (a learning disability associated with numbers)

She had also suggested some ways to overcome these hurdles—

- ✓ Mothers must teach or help with Maths at home (definitely up to primary level)
- ✓ Teachers must make extra and concerted effort in primary classes.
- ✓ Solving more unfamiliar sums.
- ✓ Not missing out in school time.
- ✓ More practice time.
- ✓ Teaching practices must improve.
- ✓ Mock tests should be held frequently.
- ✓ Improving concentration.
- ✓ Improving language
- ✓ Building up confidence.

While fully agreeing with the above observations, my point is the mode of teaching Mathematics or the syllabus proper. If Ancient Mathematics is followed systematically and methodically, and uniformly in all schools – then students who might shift from one school to another (in the same city or elsewhere) for any reason may not find it difficult to get into groove in the new school. This series is not far from the existing pattern, but definitely a pattern with some defined changes for the benefit of students.

—Baalaraman Srinivasan

Why Do Children Fear Maths?

1. **Most mothers do not teach or help with Maths at home**
   They may supervise the homework in other subject but when it comes to Maths most mothers direct the child to the father or worse the tuition teacher. Now, for a little child, Mummy is a super woman and if she can't tackle the subject, the child feels he/she is incapable of doing so too. This builds up a wrong attitude towards the subject, which becomes difficult to change.
2. **Most teachers are not comfortable teaching Maths**
   It is seen that teachers baulking at the idea of teaching Maths even to class-II. 'I am an Arts graduate' they say; conveniently forgetting that they have studied Maths up to Class X. If they are forced to teach the subject, they do so with anxiety and the fear is subconsciously passed to the students. They avoid the more complicated sums and do not explain the basic concepts in simple terms, in their own words and with many examples.
3. **Maths question paper is only unfamiliar matter**
   All other question papers ask the same questions which the students have already studied in the class, so the words, names, etc. are familiar e.g. 'Why was Akbar a great king?' or 'What is the climate of the Tundra region?' As the problems and sums in the Maths paper are not from the book (or solved earlier in the class), the entire paper appears unknown and unfamiliar, very often triggering a panic attack.

4. **Portions of successive years are linked closely**
   In most other subject like English, History, etc. the portion of the next year is not based on the present year's portion; most often it is not linked at all. So in case the student has missed out on learning some part or has not understood it, he can still tackle the next year's portion. This does not hold true for maths. If you have not understood some part or missed school, then it is extremely difficult to tackle the next year's portion – e.g. if addition is not clear, multiplication is difficult or if integers are not understood, the entire working in algebra is difficult. This difficulty keeps on mounting till the student feels buried under the weight, wants to escape and not handle Maths at all.
5. **Most Maths teachers are poor communicators**
   They are often than not impatient too. Being a good communicator is an essential quality for a teacher. This is especially true for Maths teachers. They need to make concepts easy to understand (by explaining them in simple terms) and also to develop the necessary computational skills in students.
   They also need to be sensitive to atmosphere and sense if the students have really understood the concepts or just saying so. They need immense patience too so that the students can freely clarify their doubts and ask them repeatedly until thoroughly clear.
6. **Enough practice is not given to students**
   Maths is a subject where practice is of the essence. This is especially true for weak students. But very often, their class work is incomplete due to lack of time. They avoid doing Maths at home too thus increasing the probability of errors. The duration of Maths period is not enough for practice and only practice brings proficiency.
7. **Low scores in Maths even for good students**
   Maths is a subject where the scores can be low even if the student knows the subject.
   This happens due to careless mistakes. If the mistake takes place in the first step itself or worse in noting down

the sum, then they may get a zero. This does not happen in other subjects.

8. **Maths requires continuous concentration**

   Unlike other subjects, which allows a break sometimes, Maths requires continuous concentration at each step of the sum, so as to score well and not make silly mistakes. So in a test, which requires 2 to 3 hours of concentration, it is easy for attention to waver. Then a sum goes wrong and very often, sets off the domino effect; whereby the following sums go wrong too. This can also trigger a panic attack.

9. **No command over the language in which Maths is studied**

   This happens very often in English medium schools where the students are quite often not comfortable with the language, as they don't speak it at home or at other places. So, the problems given in Maths are incomprehensible to them. They are not sure of what is to be done to solve the sum. Thus errors are committed and scores are low.

10. **Dyscalculia**

    This is a learning disability associated with numbers. If not diagnosed early, it leads to a phobia of the subject (I think some aspect of it is covered in Amir Khan's* movie 'Tare Zameen Par'). The telltale signs are - a bright child is not able to grasp the basics in maths. This, of course, is not a common condition. A psychologist should be consulted for this disability.

The above are some of the common causes that lead to fear of Maths among students. Most of these can be addressed and the difficulty can be overcome.

Suggested ways to overcome the above

In today's age of scientific and technology and information explosion, the study of Maths assumes a newer significance. It is not merely a subject but also a tool to help the learner to think, reason and articulate logically. It helps to build the scientific approach to problem solving and makes systematic thinking a way of life.

1. **Mothers must teach or help with Maths at home**
This is one of the most crucial way of making Maths appear easy and lovable. When children see their mother finding the subject easy, they too feel the same way about it. Mothers should make the effort to familiarize themselves with the portion and help children solve sums. This is not as difficult as it appears, but the will to do so have to be present. This should be done at least up to class V and ideally up to class VIII.
2. **Teachers must make extra effort in Primary Classes**
All teachers have studied Maths up to class X and so are perfectly capable of teaching at least up to class IV (even Arts Graduate). They need to take a fresh look at the subject and consult various books. They will find themselves easily able to get a new insight into the matter due to maturity. Schools should hold special workshops for these teachers on a regular basis. Emphasis must be laid on understanding the concepts and explaining them in simple terms with numerous examples from the child's environment. Up to the primary level, just building the right attitude towards maths, in fact helping the child love the subject, should be the major aim of the teacher.
3. **Solving more unfamiliar sums**
Teachers and parents must give the children, sums not only from the prescribed books but also from other books. Give them as worksheets or as homework. So that the child is used to getting different and unfamiliar sums and does not fear them in the test or exams.
4. **Not missing out on school time**
Both parent and teacher must ensure that the child does not miss schoolwork due to absence or other activities (such as sports, drama, dance etc).If some portion is missed due to unavoidable circumstances, efforts must be made to cover it at the earliest, either at home or by extra time in the school. As Maths is like brick work, (this year's portion is based on last year's); a strong foundation is a must.

5. **More practice time**

Generally, the time given for Maths in school is not adequate. Either 8 periods of 35 minutes or 7 periods of 40 minutes are given, which works out to 4 and half hours a week, if adhered to scrupulously! A child needs an hour of Maths daily, preferably in the morning hours. Schools can and should make extra time available for maths. Parents, on their part, must also give time for Maths at home, even if homework in Maths is not given. Also during holidays and vacations, Maths has to be done daily at home. It has to become an inseparable part of a child's daily routine.

6. **Teaching practices must improve**

If the subject is thrust at the child without proper and gradual introduction, it becomes unpalatable. The matter must be explained well, linked to previous knowledge and repeated often. Easy sums need to be solved first, so as to give confidence to the child. He should be encouraged to clear his doubts and these needs to be done before proceeding further. Teaching must be done with enthusiasm and joy, thus making the learning process enjoyable. This holds true for both teacher and parent and for home and school.

Holding mock tests

This needs to be done at home and at school. A test of minimum one-hour duration should be given weekly or at least fortnightly. This helps the child to get the required practice of doing Maths continuously for a longer period of time, which does not happen in classroom or homework situations. Care should be taken to set an exam-like atmosphere with proper question paper of unfamiliar sums.

Improving Concentration

As Maths requires constant concentration, this aspect of a child's ability needs to be developed, so that silly mistakes are not made. This can be done in many ways. Give the child tasks that keep him in one place e.g. colorings, stringing beads or separating mixed grains etc. Older children can be given jigsaw, crossword or Sudoku puzzles. This is to be done for short periods in the beginning and then the duration can be increased. TV time must be curtailed and should not be more than an hour or so per day.

Improving Language

As the problem sums are given in the language of instruction (in most cases English) which very often is not mother tongue, improving language skills helps the child to comprehend the sums better thus solve them correctly. The child must be encouraged to listen, speak, read and write in the language of instruction. Extra reading is very helpful as it improves the command over the language and the child grasps the intricacies of the problem easily. The adults around the child should also find time to read so as to set the right example.

Building up confidence

High confidence levels are of the essence where a subject like Maths is concerned. Without confidence, high scores in Maths are impossible. To build confidence, the adults around the child, must make concerted efforts. Every step taken by the child in the right direction needs to be praised. In the beginning simple sums should be given for solving which are well within the child's capability. Once his success rate improves, his confidence will grow. Then gradually more complex problems can be introduced. If the child commits an error, merely telling him so is not enough. The correct method has to be shown to him in a gentle manner. Then more similar sums should be given to the child so that he becomes adept to them.

The pointers given above will definitely help the child do well in maths. The parents and teachers will have to put in extra efforts for this but the results will be well worth these efforts.

—Smt. Lata Thergaonkar
(Retd. Principal)

Note: *Amir Khan's movie is quoted by the author of the book and not by the author of the article.

Contents

1

Addition (Part-I)

Do you know Addition? Posing this question seems to be silly and also we feel hurt egoistically! Is it not? We know very well that the least educated or even the illiterates know how to add numbers. They know addition from the point of view of safe-guarding themselves from being cheated from financial dealings, so do the highly educated for few more reasons and purposes. But the majority of us know the mechanical method taught to us in our schools i.e. adding from right most columns (i.e. column of units) of numbers to the left and that too adding in a chain. [Unfortunately teachers do teach even today in the same old fashion]. Let's see the following example –

Ex:1 –

```
    2 2
    7 4 9
    3 3 2
    9 6 7
    6 5 9
  -------
  2 7 0 7
  -------
```

The units are 9, 7, 2 and 9 (from bottom to top). These units are mechanically added as 9 + 7 = 16, 16 + 2 = 18, 18 + 9 = 27 and 7 of 27 is taken down as part of answer and 2 is carried over to the next column (as tens) for further addition. Then from the tens we have 5 + 6 = 11, 11 + 3 = 14, 14 + 4 = 18 and 18 + 2 (carry) = 20. Take 0 in the answer row and carry 2 (as hundreds). From hundreds we get 6 + 9 = 15, 15 + 3 = 18, 18 + 7, 25 + 2 (carry) = 27. Thus the total is 2707.

There is nothing wrong in the above method or procedure. The numbers to be added are only four 3-digit numbers and hence we did not find any difficulty in resorting to the chain method addition. As we have not been taught any other method, almost all of us do addition by the mechanical-chain-method even if the numbers are more and the digits are also more in each number. However, we can add by picking 10s and 20s as explained below –

Mental Method

We can do the sum mentally and faster as below:

1. Units: Inspect the figure 9, 2, 7, and 9 and one can immediately say 2x9 = 18 + 2 = 20. So 20 plus the remaining 7 is 27.
2. Tens: 4, 3, 6, 5 and carry 2 – you may first add 3 and carry 2 getting 5, then 5 + 5 = 10, 6 + 4 = 10 and finally 10 + 10 = 20.
3. Hundreds: 7, 3, 9, 6 and carry 2 – add 7 and 3 to get 10; add 9 and 6 to get 15; then 10 + 15 = 25 and finally add the carry 2

You may try few more alternatives depending upon the ability of mental Arithmetic. But 90% of the people (even the educated) use the chain-mechanical addition instead of picking 10s and 20s and add mentally. You may find even now a number of students and many elders who add using fingers and some of them use the phalanges of the fingers. If you follow the method of picking up 10s and 20s and a few more tips that are to follow in this lesson – your ability to add mentally is sure to increase.

Let's see an example to add seven numbers with digits varying from two to five digits (by mental method) –

Ex:2 –

```
  2 4 5 3
    4 7 8 1
      9 8 7
  5 6 7 8 0
        9 8
    7 7 8 8
  6 7 6 7 9
      2 3 3
-----------
1 3 8 3 4 6
-----------
```

1. Units: You may find three 8s including the 1 & 7, we get 3×8=24 and just add 12 (the remaining 9 and 3 in units) to get the total as 36 – take down 6 and carry 3.[Otherwise we would have added 1+7=8, 8+0=8, 8+8=16, 16+8=24, 24+9=33, 33+3=36.]
2. Tens: We have 4×8=32 + 10 (7+3) = 42 + 12 (9+carry 3) = 54. Take 4 and carry 5.
3. Hundreds: The three 7s and a 9 make 30, then the remaining 6, 2 and the carry 5 make 13 and hence total is 43. Take down 3 and carry 4.
4. Thousands: 2×7 = 14 + 10 (6 and 4) = 24 + 4 (carry) = 28 Take down 8 and carry 2
5. Ten Thousands: 6+5=11+2 (carry) =13.

In the above case we have used our knowledge of multiplication as well as addition. Also it would be of help to remember the following most important and useful tools –

- Basic pairs
- Basic triples

Basic pairs

The 'basic pairs' can be remembered with the help of following **Ten Point Circle** –

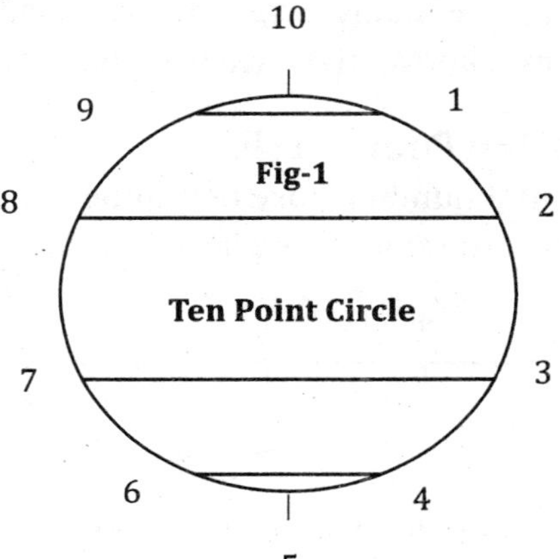

The ten point circle reveals the following **basic pairs**-

1. 9 + 1 = 10 = 1 + 9
2. 8 + 2 = 10 = 2 + 8
3. 7 + 3 = 10 = 3 + 7
4. 6 + 4 = 10 = 4 + 6
5. 5 + 5 = 10

Basic triples

Similarly the basic triple that are to be remembered are as follows –

Basic triple	Variations
1 + 1 + 8	= 1 + 8 + 1 = 8 + 1 + 1 = 10
1 + 2 + 7	= 2 + 1 + 7 = 2 + 7 + 1 = 7 + 2 + 1 = 7 + 1 +2 = 10
1 + 3 + 6	= 3 + 1 + 6 = 3 + 6 + 1 = 6 + 3 + 1 = 6 + 1 + 3 = 10
1 + 4 + 5	= 4 + 1 + 5 = 4 + 5 + 1 = 5 + 4 + 1 = 5 + 1 + 4 = 10
2 + 2 + 6	= 2 + 6 + 2 = 6 + 2 + 2 = 10
2 + 3 + 5	= 3 + 2 + 5 = 3 + 5 + 2 = 5 + 3 + 2 = 5 + 3 + 2 = 10
2 + 4 + 4	= 2 + 4 + 2 = 4 + 2 + 2 = 10
3 + 3 + 4	= 3 + 4 + 3 = 4 + 3 + 3 = 10

Note:

1. The triples which are inside the box (see above) are only basic triples and rest are its variations
2. Observe in how many ways we have used basic pairs in ex.1 and ex.2 above. Have we used basic triples so far?

Number Line vs Ten Point Circle

To add natural numbers, use of number-line was resorted to in our school. For example: to explain the addition of 1 + 4 –

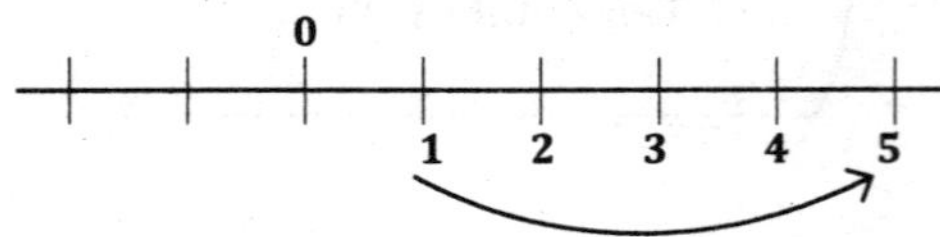

In the above number-line the part between two digits is known as units and if you move 4 units towards right from 1 we reach 5and thus the addition of 1 & 4 is being taught in our schools.

But if you are to teach the addition of 13 and 5 we have to draw another number-line, like –

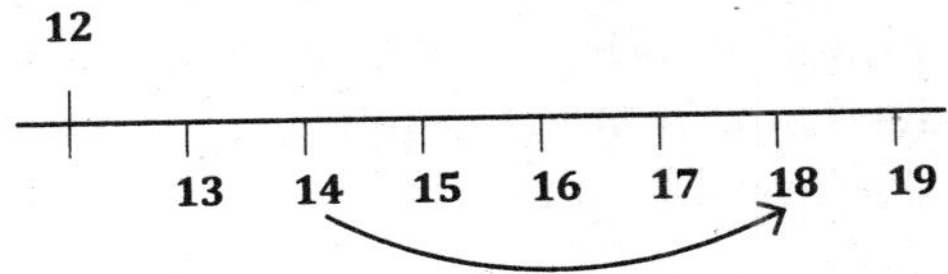

and thus explain13 + 5 = 18.

If we use a ten point circle, the repeated drawing (like number-line) is avoided and positive numbers from 1 to 100 (or even more) can be easily depicted and a single ten point circle would suffice to explain any additions

While adding positive natural numbers you have to move clockwise in the ten point circle and to subtract in the opposite direction. Combined addition or subtraction with positive as well as negative natural numbers are dealt with after 5th standard; hence we humbly opine that upto 4th standard the above ten point circle with positive numbers will be more than enough. In Fig.2 below numbers from 1 to 30 is shown in Ten Point Circle

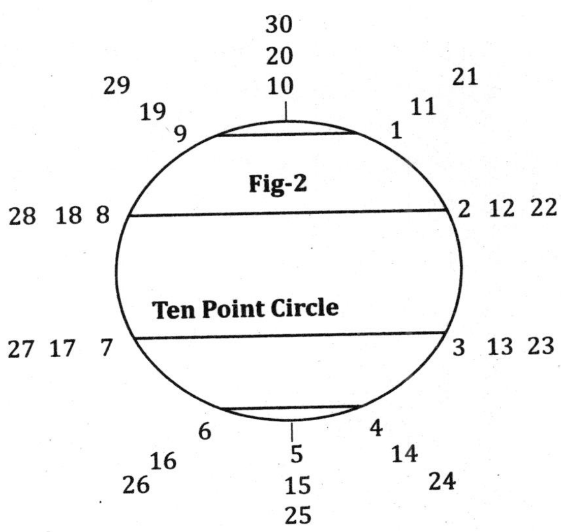

Conclusion

In this lesson we have seen the conventional method of adding and also mental method wherein we have used combination of our knowledge of multiplication as well as addition. At the end of this lesson we have seen what is ten-point circle and use of Basic pairs and Basic triples and a brief study of number-line vs ten-point circle.

□

2

Addition (Part-II)

Introduction

In the earlier part we saw addition by –

- Conventional method
- Mental method (by picking 10s and 20s)
- By using basic pairs and basic triples.

Old Habits don't die easily

Many of us may not be able to get rid of the habit of mechanical-chain addition or may not be able to adapt to the new method (i.e. picking 10s, 20s, or basic pairs, etc.); for such persons the method – ***'dropping of tens'*** and the subsequent methods that are to follow would be helpful and may ease the process of addition.

Dropping Tens Method

In this method while adding by the conventional mechanical-chain method, whenever the total exceeds ten in the intermediate stage, drop that ten, put a mark on the digit where you have just dropped ten, and then proceed with the digit left (after dropping ten). This procedure shall be continued till you reach the top of the column of addition (when you are adding from bottom to top) or till you reach the last digit (when you are adding from top to bottom). We shall re-do the example 2 in Part-1 by dropping tens.

Ex:1

$$
\begin{array}{cccccc}
 & 2 & 4 & \dot{5} & 3 & \\
 & & 4 & 7 & \dot{8} & 1 \\
 & & & \dot{9} & \dot{8} & \dot{7} \\
 & \dot{5} & \dot{6} & \dot{7} & \dot{8} & 0 \\
 & & & & \dot{9} & 8 \\
 & & \dot{7} & \dot{7} & 8 & \dot{8} \\
 & 6 & 7 & 6 & \dot{7} & \dot{9} \\
 & & & 2 & 3 & 3 \\
\hline
1 & 3 & 8 & 3 & 4 & 6 \\
\hline
\end{array}
$$

Adding from bottom to top –

1. Units -

- 3 + 9 = 12 ⇒ drop 10 ⇒ mark on 9 ⇒ move with 2
- 2 + 8 = 10 ⇒ drop 10 ⇒ mark on 8 ⇒ move with 0
- 0 + 8 + 0 + 7 = 15 ⇒ drop 10 ⇒ mark on 7 ⇒ move with 5
- 5 + 1 = 6 ⇒ take 6 to answer row; carry 3 as we dropped 3 tens

2. Tens –

- 3 + 7 = 10 ⇒ drop 10 ⇒ mark on 7 ⇒ move with 0
- 0 + 8 + 9 = 17 ⇒ drop 10 ⇒ mark on 9 ⇒ move with 7
- 7 + 8 = 15 ⇒ drop 10 ⇒ mark on 8 ⇒ move with 5
- 5 + 8 = 13 ⇒ drop 10 ⇒ mark on 8 ⇒ move with 3
- 3 + 8 = 11 ⇒ drop 10 ⇒ mark on 8 ⇒ move with 1
- 1 + 3 (carry) = 4 ⇒ take 4 to answer row; carry 5 as we dropped 5 tens.

3. Hundreds –

- 2 + 6 + 7 = 15 ⇒ drop 10 ⇒ mark on 7 ⇒ move with 5
- 5 + 7 = 12 ⇒ drop 10 ⇒ mark on 7 ⇒ move with 2
- 2 + 9 = 11 ⇒ drop 10 ⇒ mark on 9 ⇒ move with 1
- 1 + 7 + 5 (carry) = 13 ⇒ drop 10 ⇒ mark on 5 (carry) ⇒ take 3 to answer row; carry 4 as we dropped 4 tens.

4. Thousands –
- 7 + 7 = 14 ⇒ drop 10 ⇒ mark on 7 ⇒ move with 4
- 4 + 6 = 10 ⇒ drop 10 ⇒ mark on 6 ⇒ move with 0
- 0 + 4 + 4 (carry) = 8 ⇒ take 8 to answer row; carry 2 as we dropped 2 tens.

5. Ten Thousands –
- 6 + 5 = 11 ⇒ drop 10 ⇒ mark on 5 ⇒ move with 1
- 1 + 2 = 3 ⇒ take 3 to answer row; carry 1 as we dropped 1 ten.

6. Lakhs –
- Take 1 (carry) to answer row.

Thus the total is 1,38,346 as found earlier. We have explained the above procedure/method in about 20 odd lines and hence may seem to be cumbrous. But it is also one of the easy ways of adding.

Dropping Tens (slightly modified) method

Ex:2

$$
\begin{array}{rrrrrrl}
 & & 4 & 7 & \dot{8} & 1 & \\
 & & & \dot{9} & \dot{8} & \dot{7} & \\
 & \dot{5} & \dot{6} & \dot{7} & \dot{8} & ^{0} & \\
 & & & & \dot{9} & 8 & \\
 & & \dot{7} & \dot{7} & 8 & \dot{8} & \\
 & 6 & 7 & 6 & \dot{7} & \dot{9} & \\
 & & & 2 & 3 & 3 & \\
\hline
0 & 1 & 4 & 8 & 1 & 6 & \Rightarrow \text{running total} \\
1 & 2 & 3 & 5 & 3 & 0 & \Rightarrow \text{carry over} \\
\hline
1 & 3 & 8 & 3 & 4 & 6 & \Rightarrow \text{Final Total} \\
\hline
\end{array}
$$

In ex.1 above, we dropped tens at every intermediate (wherever the interim total exceeded 10) stage – whether the addition is done from top to bottom or bottom to top. After column of addition is over by this method (i.e. by dropping tens) the dropped tens were taken over as carry over at the top; but in this method we take carry over digits below the running total but a column duly shifted to left as shown in ex.2 above. That is –

While adding units (from bottom to top) –

- 3 + 9 = 12 ⇒ drop 10 ⇒ mark on 9 ⇒ move with 2
- 2 + 8 = 10 ⇒ drop 10 ⇒ mark on 8 ⇒ move with 0
- 0 + 8 + 0 + 7 = 15 ⇒ drop 10 ⇒ mark on 7 ⇒ move with 5
- 5 + 1 = 6; take 6 on the running total line. As this is the first column of addition, there is no carry over and write 0 below 6. We had dropped three tens while adding units. So we write the carry over 3 just to the left of 0.

No further explanation is needed for this method.

Dropping Tens (further modified) Method

In example 1 and 2 above the dropping of ten was marked on top of the digit where the ten was actually dropped i.e. if we had added 3 + 8 as 11, then the ten was dropped from 11 and a mark was made on 8 i.e. 8. But in the second modification of dropping tens – the mark for dropping ten is made near the immediate adjacent digit on the left. This mark is (of 10) carried from previous column, but when marked near the digit it is unity, to be added along with the digit where the marking is done. Example 3 below will illustrate this method –

Ex: 3

```
     4. 7. 8  1
     0. 9. 8. 7
  5. 6. 7. 8  0
           9  8
  0. 7. 7. 8. 8
  6  7  6. 7. 9
        2  3  3
 ----------------
1 3  8  3  4  6
 ----------------
```

Bottom to top –

1. Units—

- 3 + 9 = 12 ⇒ drop 10 ⇒ mark on left of 9 at 7 ⇒ move with 2

- 2 + 8 = 10 ⇒ drop 10 ⇒ mark on left of 8 at 8 ⇒ move with 0
- 0 + 8 + 0 + 7=15 ⇒ drop 10 ⇒ mark on left of 7 at 8 ⇒ move with 5
- 5 + 1 = 6; take 6 to answer row.

2. Tens –

- 3 + 7 + 1 (mark) = 11 ⇒ drop 10 ⇒ mark on left of 7 at 6 ⇒ move with 1
- 1 + 8 + 1 (mark) = 10 ⇒ drop 10 ⇒ mark on left of 8 at 7 ⇒ move with 0
- 0 + 9 + 8 = 17 ⇒ drop 10 ⇒ mark on left of 8 at 7 ⇒ move with 7
- 7 + 8 + 1 (mark) = 16 ⇒ drop 10 ⇒ mark on left of 8 at 9 ⇒ move with 6
- 6 + 8 = 14 ⇒ drop 10 ⇒ mark on left of 8 at 7; take 4 to answer line

3. Hundreds –

- 2 + 6 + 1 (mark) +7 + 1 (mark) = 17 ⇒ drop 10 ⇒ mark on left of 7 at 7 ⇒ move with 7
- 7 + 7 + 1 (mark) = 15 ⇒ drop 10 ⇒ mark on left of 7 at 6 ⇒ move with 5
- 5 + 9 + 1 (mark) = 15 ⇒ drop 10 ⇒ mark on left of 9 – as there is no digit add a 0 and mark at 0 ⇒ move with 5
- 5 + 7 + 1 (mark) = 13 ⇒ drop 10 ⇒ mark on left of 7 at 4; take 3 to answer line

4. Thousands –

- 7 + 7 + 1 (mark) = 15 ⇒ drop 10 ⇒ mark on left of 7 – as there is no digit write 0 and mark at 0 ⇒ move with 5
- 5 + 6 + 1 (mark) = 12 ⇒ drop 10 ⇒ mark on left of 6 at 5 ⇒ move with 2
- 2 + 0 + 1 (mark) + 4 + 1 (mark) = 8; take 8 to answer line.

5. Ten Thousands –

- 6 + 0 + 1 (mark) + 5 + 1 (mark) = 13; take 13 to answer line.

By Addition & by Subtraction Method

For mental addition this method is adopted (the same can be adopted for subtraction – then the method will be by subtraction and by addition). The procedure is –

When we add numbers like 7, 8, 9 or numbers ending in 7, 8, 9 like 37, 28, 49, etc. first we add the nearest sub-base of numbers ending in 7, 8, 9 (by addition) and then subtract the complement of the number from the added sub-base (by subtraction). See example 4 below –

Ex: 4

(a) 6 + 9

Here 10 is the base for 9; and 9 is 1 below the base 10;
So 6 + 10 (by addition) = 16 – 1 (by subtraction = 15

(b) 16 + 28

Here 30 is the sub-base of 28; and 28 is 2 below the sub-base 30;
So 16 + 30 = 46 – 2 = 44

(c) 23 + 37

Here 40 is the sub-base of 37; and 37 is 3 below the sub-base 40;
So 23 + 40 = 63 – 3 = 60

Note: This problem can be solved using basic pairs learned from 10 point circle. Here 3 and 7 are basic pairs i.e. 10. So add only the tens and then add a 10. That is 23 + 37 = 20 + 30 + 10 = 60.

Left-to-Right Method

As long as we are using paper for addition, right-to left addition is Okay. In fact this is how we learn in our schools. But it is insisted that adding two numbers, may be single-digit numbers, or two-digits or even up to four digits students should practice to add numbers mentally i.e. without using paper. A mere practice will enable you to become proficient in mental addition. The following section of this lesson will teach how to become an expert in adding mentally. We shall proceed step by step. The first and important step is to practice adding single digit numbers mentally. Once you are proficient in adding single digits, then adding multiple digit numbers are just child's play.

Adding single digit numbers is of two types; one - addition without carry over and two - addition with carry over. These two categories are shown in the following tables and it would be advisable that you become thorough with these two tables.

The row value at the beginning of the table 1 is added to each column head value to get the individual cell value. Table 2 is also prepared on the same logic.

For table 2 below you may use the technique by addition and by subtraction method explained above. Also note that the cell values in **bold** (in table 2) are the result of addition of basic pairs.

Mental Addition:

Single Digit Addition - (without carry)

$$\begin{array}{r}4\\+3\\\hline 7\end{array}\quad\begin{array}{r}5\\+2\\\hline 7\end{array}\quad\begin{array}{r}8\\+1\\\hline 9\end{array}\quad\begin{array}{r}9\\+0\\\hline 9\end{array}$$

(with carry)

$$\begin{array}{r}3\\+7\\\hline 10\end{array}\quad\begin{array}{r}5\\+6\\\hline 11\end{array}\quad\begin{array}{r}7\\+5\\\hline 12\end{array}\quad\begin{array}{r}9\\+4\\\hline 13\end{array}$$

Table: 1

	0	**1**	**2**	**3**	**4**	**5**	**6**	**7**	**8**	**9**
0	0	1	2	3	4	5	6	7	8	9
1	1	2	3	4	5	6	7	8	9	
2	2	3	4	5	6	7	8	9		
3	3	4	5	6	7	8	9			
4	4	5	6	7	8	9				
5	5	6	7	8	9					
6	6	7	8	9						
7	7	8	9							
8	8	9								
9	9									

Table: 2

	1	**2**	**3**	**4**	**5**	**6**	**7**	**8**	**9**
1									**10**
2								**10**	11
3							**10**	11	12
4						**10**	11	12	13
5					**10**	11	12	13	14
6				**10**	11	12	13	14	15
7			**10**	11	12	13	14	15	16
8		**10**	11	12	13	14	15	16	17
9	**10**	11	12	13	14	15	16	17	18

By practicing number of single digit additions the above two tables will become by heart.

Exercises:

I. Adding single digit numbers:

(1) 3 + 5 (2) 4 + 3 (3) 2 + 3 (4) 7 + 2 (5) 6 + 4

(1) 7 + 4 (2) 8 + 5 (3) 9 + 8 (4) 6 + 7 (5) 7 + 7

Two-Digit Addition

The above two tables together have 100 numbers and as we said earlier, it will not be very difficult to by heart these 100 values. In fact it becomes more or less a habit as and when we grill ourselves with more problems. Now to add say -

```
 37
+41 (40 + 1)
 37 + 40 + 1    = 78
```

Similarly—

```
 45
+23 (20 + 3)
 45 + 20 + 3    = 68
```

Instead of adding 41 to 37 add 40 to 37 which can be easily worked out as 77 (i.e. 3 + 4 in tens and 7 + 0 in units) mentally. Now add only one to 77 to get finally as 78. Similarly add 20 to 45 to get 65 and then add only 3 to get finally 68.

Extending the procedure to two-digit numbers with carry—

```
 65
+38 (30 + 8)
 65 + 30 + 8    = 95 +8 = 103
```

Here, by working from left-to right, actually the problem is shortened to adding 8 to 95. Addition of eight can also be mentally split as addition of 5 + 3. We know 95 + 5 is 100 and add 3 to 100 to get 103.

In the above there wasn't any carry in adding Tens, but only in Units. See the following two problems -

```
 48
+75 (70 + 5)
 48 + 70 + 5    = 118+ 5 = 123
```

```
 86
+54 (50 + 4)
86 + 50 + 4    = 136 +4 = 140
```

While carrying numbers you may initially stumble, but as and when you attempt more problems mentally, you may get used to it and it will be done automatically; initially view the numbers properly and visualize the carry by mere observation.

Exercises:

II. Adding two-digit numbers:

(1) 28 + 31 (2) 27 + 21 (3) 34 + 65 (4)22 + 67
(5) 33 + 26 (6) 16 + 23 (7) 34 + 46 (8) 23 + 95
(9) 27 +33
(1) 98 + 87 (2) 37 + 85 (3) 74 + 67 (4)18+19
(5) 35 + 39 (6) 49 + 48 (7) 68 + 45 (8) 58 + 47
(9) 84 + 57

Three-Digit Numbers

Addition of three-digit numbers will be on the same lines that of two-digit numbers. That is left-to-right, attain a new addition and take due care of carry, if any. For example -

Case-I: No carry in all the three digits

```
 743
+235  (200 + 30 + 5)
 978
```

With 743 first add 200; then to 943 add 30; and finally add 5 to 973 to get 978. Try the following—

```
(1)  705   (2)  512   (3)  437   (4)  346   (5)  625
    +123       +234       +342       +413       +224
```

Case-II: with carry in units

```
  847
+ 124  (100 + 20 + 7)
  971
```

Add first 100 to 847; add 20 to 947 and finally add 4 to 967 to get 971. Try the following—

(1) 714 +228 (2) 622 + 329 (3) 437 +435 (4) 346 +149 (5) 636 +335

Case-III: with carry in units and/or tens

$$\begin{array}{r} 347 \\ +\ 174 \\ \hline 521 \end{array} \quad (100 + 70 + 4)$$

Add first 100 to 347; add 70 to 447 and finally add 4 to 517 to get 521. Try the following -

(1) 137 +381 (2) 281 +134 (3) 356 +475 (4) 648 +273 (5) 222 +889

Case-IV: with carry in hundreds as well

$$\begin{array}{r} 467 \\ +756 \\ \hline 1223 \end{array} \quad (700 + 50 + 6)$$

Add first 700 to 467; add 50 to 1167 and finally add 6 to 1217 to get 1223. {Personally I would add first 800 to 467 mentally (anticipating the carry in tens) arrive at 1267 and then subtract 44 from 1267 to get 1223}

Using the same logic detailed above try the following problems

(1) 242 +137 (2) 312 +256 (3) 635 +814 (4) 457 +241 (5) 912 +475

(6) 852 +378 (7) 2700 +576 (8) 4560 +171 (9) 6120 +136 (10) 7830 +348

(11) 4240 +371 (12) 1800 +855

Conclusion

If you agree that you knew addition by mechanical-chain-addition only, then everything from **Mental Method** explained in Part-1 to the above **by addition and by subtraction** are new to you. If you practice this, then addition can be fun. Further, if you teach this to youngsters, they will have more interest towards **Mathematics.**

□

3

Checking of Arithmetic Sums (Digital Root or DR) Part-I

Introduction

The correctness of subtraction can be verified by adding subtrahend and the answer. If this sum equals the minuend, our sum is correct. Similarly,in case of divisions, multiplying divisor and quotient and then adding the remainder, if any, yields the dividend. But in other cases of Arithmetic sums, we have no other option but to redo the sum to verify its correctness. This redoing may at times be cumbrous or tedious. So we learn the checking by **digital roots** or **DR**s.

What is a DR?

If you consider a number (of multiple digits), then the sum of all its digits (till we arrive at a single digit) is called **digital root** or **digit sum**.

Suppose a number is 6138247. Its **digital root** (or **DR**) as per above definition will be 6+1+3+8+2+4+7 = 31; as 31 has two digits again 3+1 = 4. So the final single digit 4 is the DR of 6138247.

In the above to find **DR** we resorted to chain addition of the digits of given number. However, we can also convert any intermediate two-digit to single digit (i.e. intermediate **DR**) and proceed further with this intermediate **DR** till we reach the last digit. If we consider the same above number i.e. 6138247, then 6+1+3 = 10; now convert this 10 into its **DR** i.e. 1+0 = 1 and now proceed with this intermediate DR 1; 1+8+2 = 11; now convert 11 as 1+1 = 2 and proceed with 2; 2+4+7 = 13 and **DR** of 13 is 4 which is also the **DR** of the number 6138247(as found earlier)

To understand clearly, see the following examples –

No	DR
17	1+7=**8**
123	1+2+3=**6**
3121	3+1+2+1=**7**
302	3+0+2=**5**
900	9+0+0=**9**

In the above examples we got the **DR**s in a single straight addition, as the final addition straight away yields single digit. Now see the following examples –

No	DR
19*	1+9 = 10; 1+0 = **1**
93*	9+3 = 12; 1+2 = **3**
38*	3+8 = 11; 1+1 = **2**
453*	4+5+3 = 12; 1+2 = **3**
4444**	4+4+4 = 12; 1+2 = 3; 3+4 = **7**
152823**	1+5+2+8 = 16; 1+6 = 7; 7+2+3 = 12; 1+2 = **3**

*** Here the first direct total yielded two digits; it was again added to get the final *DR***

****Here we have used intermediate *DR* [12 is the intermediate DR in case of 4444 and 16 is the intermediate *DR* in case of last example].**

Before we proceed any further with the explanation of **DR**, let's first see utility of **DR** –

Utility of *DR*:

With the help of **digital root (DR)** we can check or verify any Arithmetic problems. The Arithmetic problems may be addition, subtraction, multiplication, division, squaring. Square root, cubing, etc – all these problems can be checked with the use of **DR**. Let's see a small example –

If we subtract 23 from 36 we get 13. To check with **DR** –

No		DR
36	– minuend	9
– 23	– subtrahend	– 5
13	– answer	4

As the problem is of subtraction, difference between the **DR** of minuend and **DR** of subtrahend must be equal to **DR** of answer. In the above **DR** of 36 is 3+6=9 and DR of 23 is 5. So 9 – 5 = 4, which is the **DR** of answer i.e. 13. The above subtraction can be done mentally and hence this DR check seems to be a child's play. But if you are to subtract 12347 from 30102, then checking the answer with **DR** could be of help. However, using **DR** on Arithmetic problems of addition, multiplication, etc of immense help.

Further short cut to find *DR*: *Disregarding 9s*

There is one more short cut to find **DR**. While adding across the number for finding **DR**, any 9 or 9s may be ignored (or discarded) during the chain addition and you will get the same **DR**. E.g. the **DR** of 93919 is 3+1 = 4 by ignoring the three 9s. Even if you add them we get 9+3+9+1+9 = 31; 3+1 = 4.

And if you happen to notice two (or more digits) that add upto 9, they can also be ignored. Thus **DR** of 89951 is 5 because the first digit 8 and the last digit 1 can be ignored along with other two 9s and hence **DR** of 89951 is 5.

Again in the first example i.e. immediately below the definition of **DR** – 6138247, it can be said that its **DR** is 4 immediately without any calculations because it is evident that 6-3 and 1-8 and 2-7 – all these make 9 and ignoring these 9s the remaining digit 4 is the **DR** (as we have already found).

Note:

(1) **DR** of single digit is the number itself i.e. DR of 4 is 4; DR of 6 is 6; DR of 9 is 9 or 0.

(2) Because of dropping 9, **digital root** is also known as **nines remainder**

***Digital Root* by Casting out 9s:**

See the table below –

Number	83	614	7329	26723	158232	7474777
DR	2	2	3	2	3	7

It is evident from the above table that any number of digits can ultimately abridged to a single digit as **digital root**. Keep on adding the digits; if you get a double digit add them at the intermediate stage itself, and continue adding the digits till you arrive at a single digit.

Natural Numbers and Digital roots:

Natural numbers starts from 1 and proceeds 1, 2, 3, ... 9, 10, 11, ... 18, 19, 20, ... endlessly. See table below of natural numbers and its digital roots.

No	DR	No	DR	No	DR
1	**1**	11	**2**	21	**3**
2	**2**	12	**3**	22	**4**
3	**3**	13	**4**	23	**5**
4	**4**	14	**5**	24	**6**
5	**5**	15	**6**	25	**7**
6	**6**	16	**7**	26	**8**
7	**7**	17	**8**	27	**9**
8	**8**	18	**9**	.	1
9	**9**	19	**1**	.	2
10	**1**	20	**2**	.	3

From the above table what we understand is natural numbers increase in 10s, while **DR**s repeat in ***cyclic order***. In part 1 of Addition – we have shown the natural numbers in **TEN POINT CIRCLE**. In a similar way, if we depict natural numbers in **NINE POINT CIRCLE**, let's see what conclusions can we draw –

From the **nine point circle** below we realize that –

- Along any radial branch the **DR**s are same i.e. along 3 branch – 12, 21, 30, 39, etc have the same **DR** 3.
- It is also confirmed that if we ignore or consider (i.e. subtract or add) 9 from any number, the **DR** does not change.

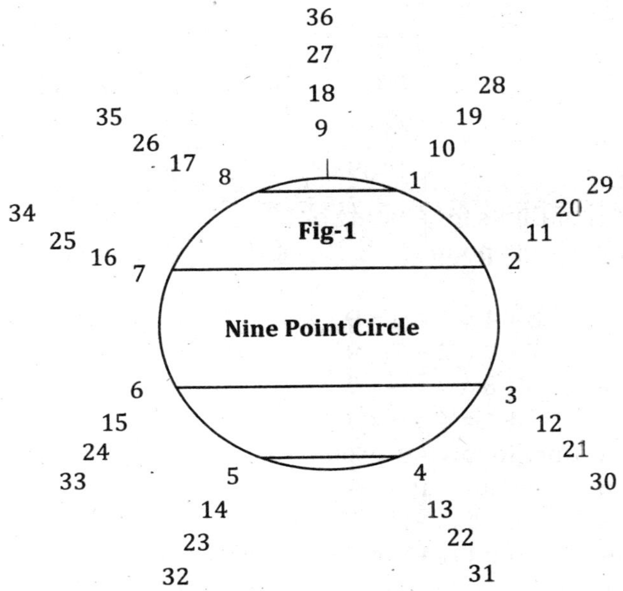

To know **DR** of 158143, we ignore 1, 5, 8 and 4 and get the **DR** from the remaining 1 & 3 as 4. In this example we have ignored 9s. Now let us see the situation where we have to consider or add 9 to **DR**. See the subtraction problem below –

Ex: Subtract 2312 from 3801 and verify the result with **DR** check –

	No	**DR**
	3801	3
	– 2312	– 8
Answer	1489	?

In the above, the **DR** of 3801 is 3 and that of 2312 is 8. We can't subtract 8 from 3. So we add 9 to the **DR** of minuend i.e. 3 to get 12 and now 12 – 8 = 4. So is the DR of answer i.e. 4.

	No	DR		
	3801	3	or	12
	– 2312	– 8		– 8
Answer	1489	?		4

Groups of Digits for Casting out 9:

From the nine point circle (from the digits joined by line) we get –

8 + 1 = 1 + 8 = 9
7 + 2 = 2 + 7 = 9
6 + 3 = 3 + 6 = 9
5 + 4 = 4 + 5 = 9

In addition following groups also total to 9 and can be considered for casting out of 9s –

1 + 1 + 7 (or 1+7+1 or 7+1+1) = 9
1 + 2 + 6 (or 1+6+2 or 2+6+1 or 6+2+1 or 6+1+2) = 9
1 + 3 + 5 (or 1+5+3 or 3+5+1 or 5+3+1 or 5+1+3) = 9
1 + 4 + 4 (or 4+1+4 or 4+4+1) = 9
2 + 2 + 5 (or 2+5+2 or 5+2+2) = 9
2 + 3 + 4 (or 2+4+3 or 4+2+3 or 3+4+2 or 4+3+2) = 9

Puzzles in finding **DRs**:

Teachers and parents, who are genuinely interested in improving their students' and wards' ability to use digital root, may get the following puzzles related to **DR** solved.

Puzzle 1:

The **DR** of a two digit number is 8 and the digits are the same. What is the number?

Puzzle 2:

The **DR** of a two digit number is 9 and the first digit is twice the second. What is the number?

Puzzle 3:

Give a two digit number that has a **DR** of 3.

Puzzle 4:

In the table below all the answers are of two digit numbers. Some have more than one answer. To solve the puzzle you are given **DR** and one more fact. You can use 9 point circle.

S.N.	DR	Additional Fact	Clue [No of answers]
1	5	Difference between the digits is 3	2
2	6	The digits are the same	1
3	6	First digit is half the second digit	1
4	7	Difference between the digits is 3	2
5	7	One digit is 4	2
6	6	Both digits are odd	3
7	5	The digits are consecutive	2
8	9	The digits are consecutive	2
9	3	One digit is double the other	4
10	8	The answer is blow 20	1
11	1	The numbers are less than 40	4
12	1	The first digit is 2	1
• Consecutive means one after another e.g. 1&2 or 2&1			

More DR Puzzles

We know that the numbers on every branch of a nine-point circle have the same DR. We can use this **nine-point circle** for quick solution. For solutions of **Puzzle 4** above and **Puzzle 5** below, a nine-point circle can be used.

Difficult Puzzles can be set on **DR** as below:

Ex: A two-digit number has a DR of 5 and the digits are the same. What is the number?

Solution:

5 is an odd number. But from the nine-point circle above we can see that 14 is in 5 branch. Now 14 being even, it can be split as 7 and 7. Therefore the required answer is 77.

Puzzle 5:

In the Puzzle below you will need to choose the right answer from the right branch of the nine-point circle. All the answers are two-digit numbers.

SN	DR	Additional clue or fact
1	5	Number is between 20 and 30
2	8	Number ends in 5
3	7	First digit is 2
4	2	Digits differ by 7
5	1	Answer is in the table of 7
6	3	First digit is three times the second
7	4	Number is in the table of 8
8	6	Digits are the same
9	8	Last digit is three times the first
10	5	Number is in the table of 8
11	9	Ends in 7
12	3	Both digits are odd

□

4

Addition (Part-III)

Dropping of Elevens

This method was developed by a Russian born mining engineer and a genius –Jackow Trachtenberg, when he was in German detention camp during World War I. This method of addition can be done from left to right also. This method almost pin-point the mistake i.e. we can know in which column of addition the mistake has occurred.

In this method, instead of dropping the 10s (as was explained in Part 2 of Addition), we would be dropping 11s in the process of column-wise chain addition. Let's see an example –

Ex: 1

						DR[*]
	4	6	7	8		7
			3	$\dot{9}$		3
		$\dot{8}$	$\dot{9}$	0		8
	$\dot{9}$	6	$\dot{9}$	$\dot{8}$		5
		$\dot{8}$	$\dot{7}$	$\dot{9}$		6
		$\dot{5}$	4	7		7
	7	4	1	$\dot{9}$		3
		2	3	4		9
	$\dot{8}$	1	$\dot{6}$	$\dot{3}$		9
	3	$\dot{4}$	$\dot{6}$	7		2
0	9	0	0	9	→ Running Total	
0	2	4	5	5	→ Elevens (or marks)	
3	6	0	1	4	→ Total	→5

This method is similar to dropping of tens. Instead of dropping 10s, we drop 11s while adding along the column. Dropping 10 was easy in the sense that while adding if we happen to get two digits, the left digit is dropped and we proceed with the units digits, i.e. if the running total is 16 then 1 is dropped and we proceed with 6.

But while dropping 11,drop 1 of left digit and reduce the units digit by 1 i.e. if our running total is 16, then drop the left digit 1 and reduce the units digit 6 by 1 and proceed with the resultant 5. Again if the running total is 14, drop 1 and reduce 4 to 3 and proceed further with 3. If the running total is 11 drop the entire 11 and proceed with 0.

However, as in the previous case whenever you drop eleven make a mark on the top of the number. In the Ex. 1 above, ten numbers are added from top to bottom (it can be added from bottom to top also) and from left to right (it can be added in the conventional way i.e. from right to left also). Starting from top to bottom and from left most column –.

Column 1:

- 4 + 9 = 13 ⇒ drop 11 ⇒ mark on top of 9 and proceed with 3-1=2
- 2 + 7 + 8 = 17⇒drop 11 ⇒ mark on 8 and proceed with 7-1=6
- 6 + 3 = 9 ⇒ write 9 in the running total row and below this write 2 which is the number of marks or elevens dropped in this column.

Column 2:

- 6 + 8 = 14 ⇒ drop 11 ⇒ mark on 8 and proceed with 4-1=3
- 3 + 6 + 8 = 17 ⇒ drop 11 ⇒ mark on 8 and proceed with 7-1=6
- 6 + 5 = 11 ⇒ drop 11 ⇒ mark on 5 and proceed with 0
- 0 + 4 + 2 + 1 + 4 = 11 ⇒ drop 11⇒ mark on 4 ⇒ write 0 in the running total row and below this write 4 which is the number of marks or eleven in this column.

Column 3:

- 7 + 3 + 9 = 19 ⇒ drop 11 ⇒ mark on 9, proceed with 9-1=8
- 8 + 9 = 17 ⇒ drop 11 ⇒ mark on 9, proceed with 7-1=6
- 6 + 7 = 13 ⇒ drop 11 ⇒ mark on 7, proceed with 3-1=2
- 2 + 4 + 1 + 3 + 6 = 16 ⇒ drop 11 ⇒ mark on 6, proceed with 6-1=5
- 5 + 6 = 11 ⇒ drop 11 ⇒ mark on 6, write 0 in the answer row and 5 below it as there are five marks or elevens dropped in this column.

Column 4:

- 8 + 9 = 17 ⇒ drop 11 ⇒ mark on 9 , proceed with 6
- 6 + 0 + 8 = 14 ⇒ drop 11 ⇒ mark on 8, proceed with 3
- 3 + 9 = 12 ⇒ drop 11 ⇒ mark on 9, proceed with 1
- 1 + 7 + 9 = 17 ⇒ drop 11 ⇒ mark on 9, proceed with 6
- 6 + 4 + 3 = 13 ⇒ drop 11 ⇒ mark on 3, proceed with 2
- 2 + 7 = 9 ⇒ write 9 in the answer row and 5 below it.

We have running total (after dropping elevens) and the number of elevens dropped in each column. To arrive at the final total, the addition of the above two rows is done in a special way. It is started conventionally from the units; that is, 9 + 5 = 14. Write 4 on the total line with a dot for carry over 1. From next step we add in **'L'** shape as explained below –

0	9	0	0	9	⇒ Running total
0	2	4	5	5	⇒ Elevens or marks
3	•6	•0	•1	•4	

i.e.

T	U	
		⇒ Tens Units
0	9	⇒ Running total
5	5	⇒ elevens or marks
•1	•4	⇒ 5 + 5 + 0 + 1 (carry) = 11

H	T	U	
			⇒ Hundreds Tens Units
0	0	9	⇒ Running total
4	5	5	⇒ elevens or marks
•0	•1		⇒ 5 + 4 + 0 + 1 (carry) = 10

Th	H	T	U	
				⇒ Thousands Hundreds Tens Units
9	0	0	9	⇒ Running total
2	4	5	5	⇒ elevens or marks
•6	•0			⇒ 4 + 2 + 9 + 1 (carry) = 16

As we still have carry over of 1, we do the last step by imagining two 0s in the running total and in elevens dropped in the Ten Thousands column and again add in the same **'L'** shape as below –

TTh	Th	H	T	U	
					⇒ Ten Thousands Thousands Hundreds Tens Units
0	9	0	0	9	
0	2	4	5	5	
3	•6				⇒ 2 + 0 + 0 + 1 (carry) = 3

∴ **The Total is 36014.**

Checking in Dropping 11s method

In this method check can be exercised with **DR** in such a way that we can check column wise totals as explained below –

9	0	0	9	⇒ Running total	... A
2	4	5	5	⇒ Elevens	... B
2	4	5	5	⇒ Elevens (repeated)	... C
13	8	10	19	⇒ Total of A + B + C	... D
4	8	1	1	⇒ **DR** of row D	... E
31	44	55	64	⇒ Total of each column of Addends	... F
4	8	1	1	⇒ **DR** of row F	... G

For the addition to be correct row E and row G should tally. If it does so, then the addition is correct, else recheck only that column where the DR does not tally.

This method i.e. dropping of 11is explained in 4 pages. But once you practice this method, you can adopt this method with lots of ease and confidence.

* What is **DR** (Digital Root) and how it is calculated and utilized, is explained in **Checking of Arithmetic Sums (Part-I).**

DR or Digital root is also known as **Nines Remainder** and instead of checking by nines remainder, we can also check by elevens remainder; this is explained in **Checking of Arithmetic Sums (Part-II)**.

□

5

Checking of Arithmetic Sums (Eleven's Remainder) Part-II

Checking by the elevens Remainder

Instead of the **digital-root** (explained in **Checking Arithmetic Sums Part-I)** method, checking by elevens remainder can be used as an alternative method either as double check, if such a thing is desired, or simply for the sake of change. In this elevens remainder method we do not divide anything by 11. The method is –

I-Case: Two digit numbers

To find the elevens remainder of a two digit number, like 59, we subtract the tens-digit from the units-digit: for 59 we have 9 minus 5 is 4. The elevens remainder of 59 is 4. This is what we would have found if we had actually divided 59 by 11.

Sometimes we can't subtract because the tens-digit may be larger than units-digit, as in 73 for instance. In such a case, we make the units-digit big enough by adding 11 to it. For 73 we have 3 plus 11 is 14, and from this 14 now minus 7 is 7. For 41 the elevens remainder would be 1 plus 11 is 12 minus 4 is 8.

II-Case: All numbers longer than two digits

The method here is to use every alternate digit. That is to say, we start at the right-hand end of the number, and work back to the left adding every alternate digits; after this is done with; we pick up the skipped digits and finally subtract them.

Consider 4 9 7 3 1 2 5 0 8. Start at the right-hand end, the 8, and work back to the left adding up every alternate digit:

8 + 5 + 1 + 7 + 4 = 25

Then the skipped numbers from right are –

0 + 2 + 3 + 9 = 14

The subtract –

25 – 14 = 11

This 11 can be further reduced to 1 – 1 = 0. Therefore the elevens remainder of the long number 497312508 is 0 or 11.

We had 25 – 14 in the above case. Suppose in another case we could have something like 25 minus 34 (i.e. the sum of first set of alternate numbers starting from the extreme right digit is smaller than the skipped numbers), so that the subtraction is not possible (since it yield negative value). In such a case add 11 (or 11s) to the smaller number to bring to a stage where we could subtract yielding positive value; here 25 minus 34 would become 25+11 = 36 minus 34 equals 2. ***It may be remembered that the first set of addition has to start from right end only without any exception.***

If these numbers seem large and uncomfortable, 25 and 34, then they can be easily avoided by using a little shortcut. After you have found the first total like the 25 in this case, do not set aside to find 34. Instead, you will now work down from the 25, or whatever number it is. That is after you find the total of every alternate number (from the right-hand end), go back to the penultimate (next-to-last number) and subtract it from the total i.e. 25. Continue subtracting every alternate number to the left (these numbers skipped to arrive at the first total i.e. 25). It amounts to subtracting the second total a little piece at a time.

For example: 4 9 0 8 6 3 2. Start at the right end and add all the underlined digits:

4 9 0 8 6 3 2

i.e. add 2 plus 6 is 8, plus 0 is 8, plus 4 is 12. Then go back to right end and from 12 subtract the skipped digits one by one –

4 9 0 8 6 3 2

i.e. 12 minus 3 is 9, then 9 minus 8 is 1, and 1 minus 9 won't go, so we increase 1 by 11 and say: 1 plus 11 is 12 minus 9 is 3. So, the elevens remainder for 4908632 is 3.

Another shortcut, very effective, is to go across the number using adjacent pairs of figures. In each pair we subtract one figure from the other, because one of them is an 'even' figure and the other one is an 'odd' one (in order of position, of course). For instance, take 5 7 0 4 3 7 1 9 2 8. Write the numbers in groups of digits in pairs, as we have shown below –

$$\frac{57}{2}\ \frac{04}{4}\ \frac{37}{4}\ \frac{19}{8}\ \frac{28}{6}$$ the bottom figures are subtracting the pairs (left digit from right)

Now we add the figures at the bottom (the digits we had after subtracting the pairs) – 2 plus 4 is 6, plus 4 is 10, plus 8 is 18 which is 7 (after 8 minus 1), plus 6 is 13 which is 2. So, the elevens remainder of 5704371928 is 2.

In case of long numbers (such as above), if it has odd number of digits – to make pairs out of it as above, add a leading zero and make the number of digits even.

Application

We apply the elevens remainder to calculations as a check as we did with nines remainder (or digital root) previously. The principal involved are same as before.

Whatever operations we perform on the given numbers, we do the same operation (like addition, subtraction, multiplication, etc)on the elevens remainder. Then the result of operation on the elevens remainder must be the same as the elevens remainder of the answer, if the operation is correct.

Let us take an example on addition –

302 + 114 + 273 + 154 = 843
(5) + (4) + (9) + (0) = (7)

The operation being addition, the summation of elevens remainders(inside the brackets) must be equal to elevens remainder of answer i.e. 5 + 4 + 9 + 0 = 18 which is 8 – 1 =7; so is the elevens remainder of 843.

□

6

Addition (Part-IV)

Some Interesting aspects in addition

I. **Sum of sequence of 'n' natural numbers.**

$$-\frac{1}{2}\times n\times(n+1)$$

E.g.1: Sum of all numbers upto 25

Ans: here n = 25

$$\therefore \text{Sum} = \frac{1}{2}\times 25\times(25+1) = \frac{1}{2}\times 25\times 26 = 25 \times 13 = 325$$

II. **Sum of sequence of consecutive odd numbers.**

$$-\left[\frac{n+1}{2}\right]^2$$

E.g.2: Sum of all odd numbers 1 to 25

Ans: here n = 25

$$\therefore \text{Sum} = \left[\frac{25+1}{2}\right]^2 = \left(\frac{26}{2}\right)^2 = 13^2 = 169$$

III. **Sum of sequence of consecutive even numbers.**

$$-\frac{1}{4}\times n(n+2)$$

E.g.3: Sum of all even numbers from 2 to 26

Ans: here n = 26

$$\therefore \text{Sum} = \frac{1}{4}\times 26\times(26+2) = 26 \text{ X } 7 = 182$$

IV. Sum of sequence of consecutive numbers between any two numbers.

$$- \frac{1}{2}\times(n_1+n_2)\times(n_2-n_1+1) \text{ where } n_2 > n_1$$

E.g.4: Sum of all numbers between 6 and 27

Ans: here n1 = 6 and n_2 = 27

$\therefore$ Sum =

$$\frac{1}{2}\times(6+27)\times(27-6+1) = \frac{1}{2}\times 33\times 22 = 33\times 11 = 363$$

V. Sum of digits of squares of repeated ones.

– (number of digits in repeated ones)^2

E.g.5 (a): Sum of digits of $(1111)^2$

Ans: $(1111)^2$ = 1234321

Or 1+2+3+4+3+2+1 = 16 = 4^2

i.e. there are 4 ones in 1111 and hence sum of digits in its square is 4^2 = 16

E.g.5 (b): Sum of digits of $(111)^2$

Ans: there are 3 ones in 111 and hence 3^2 = 9

i.e. $(111)^2$ = 12321 and 1+2+3+2+1 = 9 = 3^2

VI. Sum of sequence of numbers from 1 to a desired one-digit number and back. (This is corollary of E.g. 5(a) and 5(b) above.)

– n^2 where n is the desired number

E.g.6: Sum of digits 1 to 7 and back

Ans: The desired number is 7 and the required sum is 1+2+3+4+5+6+7+6+5+4+3+2+1 = 7^2 = 49

VII. Sum of sequence of numbers in 10s upto a desired number also in 10s and back upto 10.

– If the desired number in 10s is say 15 and the sum required is from 10 to 15 and back, then follow the following steps -

Step 1: Square the unit digits of desired number – in this case it is 5 of 15 and 5^2 is 25. Take 5 and carry 2.

Step 2: The number of terms will be 2 × unit digit of chosen number + 1 = 2 × 5 + 1 = 11

Step 3: Number of terms (found in step 2) + carry in step 1 = 11+2 = 13; so sum of sequence = 135

∴ 10+11+12+13+14+15+14+13+12+11+10 = 135

E.g.7: Sum of numbers 10 to 17 and back to 10

Ans: The chosen number is 17

Step 1: Square of unit digit of 17 i.e. 7 is 49. Take 9 and carry 4.

Step 2: No of terms = 2 × 7 +1 = 15

Step 3: No of terms + carry in step 1 = 15 + 4 = 19

∴ 10+11+12+13+14+15+16+17+16+15+14+13+12+11+10=199

VIII. Sum of sequence of numbers in 20s upto a desired number also in 20s and back upto 20.

E.g.8: If the desired number in 20s is say 24 and the sum required is from 20 to 24 and back, then follow the following steps-

Step 1: Square the unit digits of desired number – in this case it is 4 of 24 and 4^2 is 16. Take 6 and carry 1.

Step 2: The number of terms will be 2 × unit digit of chosen number + 1 = 2 × 4 + 1 = 9

Step 3: 2 × Number of terms (found in step 2) + carry in step 1 = 2 × 9 + 1 = 19; so sum of sequence = 196

∴ 20+21+22+23+24+23+22+21+20 = 196

IX. Sum of sequence of numbers in 30s upto a desired number also in 30s and back upto 30.

E.g.9: – If the desired number in 30s is say 36 and the sum required is from 30 to 36 and back, then follow the following steps-

Step 1: Square the unit digits of desired number – in this case it is 6 of 36 and 6^2 is 36. Take 6 and carry 3.

Step 2: The number of terms will be 2 × unit digit of chosen number + 1 = 2 × 6 + 1 = 13

Step 3: 3 × Number of terms (found in step 2) + carry in step 1 = 3 × 13 + 3 = 42; so sum of sequence = 426

∴ 30+31+32+33+34+35+36+35+34+33+32+31+30 = 426

X. For numbers in 40s, 50s, 60s, 70s, 80s and 90s the sum can be found on the logic explained in VIII and IX above

Sequence of numbers	Step 1	Step 2	Step 3
10 to 19	Square the unit digit	No of terms is twice unit digit + 1	1 x (Step 2 + carry in step 1)
20 to 29	---- do ----	---- do ----	2 x (---- do ----)
30 to 39	---- do ----	---- do ----	3 x (---- do ----)
40 to 49	---- do ----	---- do ----	4 x (---- do ----)
50 to 59	---- do ----	---- do ----	5 x (---- do ----)
60 to 60	---- do ----	---- do ----	6 x (---- do ----)
70 to 79	---- do ----	---- do ----	7 x (---- do ----)
80 to 89	---- do ----	---- do ----	8 x (---- do ----)
90 to 99	---- do ----	---- do ----	9 x (---- do ----)

XI. Sum of sequence of doubles

The following steps are involved –

1. Choose a number
2. Jot down the series of doubles – i.e. each successive term is twice of the previous.
3. The sum of all the numbers in this sequence is 2 times the last term minus the first term

E.g.11:

1. Suppose the number chosen is 7.
2. Doubles are 7, 14, 28, 56, 112, 224, 448
3. Sum $\rightarrow 2 \times 448 - 7 = 889$.

XII. To add a sequence of quadruples.

The following steps are involved –

1. Choose a number
2. Generate a series of quadruples by multiplying each by 4 to get the next number in the series.
3. The sum of all the numbers in this sequence is 4 times the last term minus the first term and then divided by 3.

E.g. 12(a):

1. Suppose the number is 3.
2. The sequence is 3, 12, 48, 192, 768, and 3072
3. Sum → (4 × 3072 – 3)/3 = 4095.

E.g. 12(b):

1. Let the number be 24
2. The sequence is 24, 96, 384, 1536, and 6144
3. Sum → (4 × 6144 – 24)/3 = 8184.

□

7

Subtraction (Part-1)

Conventional Borrowing Method

Almost all over the globe I think subtraction is taught to us to be done from right to left (if I am wrong any one may correct me) as shown in example 1 below –

Example 1: Subtract 691 from 864 –

Ans: The sum can be set as below –

```
  7
  8̸ ¹6 4    – minuend
 –6  9 1    – subtrahend
 ---------
  1  7 3    – difference or answer
 ---------
```

Here we do the subtraction from right to left as per steps below:

1. 4 – 1 = 3
2. 6 – 9 is not possible; so we borrow 1 from left side i.e. from 8 and make the 6 as 16. ∴ 16 – 9 = 7
3. As we have borrowed 1 from 8 in step 2 we have now 7 in hundredth's place and 7 – 6 = 1
4. So finally **864 – 691 = 173.**

This is how we conventionally do the subtraction. **But do you know that subtraction can be done by five different methods including the conventional one we have discussed above?** This means that we are yet to know four more methods. I am sure majority of us do not know these four new methods.

What is interesting is (you would definitely agree with me at the end of this discussion) that all the four methods (which we are yet to know) are simpler and faster than the conventional method, provided you practice for some time (even a day or two of concerted effort will be enough to gain expertise in any of the methods).

So shall we go ahead with new methods? –

Give away method

Alternatively we do the subtraction from left to right (as against the right to left method) and also instead of ***borrowing*** from the immediate left digit (whenever subtraction is not possible) we can **give-away** to the immediate right digit where subtraction is not possible. See example 2 below –

Example 2: Subtract 47948 from 60874

(a) First we shall solve the sum by the conventional borrow method and then by the give-away method so that application of two different method on the same problem gives a stronger and louder impact on the difference in the two methods as well as gives you an opportunity to judge (without any bias) as to which method is less cumbrous and easier.

Ans:

```
         9
  5     10    6
  6̸   0̸ ¹8  7̸ ¹4  - minuend
  4    7  9  4  8  - subtrahend
  ----------------
  1    2  9  2  6  - answer
  ----------------
```

The right to left subtraction is as below –

1. 4 – 8 is not possible. So we borrow 1 from 7 in the minuend.
   So 14 – 8 = 6
2. The 7 in the tens place of the minuend is now 6 as we have borrowed 1 in the earlier step; so 6 – 4 = 2.
3. Moving left 8 – 9 is not possible; so borrow 1 from left. But we cannot borrow form zero and hence move further left and from the leftmost digit i.e. 6 we borrow 1 and make the 0 in the minuend as 10 and from this 10 we borrow 1 and make the 8 in the hundreds place as 18 and hence 18 – 9 = 9.

4. Moving further left the 0 here was first made as 10 due to borrow from leftmost digit 6 and further borrow in step 3 above the 10 now stays as 9 and 9 – 7 = 2.
5. Finally the left most digit now being 5 due to borrow in step 3, 5 – 4 = 1.
6. So **60874 – 47948 = 12926.**

(b) We shall now solve the problem by give-away method –

Ans:

$$\begin{array}{rl} \mathbf{6\ {}^{1}0\ {}^{1}8\ 7\ {}^{1}4} & \textbf{– minuend} \\ \mathbf{-\,4\ 7\ 9\ 4\ 8} & \textbf{– subtrahend} \\ \hline \not{2}\ \not{3}\ 9\ \not{3}\ 6 & \\ \mathbf{1\ \ 2\ 9\ 2\ 6} & \textbf{– answer} \\ \hline \end{array}$$

Starting from leftmost digit –

1. 6 – 4 = 2; however before taking the answer as 2 verify the immediate right column and if the subtraction is possible retain 2 otherwise give-away 1 to the 0 in minuend and retain 1 as the answer for this step. 0 – 7 is not possible so 1 is given away from 2 and only 1 is retained.
2. Moving right, the zero in the minuend is now 10 due to step 1 above and 10 – 7 = 3; but before taking 3 as the answer, verify the subtraction in the immediate right is possible or not. 8 – 9 is not possible; so give-away 1 to 8 in the minuend and take 2 as the answer.
3. Moving right, the 8 in minuend is now 18 due to step 2 above and 18 – 9 = 9; before taking 9 as the answer, verify the subtraction in the immediate right is possible or not. 7 – 4 is possible and hence retain 9 as the answer.
4. Moving right, 7 – 4 = 3; before taking 3 as the answer verify in the immediate right (rightmost column in this case)subtraction is possible or not. 4 – 8 is not possible; so give-away 1 from 3 and retain 2 as the answer.
5. The right most digit is now 14 due to step 4 above and 14 – 8 = 6
6. So finally **60874 – 47948 = 12926**. Same as the result obtained from borrow method.

The number of zeros involved was just one and if there would have been more zeros the borrow method is definitely cumbrous. Let us see example 3 below –

Example 3: Subtract 79248 from 100086

Ans:

$$
\begin{array}{cccccc}
1 & ^{1}0 & ^{1}0 & ^{1}0 & 8 & ^{1}6 \\
-0 & 7 & 9 & 2 & 4 & 8 \\
\hline
\not{1} & \not{3} & \not{1} & 8 & \not{4} & 8 \\
0 & 2 & 0 & 8 & 3 & 8 \\
\hline
\end{array}
$$

From leftmost digit, Steps

1. 1 – 0 = 1; but as 7 cannot be taken away from 0 give-away this 1 to next column.
2. 10 – 7 = 3; but again 9 cannot be taken away from 0 in the third column (from left). So give-away 1 from the 3 and write 2 below 7.
3. 10 – 9 =1; again 2 cannot be taken away from 0 in the fourth column. Hence, give-away this 1 and write 0 below 9.
4. 10 – 2 = 8; as 4 can be taken away from 8 in the fifth column write 8 below 2.
5. 8 – 4 = 4; but 8 cannot be taken away from 6 in the rightmost column. Hence give-away 1 from 4 and write 3 below 4.
6. 16 – 8 = 8.
7. **∴ Answer is 20838**

With examples 2 & 3 above, we are almost done with give-away method. However, there is a special case where the same digit may be subtracted from one another. In such cases (whether it is a single column of same digits or a series of consecutive columns of same digits) go further to the right till you reach a column where the digits are different. At this stage decide whether subtraction is possible or not. If subtraction is not possible then give-away in each of the earlier column where the digits are same (see example 4 below). Otherwise mark zero for the columns where the digits are same (see example 5 below).

Example 4: Subtract 34484 from 74457

Ans:

	7	**^{1}4**	**^{1}4**	**^{1}5**	**7**	**– minuend**
-	**3**	**4**	**4**	**8**	**4**	**– subtrahend**
	~~4~~	~~10~~	~~10~~	7	3	**– intermediate values**
	3	**9**	**9**	**7**	**3**	**– answer**

1. 7 – 3 = 4; give-away 1 and take 3
2. 14 – 4 = 10; give-away 1 and take 9
3. 14 – 4 = 10; give-away 1 and take 9
4. 15 – 8 = 7
5. 7 – 4 = 3.
6. The answer is **39973**

In the above example, the second and third columns from the left have same digits (4 in this case). But the fourth column has 5 and 8 which cannot be subtracted. So even though 7 – 3 = 4 in the left most column, we write 3 and give-away 1 to the 4 on the right. Then 14 – 4 =10; but again we give-away 1 from this 10 to the right which is 4 again and write down 9 below 4 in the second column. Again 14 – 4 = 10; by giving 1 to 5 in the fourth column and so on ...

Example 5: subtract 33338 from 53386

Ans:

	5	**3**	**3**	**8**	**^{1}6**
-	**3**	**3**	**3**	**3**	**8**
	2	**0**	**0**	**4**	**8**

1. 5 – 3 = 2
2. 3 – 3 = 0
3. 3 – 3 = 0
4. 8 – 3 = 5; give-away 1 and write 4
5. 16 – 8 = 8.
6. The answer is **20048.**

This is all about give-away method and if you are not biased you would agree with me that this method is easier than the conventional method, nevertheless at least a day or two's practice is necessary. We shall see about other unknown methods of subtraction in the next lesson.

□

8

Subtraction (Part-II)

We reviewed first the conventional borrow method in Subtraction (1) and then learnt about subtraction by give-away method and that too the subtraction was done from left to right as against the conventional way i.e. from right to left.

Those who feel inconvenient in doing subtraction from left to right and still wants to do away with borrowing – Well! here is a novel method known as **Complement Method of Subtraction** and in this method you continue to subtract from right to left, however instead of borrowing from left when subtraction is not possible (i.e. the digit in subtrahend is more than the digit in minuend) we use complement as explained in example 1 below. But before we learn to use complement method for subtraction lets just review what complement is?

Complement

Complement of a number is nothing but the difference between the number and its base. The base of a number (normally) is 10 for single digit number, 100 for double digit number, 1000 for triple digit number, and so on. As subtraction is done digit by digit, we shall first restrict our selves to complement of single digit numbers and it is tabulated as below –

Number	**1**	**2**	**3**	**4**	**5**	**6**	**7**	**8**	**9**	**0**
Complement	**9**	**8**	**7**	**6**	**5**	**4**	**3**	**2**	**1**	**0**

So Complement of a single digit number is the difference between 10 and the number. Zero is neutral and its complement is also zero. [Finding complement of two or more digits will be done with a formula – All from NINE and the last from TEN – which is also a method of subtraction and will be explained in the next lesson].

Complement Method of subtraction:

The steps in the following example will illustrate this method.

Example 1: Subtract 4758 from 8123

Ans:

$$\begin{array}{r} 8\ 1\ 2\ 3 \\ -4\ 7\ 5\ 8 \end{array}$$

From rightmost digit –

Step 1: 3 – 8 is not possible; so take complement of 8 in the subtrahend, which is 2 and add the same to 3 in the minuend and write 5 in the answer-row. As we have used complement in this column place a dot to the left above 5 in the subtrahend (this dot is equivalent to a carry-over 1) as shown below –

$$\begin{array}{r} 8\ 1\ 2\ 3 \\ -4\ 7\ \dot{5}\ 8 \\ \hline 5 \\ \hline \end{array}$$

Step 2: 2 minus(5+dot) is not possible; so take complement of 5+dot i.e. complement of 6, which is 4 and add to 2 in the minuend and write 6 in the answer-row, below 5 of subtrahend. Mark a dot above 7.

$$\begin{array}{r} 8\ 1\ 2\ 3 \\ -4\ \dot{7}\ \dot{5}\ 8 \\ \hline 6\ 5 \\ \hline \end{array}$$

Step 3: 1 minus (7+dot) is not possible; so take complement of 7+dot i.e. complement of 8, which is 2 and add to 1 in the minuend and write 3 in the answer-row, below 7 of subtrahend. Mark a dot above 4.

$$\begin{array}{r} 8\ 1\ 2\ 3 \\ -\ \dot{4}\ \dot{7}\ \dot{5}\ 8 \\ \hline 3\ 6\ 5 \\ \hline \end{array}$$

Step 4: 8 minus (4+dot) is 8 – 5 = 3; write 3 in answer-row as the leftmost digit.

∴ **8123 – 4758 = 3365.**

Example 2: Subtract 5989 from 8763

Ans:

$$\begin{array}{r} 8\ 7\ 6\ 3 \\ -\dot{5}\ \dot{9}\ \dot{8}\ 9 \\ \hline 2\ 7\ 7\ 4 \\ \hline \end{array}$$

Step 1: 3 – 9 not possible; dot over 8; 9's complement plus 3 – write down 4

Step 2: 6 – (8+dot) not possible; dot over 9 on the left; (8+dots)'s complement + 6 – write down 7

Step 3: 7 – (9+dot) not possible; dot over 5; (9+dot)'s complement + 7 – write down 7

Step 5: 8 – (5+dot) = 2.

Answer:8763 – 5989 = 2774

This is all about complement method. As said earlier with practice this method becomes easier than conventional method and also a simple method of dropping of tens enable checking of subtraction done by complement method (as explained below)

Checking:

$$\begin{array}{rl} 8\ 7\ 6\ 3 & \text{- (minuend)} \\ -\dot{5}\ \dot{9}\ \dot{8}\ 9 & \text{- (subtrahend)} \\ \hline 2\ 7\ 7\ 4 & \text{- (Difference/answer)} \\ \hline \end{array}$$

In the above case from left to right –

Col.1 → 2 + 5 + dot = 8 tallies with digit in minuend

Col.2 → 7 + 9 + dot = 17 – dropping ten = 7 tallies with digit in minuend

Col.3 → 7 + 8 + dot = 16 – dropping ten = 6 tallies with digit in minuend

Col.4 → 4 + 9 = 13 dropping ten = 3 tallies with digit in minuend.

Let's see about the next method in the next lesson.

Note: Complement of single digit numbers can be picked-up easily from **TEN POINT CIRCLE** – which is reproduced below. The digits at either end of the straight line in **Fig.1**(below) are compliment to each other, i.e. 9–1, 8–2, 7–3, 6–4 (of course 5–5)

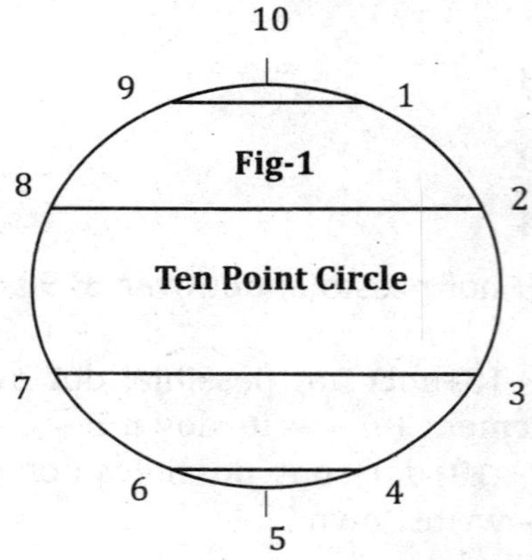

Fig-1

Ten Point Circle

□

9

Subtraction (Part-III)

Vinculum Method

Before we deal with **Vinculum method,** let us first see what is **Vinculum**? Many of you would have learned in algebra – that there are four different types of brackets with which we can alter the hierarchy of Arithmetic operations. The four brackets are –

- ☑ Vinculum (or bar) ——
- ☑ Single (or round) bracket ( )
- ☑ Square bracket and lastly [ ]
- ☑ Double (or curly) bracket. { }

The sequence of operations (when all the four brackets are used) is as follows –

- First perform all operation in the vinculum (or bar bracket) in the indicated order; remember to use BODMAS or **PEMDAS***
- Then perform all the operation in the single bracket by the same rule
- Then all operations in the square bracket
- The all operations in curly bracket
- And finally the remaining operations, if any are to be performed.

***PEMDAS** – This *acronym* is used in British Schools where **PEMDAS** means Parenthesis, Exponentiation, Multiplication, Division, Addition, and Subtraction

The above explanation holds good for Algebra; but in case of Arithmetic, the vinculum over a single digit indicates a minus quantity or deficiency. For example, the number $\mathbf{8\,\bar{6}\,7}$ indicates the digit in tens place is negative while the other two digit i.e. 8 in hundreds place and 7 in units place are positive. Now if we write $\mathbf{8\,\bar{6}\,7}$in the extended form it will actually be 800 – 60 + 7 = 747. On the same logic $\mathbf{8\,6\,\bar{7}}$ will be 800 + 60 – 7 = 853; and so on.

From the above paragraph we evolve a very simple formula for converting a vinculum number to non-vinculum –

we take the complement of the number over which vinculum is marked and then reduce the immediate left digit by unity. In case of $\mathbf{8\,\bar{6}\,7}$, the vinculum is on 6; its complement is 4 and reducing unity from the immediate left digit i.e. 8 is 7 and hence $8\bar{6}7$ = 747.

In **Subtraction (2)**, we mentioned about using the formula – **All from NINE and last from TEN** – for finding complement of two or more digits. This is the time to know about this.

All from NINE and last from TEN

Suppose our number with vinculum is $\mathbf{3\,\overline{8\,9\,7}\,2}$; the complement of 897 is found by using the formula – All from NINE ... i.e. subtract all numbers from right from nine and the last digit from ten. So the complement of 897 is 103 and as was in the case of single digit reduce immediate left digit i.e. 3 by unity to get 2. So conversion of vinculum number $\mathbf{3\overline{897}2}$ will be **21032**.

It is obvious that converting a non-vinculum number to vinculum, the rule is just the reverse i.e. first take the complement of the number to be made vinculum; mark on the complement with a bar; and then increase the immediate left digit by unity. So, if the digit 8 is to be converted as vinculum in the number 482, then complement of 8 i.e. 2; mark vinculum sign over 2 and increase the immediate left digit i.e. 4 by unity. Hence $\mathbf{482 = 5\bar{2}2}$. If two or more consecutive digits are to be marked with vinculum use the formula All from NINE...

Now let us see how to do subtraction using vinculum –

Example 1: Subtract 985 from 2468

Ans:

$$\begin{array}{r l} 2\;4\;6\;8 & \text{- Minuend} \\ -\,0\;9\;8\;5 & \text{- Subtrahend} \\ \hline 2\;\bar{5}\;\bar{2}\;3 & \text{- Answer or 1483 (non-vinculum)} \end{array}$$

From rightmost or leftmost digit

Step 1: 8 – 5 = 3; take 3 in the answer row.

Step 2: moving left 6 – 8 is not possible; but 8 – 6 = 2; take this 2 with a vinculum sign in the answer row.

Step 3: moving left 4 – 9 is not possible; but 9 – 4 = 5; take this 5 with a vinculum sign in the answer row.

Step 4: moving further left i.e. left most column 2 – 0 = 2; take 2 in the answer row.

Step 5: we now know how to convert vinculum number $2\,\bar{5}\,\bar{2}\,3$ (by using All from NINE ... formula). So, **2468 – 983 = 1483.**

Example 2: subtract 37869 from 46750

Ans:

$$\begin{array}{r} 4\ 6\ 7\ 5\ 0 \\ -3\ 7\ 8\ 6\ 9 \\ \hline 1\ \bar{1}\ \bar{1}\ \bar{1}\ \bar{9} \\ \hline \end{array}$$

So $\mathbf{1\,\bar{1}\,\bar{1}\,\bar{1}\,\bar{9} = 8881}$

As we can easily remember the complement of single digit and also finding complement of multiple digits is also very simple by using 'All from NINE'formula and also as neither borrowing nor give-away is involved, don't you agree that using vinculum is also easy and faster way of subtraction as compared to conventional method.

By subtraction and/or by addition

We have another method known as **'by subtraction and/or by addition'** and for mental subtraction this method can be used. The method works as explained below –

When we subtract large numbers like 7, 8, 9 or numbers ending in 7, 8, 9 like 37, 29, 48, etc. first subtract the nearest sub-base and then add the complement from the subtracted base. **[The 'and/or' is used because in case of addition, we first add the nearest sub-base and then subtract the complement from the added base].** See example 3, 4 and 5 below –

Example 3: Subtract 29 from 243

Ans: 243 – 30 = 213 + 1 = 214[Here 30 is the sub base for 29, which is first subtracted and 1 being the complement of 29 of the sub base 30, it is added]

Example 4: Subtract 38 from 76

Ans: 86 - 40 = 46 + 2 = 48 [Here 40 is the sub base for 38,which is first subtracted and 2 being the complement of 38 of the sub base 40, it is added]

Example 5: Subtract 197 from 518

Ans: 518 – 200 = 318 + 3 = 321 [here 200 is the sub base for 197, which is first subtracted and 3 being the complement of 197 of the sub base 200, it is added]

All from NINE and last from TEN

Finally to end the **Subtraction (3)** the last known method is 'All from NINE' formula. Readers already know this method which we have explained in the previous section i.e. Vinculum Method of Subtraction. In the previous section we have explained this for finding complement. But to use as a method of subtraction this will be useful when we are to know what amount we have to get back after made a purchase of Rs.847.85 and tendered a Rs.1000 note. Forgetting the decimal point in 847.85, apply 'All from NINE' formula on 847.85 i.e. subtract all the digits from left from NINE and the rightmost digit from TEN. Bingo! The answer is 152.15.

Extension of AFNLFT

Readers may note that "All from NINE ... (AFNLFT)" formula will be used in multiplication as well as in division (while finding complements). However, let us see how we can subtract a number which is just below a base from a number which is just above base. For example 7, 88, 982, 9978 (which are just below the base 10,100,1000,10000, respectively) are to be subtracted from say, 13,123, 1023,12223 (which are just above the base 10,100,1000,10000, respectively), then the excess of minuend from the base and the deficiency of the subtrahend from the base are to be added to get the result of subtraction.

For finding the excess simply subtract the base and for finding deficiency use AFNLFT formula i.e. All From Nine and Last From Ten formula. E.g.

1. **13-7 = 3 + 3 = 6**

   (Here 3 and 3 are excess and deficiency of 13 and 7 respectively from its base 10 and they are added to get the result of subtraction of 13 –7)

2. **123-88 = 23 + 12 = 35**
   (Here 23 and 12 are the excess and deficiency of 123 and 88 respectively from its base 100)
3. **1023 - 982 = 23 + 18 = 23 + 20 - 2 = 41**
   (Here 23 and 18 are excess and deficiency from base 1000)
4. **12223-9978 = 2223 + 22 = 2245**
   (Here 2223 and 22 are the excess and deficiency of 12223 and 9978 from their base 10000)

Try these for yourself:

1. 114 – 87 2. 142 – 88 3. 163 – 76 4. 123 – 69
5. 112 – 86 6. 152 – 87 7. 136 – 57 8. 134 – 76

This method works with numbers near sub-bases also—

E.g. **5. 462 – 276 = 162 + 24 = 186**
(Here the sub-base considered is 300 – which is nearest to subtrahend 276 and 162 and 24 are excess and deficiency respectively from sub-base 300)
6. 541 – 187 = 341 + 13 = 354
(Here 341 and 13 are the excess and deficiency from sub-base 200)

Try these for yourself

(a) 263 – 198 (b)834 – 286
(c) 429 – 168 (d)724 – 375

Mental Subtraction

Based on some of the tools/procedures we have learnt we can practice to improve our mental ability to subtract any number, of any digits. These mental subtractions can be done left to right and few examples on two-digit numbers, and three-digit subtraction are shown below -

Subtraction of Two-digit numbers:

Case-I: *Split and subtract*

$$\begin{array}{r} 76 \\ -\ 34 \\ \hline 42 \end{array} \quad (30, 4)$$

42 Here we have split the subtrahend 34, as 30 & 4 and first we deducted 30 from the minuend 76 to get 46 and now our problem is simplified to subtraction of single digit 4 from 46 to finally get 42. Case-II: by subtraction and addition

$$\begin{array}{r} 84 \\ -\ 59 \\ \hline 25 \end{array} \quad (-60, +1)$$

Here we have first subtracted the immediate sub-base of the subtrahend (60 in AI this example) from the minuend and then added the complement of sub-base and subtrahend. In fact this method can be used very easily for subtraction of three-digit or even larger numbers. For example –

$$\begin{array}{r} 5678 \\ -\ 3729 \\ \hline 1949 \end{array} \quad (-4000, +271)$$

Here 4000 is the sub-base of the subtrahend 3729, and 271 is the complement of 3729 from the sub-base 4000.

For finding the complement of a number we can use AFNLFT (All From Nine and Last From Ten) already explained above, with slight modification to subtract from sub-base.

Modified AFNLFT

I. If the number digits in sub-base and subtrahend are same then the difference between the left most digit minus one and the remaining digits from left to right are as per AFNLFT. Example –

1. 40 – 26; 4 – 2 – 1 = 1 and 10 – 6 = 4. Therefore 40 – 26 = 14. Here as there are only two digits the left most is found by their difference minus one. And the digit left being one and last we use the later part of AFNLFT i.e. the LFT (Last From Ten) part only
2. 70 – 23; 7 – 2 – 1 = 4 and 10 – 3 = 7. Therefore 70 – 23 = 47.
3. 800 – 356; 8 – 3 – 1 = 4 & for 56 use AFNLFT i.e. 9 – 5 = 4 & 10-6 = 4. Therefore 800 – 356 = 444.
4. 500-173; 5-1-1 = 3 & ANLFTon 73 will be 9-7 = 2 and 10-3 = 7. Therefore 500 – 173 = 327.
5. 4000 – 2413; 4 – 2 – 1 = 1 and AFNLFT on 413 is 9 – 4 = 5, 9 – 1 = 8, and 10 – 3 = 7. Therefore 4000 – 2413 = 1587.
6. 70000 – 60107; 7 – 6 – 1 = 0 & AFNLFT on 0107 is 9 – 0 = 9, 9 – 1 = 8, 9 – 0 = 9, and 10 – 7 = 3. Therefore 70000 – 60107 = 09893 or 9893.

II. If the number of digits in the subtrahend is less than the digits in sub-base, then reduce the left most digit of sub-base by one and then apply AFNLFT on the subtrahend. Examples –

a. 20 – 9; 2 – 1 = 1 and AFNLFT on 9 is 10 – 9 = 1 (being last digit only LFT is applied). Therefore 20 – 9 = 11

b. 300 – 27; 3 – 1 = 2 and applying AFNLFT on 27, 9 – 2 = 7 and 10 – 7 = 3 Therefore 300 – 27 = 273.

c. 7000 – 786; 7 – 1 = 6 and AFNLFT on 786 is 9 – 7 = 2, 9 – 8 = 1 and 10 – 6 = 4. Therefore 7000 – 786 = 6216.

d. 4000 – 34; 4 – 1 = 3 and now consider the subtrahend 34 as 034 and AFNLFT on 034 is 9 – 0 = 9, 9 – 3 = 6 and 10 – 4 = 6. Therefore 4000 – 34 = 3966.

Try the following examples to become at home with mental subtraction:

(a)	(b)	(c)	(d)
86 - 25	86 - 47	81 - 39	38 - 23
(e) 148 - 86	(f) 125 - 79		

□

10

Multiplication (Part-I)

Introduction

There are innumerable methods of multiplication compared to addition and subtraction. Efforts have been made to illustrate all methods including obsolete methods like lattice method and Russian Peasant's Algorithm.

Before doing multiplication by any method, teachers/parents must ensure that all their students/wards know tables upto 30 thoroughly. For almost all chores of works in our life like brushing teeth, taking bath, eating food, etc. we never give a break. Similarly every day (including weekly holidays and vacations) at least upto 10 std. students must practice tables, however bright they might be in Mathematics.

How to prepare tables for any number is explained in Appendix - A at the end of this book.

Some Old Special Cases of Multiplication

Lattice Method

In this method the intermediate and individual multiplication of each digit of the multiplicand and multiplier are arranged in a lattice and then added along the diagonals to arrive at the answer of multiplication. Teachers/parents may realize that, till proficiency is achieved by students/wards in learning tables beyond 10, this method of multiplying may yield better understanding.

The lattice method of multiplication is explained in example 1 and 2 below:

Example. 1: 26 × 58

Procedure: As both numbers are two digit numbers, a 2 × 2 lattice can be setout as below:

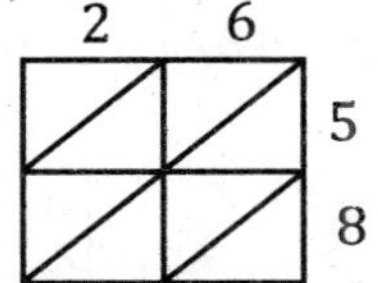

Fig.1: 2 × 2 lattice

The multiplicand 26 is put above the lattice i.e. the 2 above the first column of lattice and 6 above the second column. The multiplier 58 is written along the right side of the lattice i.e. 5 along the first row of lattice and 8 along the second row as shown above.

The individual product of each digit is marked in corresponding cells, with the tens above the diagonal and units below. E.g. the individual products of 26 × 58 are –

5 × 6 = 3/0; 5 × 2 = 1/0; 8 × 6 = 4/8; 8 × 2 = 1/6

These are entered into the lattice as shown below –

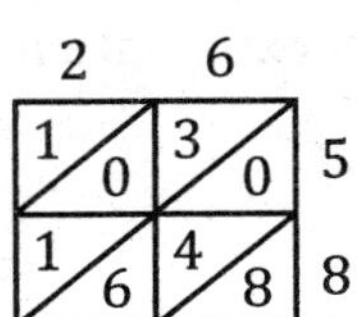

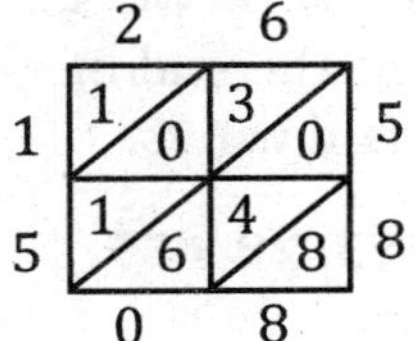

Fig.2: 2 × 2 lattice

The addition along each diagonal are marked. The final answer i.e. 1508 is shown along the left of lattice and at bottom.

So 26 × 58 = 1508

{8} × {4} {5}

Note: Readers may remember that the figures in curly brackets are DRs. [DR i.e. Digital Root of a number is the sum of all digits in the number till we reach a single digit. So DR of 26 is 2+6→8; DR of 58 is 5+8→13→1+3→4; and DR of 1508→1+5+0+8→14→1+4→5. Here the sum to be correct, the DR of 26 multiplied by DR of 58 should be equal to DR of 1508 – for details about finding DR please refer to lesson **Arithmetic Checking part I**]

3 digit × 2 digit

For 3 × 2 digit multiplication, we use a lattice of 3 columns and 2 rows. The procedure is similar to 2 × 2. See example 2 below–

Example. 2: **206 × 48**

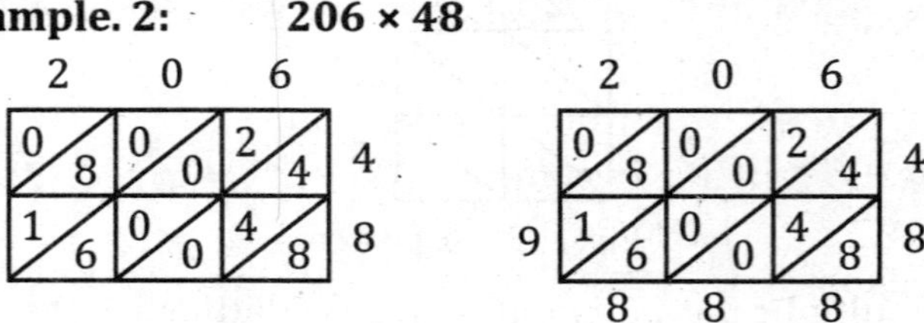

Fig.3: 3 × 2 lattice

So 206 × 48 = 9888

{8} × {3} {6}

Russian Peasant Algorithm:

Or binary method of multiplication:

The 'binary method of multiplication' also known as Russian Peasant Algorithm is also an easy method of multiplication and lets first see how it works. Teachers/parents should know this method and at the end of example 4, an explanation is given as why this method works.

Example 3: 28 × 57

Procedure:

	LHS	× RHS
Step 1: Divide the left hand side number	28	57×
i.e. multiplicand, 28 by 2, omitting fractions if any;	14	114×
and multiply the right hand side number i.e.	7	228✓
multiplier, 57 by 2. Continue this division and	3	456✓
multiplication till LHS becomes 1	1	912✓

Step 2: Ignore all the even numbers of LHS and corresponding RHS also (×). Retain (✓) the other numbers.

Step 3: Add the retained RHS numbers i.e. 228, 456 and 912

So 28 × 57 = sum of retained numbers on RHS

= 228 + 456 + 912 = 1596

{1} × {3} {3}

Note: Now even if we interchange the multiplicand and multiplier we will get the same result as shown in example 4 below –

Example 4:

Procedure:

	LHS × RHS	
Step 1: Divide the left hand side number i.e. multiplicand, 57 by 2, omitting fractions if any; and multiply the right hand side number i.e. multiplier, 28 by 2. Continue this division and multiplication till LHS becomes 1	57	28✓
	28	56×
	14	112×
	7	224✓
	3	448✓
	1	896✓

Step 2: Ignore all the even numbers of LHS and corresponding RHS also (×). Retain (✓) the other numbers.

Step 3: Add the retained RHS numbers i.e. 28, 224, 448, and 896

So 57 x 28 = sum of retained numbers on RHS

= 28 + 224 + 448 + 896 = 1596

{3} × {1} {3}

Same as before.

Why does it work?

From ex. 3 & 4 above we have seen how this binary method of multiplication works. But we should also know as to why it works?

The method is easy and simple to workout. But people always wonder as why it works. While the principle of dividing the multiplicand by 2 and multiplying the multiplier by 2 is logical, ignoring the remainder (while dividing) and some of the rows while summing need to be observed critically to understand why it works.

- ☑ The method is counterbalancing as with each step a factor 2 is moved from the number in the left column to the number in the right column.
- ☑ The numbers on RHS contains 1, 2, 4, 8, 16 times of 57 at each stage

LHS × RHS	**2^n × 57**	
28 × 57	$2^0 \times 57$	1 × 57
14 × 114	$2^1 \times 57$	2 × 57
7 × 228	$2^2 \times 57$	4 × 57
3 × 456	$2^3 \times 57$	8 × 57
1 × 912	$2^4 \times 57$	16 × 57

In the above right hand column contains 1, 2, 4, 8, 16 times of 57; ascertaining relation of binary system of numeration.

☑ In the above example 3, the retained rows contain 4 times, 8 times, and 16 times of 57 resulting in 4+8+16 = 28 times of 57 i.e. 28 × 57. The retained numbers correspond to binary expansion of 28 i.e. $2^2+2^3+2^4 = 4 + 8 + 16 = 28$.

☑ In example 4 above, the retained rows contain 1 time, 8 times, 16 times, and 32 times of 28 which tends to 57 x 28. Here the retained numbers correspond to binary expansion of 57 i.e. $2^0+2^3+2^4+2^5 = 1+8+16+32 = 57$.

Trachtenberg's Speed Method

Trachtenberg, founder of Mathematical Institute in Zurich, Switzerland, has advocated speed method for multiplying by single digits. This is based on **All from NINE and last from TEN** –

All from NINE and last from TEN is a formula used when we have to subtract number from base like – 10, 100, 1000, 10000, etc. and explained in the earlier **lesson 8 & 9** of **'Subtraction – II & III'**. Just for refreshing – one example from the previous lesson.

Example: Subtract from base

(i) 65 → 35 (3 is 6 from 9 and 5 is 5 from 10)

(ii) 347 → 653 (6 is 3 from 9, 5 is 4 from 9 and 3 is 7 fro 10)

(iii) 2088 → 7912 (7 is 2 from 9, 9 is 0 from 9, 1 is 8 from 9 and 2 is 8 from 10)

So to subtract any number from its base simply subtract all the digits from 9 and the right most digit from 10. The resulting answer is also known as complement of the given number i.e. in case (i) above 35 is the complement of 65; in case (ii) above 653 is the complement of 347 and so on. And the sum of the given number and its complement always works out to its base. That is 65 + 35 = 100; 347 + 653 = 1000; and 2088 + 7912 = 10000.

Trachtenberg's Method (Part-I)

(a) Multiplication by 9: Rules:

First Step: Subtract from 10

Middle Steps: Subtract from 9 and add the neighbour

Last Step: Reduce the left most digit of the multiplicand by 1

Example 1: 25678 x 9

$$\begin{array}{ccccc} 9 & 9 & 9 & 9 & 10 \\ \downarrow & \downarrow & \downarrow & \downarrow & \downarrow \\ 2 & 5 & 6 & 7 & 8 \end{array} \times 9$$

$$2\ {}^{1}3\ {}^{1}1\ {}^{1}1\ {}^{1}0\ 2$$

$\therefore$ **25678 × 9 = 231102**

{1} × {9} {9}

Note: Please see part-III below for multiplication by 9 in a different way. Also multiplication by 9s i.e. 99, 999, etc are explained.

(b) by 8: Rules

First Step: Subtract from 10 and double

Middle Steps: Subtract from 9, double and add the neighbour

Last Step: Reduce the left most digit of the multiplicand by 2

Example 2: 13121 x 8

$$\begin{array}{ccccc} 9 & 9 & 9 & 9 & 10 \\ \downarrow & \downarrow & \downarrow & \downarrow & \downarrow \\ 1 & 3 & 1 & 2 & 1 \end{array} \times 8$$

$$1^{2}0\ {}^{1}4\ {}^{1}9\ {}^{1}6\ {}^{1}8$$

$\therefore$ **13121 × 8 = 104968**

{8} {8} {1}

(c) by 4: Rules

1st Step: Subtract from 10, and add 5 if the number is odd

Middle Steps: Subtract from 9 and add ½ the neighbour, plus 5 if the number is odd.

Last Step: take ½ the left most digit of the multiplicand and reduce by 1.

Note: While halving odd numbers we ignore remainder as was done in ***Binary Multiplication***

Example 3(a): 40246x4

$$\frac{4\,0\,2\,4\,6 \times 4}{4}$$ → 4 is 6 from 10

$$\frac{4\,0\,2\,4\,6 \times 4}{8\,4}$$ → 8 is 4 from 9 plus half of 6

$$\frac{4\,0\,2\,4\,6 \times 4}{9\,8\,4}$$ → 9 is 2 from 9 plus half of 4

$$\frac{4\,0\,2\,4\,6 \times 4}{{}^{1}0\,9\,8\,4}$$ → 10 is 0 from 9 plus half of 2

$$\frac{4\,0\,2\,4\,6 \times 4}{6\,{}^{1}0\,9\,8\,4}$$ → 6 is 4 from 9 plus half of 0 plus carry 1

$$\frac{4\,0\,2\,4\,6 \times 4}{1\,6\,{}^{1}0\,9\,8\,4}$$ → 1 is half of 4 minus 1

∴ **40246 × 4 = 160984**

{7} × {4} {1}

Note: Need to add 5 did not arise in example 3(a), because all digits of 40246 are even. Now see example 3(b) below.

Example 3(b): 163581 x 4

$$\frac{1\,6\,3\,5\,8\,1 \times 4}{{}^{1}4}$$ → 14 is 1 from 10 plus 5 (since 1 being odd)

$$\frac{1\,6\,3\,5\,8\,1 \times 4}{2\,{}^{1}4}$$ → 2 is 8 from 9 plus half of 1 plus carry 1

$$\frac{1\,6\,3\,5\,8\,1 \times 4}{{}^{1}3\,2\,{}^{1}4}$$ → 13 is 5 from 9 plus 5 (5 being odd) plus half of 8

$$\frac{1\,6\,3\,5\,8\,1 \times 4}{{}^{1}4\,{}^{1}3\,2\,{}^{1}4}$$ → 14 is 3 from 9 plus 5 (3 being odd) plus half of 5 plus carry 1

$$\frac{1\,6\,3\,5\,8\,1 \times 4}{5\,{}^{1}4\,{}^{1}3\,2\,{}^{1}4}$$ → 5 is 6 from 9 plus half of 3 plus carry 1

$$\frac{1\,6\,3\,5\,8\,1 \times 4}{{}^{1}6\,5\,{}^{1}4\,{}^{1}3\,2\,{}^{1}4}$$ → 16 is 1 from 9 plus 5 (1 being odd) plus half of 6 plus carry 1

$$\begin{array}{r} 1\ 6\ 3\ 5\ 8\ 1 \times 4 \\ \hline 0\ {}^{1}6\ 5{}^{1}4\ {}^{1}3\ 2\ {}^{1}4 \end{array}$$ → 0 is half of 1 minus 1 plus carry1

∴ **163581 × 4 = 654324**

{6} × {4} {6}

Note: At odd numbers we have added 5 as per demand of the rule.

(d) by3: Rules

1st Step: Subtract from 10, double and add 5 if the number is odd

Middle Steps: Subtract from 9, double and add ½ the neighbour, plus 5 if the number is odd.

Last Step: take ½ the left most digit of the multiplicand and reduce by 2.

Example 4: 3147 × 3

$$\begin{array}{r} 3\ 1\ 4\ 7 \times 3 \\ \hline {}^{1}1 \end{array}$$ → 11 is 7 from 10, double plus 5 (7 being odd)

$$\begin{array}{r} 3\ 1\ 4\ 7 \times 3 \\ \hline {}^{1}4\ {}^{1}1 \end{array}$$ → 14is 4 from 9, double plus half of 7 plus carry1

$$\begin{array}{r} 3\ 1\ 4\ 7 \times 3 \\ \hline {}^{2}4{}^{1}4\ {}^{1}1 \end{array}$$ → 24 is 1 from 9, double plus 5 plus half of 4 plus carry 1

$$\begin{array}{r} 3\ 1\ 4\ 7 \times 3 \\ \hline {}^{1}9\ {}^{2}4\ {}^{1}4\ {}^{1}1 \end{array}$$ → 19 is 3 from 9, double plus 5 plus half of 1 plus carry 2

$$\begin{array}{r} 3\ 1\ 4\ 7 \times 3 \\ \hline 0\ {}^{1}9\ {}^{2}4\ {}^{1}4\ {}^{1}1 \end{array}$$ → 0 is half of 3 minus 2 plus carry1

∴ **3147 × 3 = 9441**

{6} × {3} {9}

Note: Trachtenberg evolved methods for multiplying by other numbers like, 5, 6, 7, 11 and 12; but it is not covered under this section as they don't follow the formula 'ALL from NINE and last from TEN' in any way.

Trachtenberg's Speed Method (Part-II)

We shall see now Trachtenberg's method of multiplication by – 11 and 12; as an offshoot of multiplication by 12 we shall see multiplication by 13 and 21.

I. by 11: **Rule**

One line rule: Add the neighbour

Example 5: 23145 × 11

$$\frac{0\,2\,3\,1\,4\,5 \times 11}{2\,5\,4\,5\,9\,5}$$

Note: Here a leading zero is placed to complete the multiplication

∴ **23145 × 11 = 254595** {6} × {2} = {3}

II. by 12: **Rule**

One line rule: Double the digit and add the neighbour.

Example 6: 456789 × 12

$$\frac{0\ 4\ 5\ 6\ 7\ 8\ \ 9 \times 12}{5\ {}^{1}4\ {}^{1}8\ {}^{2}1\ {}^{2}4\ {}^{2}6\ {}^{1}8}$$

∴ **456789 × 12 = 5481468**

{3} × {3} {9}

As an offshoot of multiplication by 12, we do the multiplication by 13 as well as 21 as explained below –

III. by 13: **Rule**

One line rule: Triple the digit and add the neighbour.

Example 7: 35609 × 13

$$\frac{0\ 3\ 5\ 6\ 0\ 9 \times 13}{4\ {}^{1}6\ {}^{2}2\ {}^{1}9\ {}^{1}1\ {}^{2}7}$$

∴ **35609 × 13 = 462917** {5} × {4} = {2}

IV. by 21: **Rule**

One line rule: Add double the neighbour

Example 8: **3241 × 21**

$$\frac{0\ 3\ 2\ 4\ 1 \times 21}{6\ 8^{1}0\ 6\ 1}$$

∴ **3241 × 21 = 68061**

{1} × {3} {3}

Part-III

A: Another method for multiplication by 9: -

Example 9(a): 2372 × 9

Ans: presume 0s (zeros) on either side of the multiplicand i.e. 023720.

Now starting from the first significant digit i.e. 2 – subtract each previous digit in turn – i.e.

$2 - 0 = 2$

$3 - 2 = 1$

$7 - 3 = 4$

$2 - 7 = -5 = \overline{5}$

$0 - 2 = -2 = \overline{2}$

$\therefore$ $2372 \times 9 = 214\overline{52} = 21348$

Note: $\overline{52}$ is –52 i.e. vinculum number and we know from **'Subtraction -3'** about vinculum.

Example 9(b): 94 × 9

Ans: $94 = 0940$

$9 - 0 = 9$

$4 - 9 = -5 = \overline{5}$

$0 - 4 = -4 = \overline{4}$

$\therefore 94 \times 9 = 9\overline{54} = 846.$

B: Multiplication by 9s i.e. by 99, 999, etc.

Example 10(a): 367 × 999

Ans: Here first the multiplicand, 367 is reduced by 1 i.e. 367 – 1 = 366; then the value of 'All from NINE ... of multiplicand is annexed to 366. All from NINE ... for 367 is 633;

$\therefore$ **367 × 999 = 366633** {7} × {9} = {9}

Example 10(b): 7861 × 99999

Ans: Here the multiplicand has 4 digits while the multiplier has 5 – 9s. So assume a leading zero to the multiplicand i.e. 7861 = 07861 and then follow the same procedure as explained in example 10(a) above. 07861 – 1 = 07860; and All from NINE ... of 07861 is 92139.

$\therefore$**7861 × 99999 = 786092139** {4} × {9} {9}

Note: This method will not be applicable if the number of 9s in the multiplier is less than the number of digits in the multiplicand.

□

11

Multiplication (Part-II)

Introduction

In this Lesson we shall see some simple methods to enhance our ability to multiply mentally. A little bit of practice will make you an expert and it may become a habit. The methods explained are –

- Doubling
- Breaking and doubling
- Halving
- Doubling, halving & splitting
- Squaring 2 digit numbers ending in 5
- Squaring Numbers between 50 to 59
- Multiplication of numbers whose last digits add upto 10 and their first digit is same
- Multiplication of numbers whose last digit are same and their first digits add upto 10.

Doubling

When we are to multiply by numbers like 4, 8, 16, etc. we can resort to doubling the multiplicand required number of times, as doubling is an easy process. So if we are to multiply a number by say 4, then we double the multiplicand twice (2 × 2 = 4) and for 8 we double the multiplicand thrice (2 × 2 × 2 = 8) and so on.

Example 1: 63 × 4

Ans: 63 x4: → we double 63 → 126 → double again → 252
{9} x{4} {9}

Note: The figures in curly brackets are DRs.

Example 2: 325 × 8

Ans: 325 × 8: 325 → 650 → 1300 → 2600
{1} × {8} {8}

Example 3: 26 × 16

Ans: 26 × 16: 26 → 52 → 104 → 208 → 416
{8} × {7} {2}

Example 4: 76 × 32

Ans: 76 × 32: 76 → 152 → 304 → 608 → 1216 → 2432
{4} × {5} {2}

Note: In the above examples DRs of multiplicand, multiplier, and the answer are shown for each number in curly brackets. Teachers/parents should constantly remind their students/wards to apply **DR** check in the class/in the examinations/in home works.

Breaking & Doubling

If we are to double, say 164, it can be mentally broken or split as 16 & 4 (16/4); then double of 16 → 32 and 4 → 8, hence 164 → 328. Similarly 243 can be split as 24 & 3 (or 2 & 43) to get 48 & 6 (or 4 &86) getting (either way) 486. In case of 164 we have not split as 1 & 64 since doubling 64 involves a carry to left. So this judicious breaking is effective and will be regularly used in further sums (wherever necessary).

Also multipliers like 40, 800, etc can be split as 4 x 10, 8 x 100; then double twice or thrice (for 4 or 8 respectively) and finally add required numbers of naught in the end.

Example 5: 14 × 40

Ans: 14 × 40 : 14 → 28 → 56 → 560
{5} × {4} {2}

Converting to Smaller Known Tables

If we are to multiply 16 by 14 – and if we are not good at table 16 and 14, then we may convert 16 × 14 as (2x8) and (2 × 7). Here we know that 8 × 7 = 56 and double 56 twice to get the desired result.

Example 6: 16 × 14

Ans: 16 × 14: 2 × 8 × 2 × 7 or 8 × 7 × 2 × 2 → 56 → 112 → 224

{7} × {5} {8}

Example 7: 28 × 16

Ans: 28 × 16: 2 × 2 × 7 × 2 × 2 × 2 × 2 → 7 → 14 → 28 → 56 → 112 → 224 → 448

{1} × {7} {7}

Checking:

In the above problem we have doubled 7 – 6 times. It may so happen that we may forget the number of times we have already doubled or the number of times still to double (when we tackle such problems mentally). In such cases we do two mental checks –

Check 1 - 28 × 16 ≅ 30 × 15 = 450. So our answer should hover around 450 (448 is near to 450)

Check 2 - 8 of 28 and 6 of 16 (unit digits) yield 48 as their product and hence the right most digit (unit digit) of the answer should be 8. (So is the case in our answer.)

Halving (with multipliers 5, 50, 25, etc)

As 5 is half of 10 and whenever we are to multiply by 5 – put a zero to the multiplicand (which equals to multiplying by 10) and then halve it once. Similarly while multiplying by 50 put two zeros to multiplicand (which amounts to multiplying by 100) and then halve it once. In case of multiplying by 25 put two zeros to multiplicand and then halve the result twice. Like the doubling seen in the previous section halving is also equally easy to work with. See examples 8 to 13below –

Example 8: 66 x 5

Ans: 66 x 5 → put a zero to 66 → 660 → half of 660 → 330

{3} x {5} {6}

Example 9: 87 x 5

Ans: 87 x 5 → put a zero to 87 → 870 → half of 870 → 435

{6} x {5} {3}

Example 10: 626 x 5

Ans: 626 × 5 → put a zero to 626 → 6260 → half → 3130
{5} × {5} {7}

Note: In example 9 and 10 above we mentally split the 10s products viz. 870 and 6260 as 8/70 and 62/60 (6/26/0) respectively and then wrote half of it as 4/35 and 31/30 (or 3/13/0) respectively.

Example 11: 29 × 50

Ans: 29 × 50 → put two zeros → 2900 → half → 1450
{2} × {5} {1}

Note: Here also we mentally break 2900 as 2/90/0 to get half of it as 1/45/0. We break in this fashion by bringing **even** numbers in each part, because halving **even** numbers is more preferable than **odd** numbers. Hence we split 2900 as 2/90/0 and not as 29/00 – as halving the **odd** number **29** creates a mental block because a 50 has to be carried over (after halving 29) to further right.

In case of multiplier 25, we add two zeros to multiplicand and halve twice as shown in example 12 & 13 below –

Example 12: 29 × 25

Ans: 29 × 25 → put two 00s → 2900 → half → 1450 → half → 725
{2} × {7} {5}
[Split 2900 as 2/90/0 and 1450 as 14/50]

Example 13: 82 × 25

Ans: 82 × 25 → put two 00s → 8200 → half → 4100 → half → 2050
{1} × {7} {7}
[Split 8200 as 82/00 (or 8/200) and 4100 as 4/10/0]

Doubling, Halving & Splitting (with multipliers ending in 5, 25, 75, etc)

We have seen multiplication by 5, 25, 50, etc. in the earlier section. Now we shall see multiplication by multipliers ending in 5 (such as 35, 45 ...), ending in 25 (such as 125, 225 ...), ending in 75 (such as 175, 275 ...). Here we may resort to doubling, halving, splitting, etc. as may be necessary.

Example 14: 46 × 45

Ans: 46 × 45 → here by halving the first & doubling the second we get 23 × 90.

So we arrive at multiplying by 9 and then annexing a zero. And this can be done either as shown in example 1 or example 9(a) of lesson 10.

46 × 45 →23 × 90 → 2070

{1} × {9} {5} × {9} {9}

Example 15: 44 × 15

Ans: 44 × 15 → 22 × 30 → 11 × 60 → 660

{8} × {6} {4} × {3} {2} × {6} {3}

Example 16: 124 × 125

Ans: 124 × 125 → 62 × 250 → 31 × 500 → put three 0s to 31 → 31000 → half → 15500

{7} × {8} {8} × {7} {4} × {5} {2}

Example 17: 448 × 175

Ans: 448 × 175 → 224 × 350 → 112 × 700 → 78400

{7} × {4} {8} × {8} {4}x{7} {1}

Note: In examples 14, 15, 16, and 17 the multiplicands were multiples of 2, 4 (as the case may be). Otherwise this method will not work.

Squaring Numbers ending in 5

Here we use the axiom – 'by one more than the one before' and this gives a simple way of multiplying a number (that ends in 5) by itself i.e. squaring a number that ends in 5.

Suppose 65 is to be multiplied by itself i.e. 65 is to be squared; hence one more the one before the number 5 i.e. 6 is 7; multiply 6 and 7 to get 42;and this is the left hand part of the answer and simply suffix 25 (being square of 5 – as the number ends in 5) to 42 and you have the answer.

Example 18: 65^2

Ans: 65^2→ 4225 → (42 is 6 × 7 and 25 is 5^2)

{2^2} {4}

Example 19: 25^2

Ans: $25^2 \rightarrow 625 \rightarrow$ (6 is 2 × 3 and 25 is 5^2)

{7^2} {4}

Example 20: 305^2

Ans: $305^2 \rightarrow 93025 \rightarrow$ (930 is 30 × 31 and 25 is 5^2)

{8^2} {1}

Example 21: $(8½)^2$

Ans: $(8½)^2 \rightarrow 8.5^2 \rightarrow 72.25 \rightarrow$ (72 is 8 × 9 and →25 is →5^2)

{4^2} {7}

Note: We can combine some of the methods explained above – such as splitting, doubling, halving, and one more than the one before.

Example 22: 35 × 175

Ans: 35 × 175 → 35 × (35 × 5) → 35^2 × 5 → 1225 × 5 →
→ 1225 × 10 → 12250
→ 12250 → half → 6125

{8} × {4} {5}

Example 23: 435^2

Ans: $435^2 \rightarrow 189225 \rightarrow$ (1892 is 43 x 44 and 25 is 5^2)

{3^2} {9}

Note: It is easier to multiply 43 by 44 rather than 435^2; this 43 x 44 can be done mentally by **VC-method** which is dealt with in lesson 14.

Squaring Numbers 50 to 59

These numbers begin in 5. The method followed is a corollary of the above method i.e. one more than the one before. Here square of the left i.e. 25 is added to the unit digit and thus we get the left part of the answer and to it the square of the unit digit is annexed to get the entire answer.

Example 24:

(i) $50^2 \rightarrow 2500 \rightarrow$ (25 is 5^2 + 00 and 00 is 0^2) {5^2} →{7}

(ii) $51^2 \rightarrow 2601 \rightarrow$ (26 is 5^2 + 1 and 01 is 1^2) {6^2} →{9}

(iii) $52^2 \rightarrow 2704 \rightarrow$ (27 is $5^2 + 2$ and 04 is 2^2) $\{7^2\} \rightarrow \{4\}$
(iv) $53^2 \rightarrow 2809 \rightarrow$ (28 is $5^2 + 3$ and 09 is 3^2) $\{8^2\} \rightarrow \{1\}$
(v) $54^2 \rightarrow 2916 \rightarrow$ (29 is $5^2 + 4$ and 16 is 4^2) $\{9^2\} \rightarrow \{9\}$
(vi) $55^2 \rightarrow 3025 \rightarrow$ (30 is $5^2 + 5$ and 25 is 5^2) $\{1^2\} \rightarrow \{1\}$
(vii) $56^2 \rightarrow 3136 \rightarrow$ (31 is $5^2 + 6$ and 36 is 6^2) $\{2^2\} \rightarrow \{4\}$
(viii) $57^2 \rightarrow 3249 \rightarrow$ (32 is $5^2 + 7$ and 49 is 7^2) $\{3^2\} \rightarrow \{9\}$
(ix) $58^2 \rightarrow 3364 \rightarrow$ (33 is $5^2 + 8$ and 64 is 8^2) $\{4^2\} \rightarrow \{7\}$
(x) $59^2 \rightarrow 3481 \rightarrow$ (34 is $5^2 + 9$ and 81 is 9^2) $\{5^2\} \rightarrow \{7\}$

Note:

1. Please note 00, 01, 04, 09 in (i), (ii), (iii), (iv) above
2. 55^2 can be done by earlier method i.e. one more than ...

Multiplication of numbers whose last digits add upto 10 and first digits are the same

This is also an upshot of squaring numbers ending in 5. In this case also the rule – one more than the one before – can be applied.

Example 25:

(1) $41 \times 49 \rightarrow 2009 \rightarrow$ (20 is 4×5 and 09 is 1×9)
$\{5\} \times \{4\}$ $\{2\}$ (note the 0 in the 09 above)

(2) $76 \times 74 \rightarrow 5624 \rightarrow$ (56 is 7×8 and 24 is 6×4)
$\{4\} \times \{2\}$ $\{8\}$

(3) $103 \times 107 \rightarrow 11021 \rightarrow$ (110 is 10×11 and 21 is 3×7)
$\{4\} \times \{8\}$ $\{5\}$

(4) $498 \times 402 \rightarrow 200196 \rightarrow$ (20 is 4×5 and 0196 is 98×2)
$\{3\} \times \{6\}$ $\{9\}$ (note the 0 in the 0196 above)

Note: In the above examples the first digits are same and the sum of the second digits works out to 10.

A slight extension of the above **by splitting** is –

(5) $93 \times 39 \rightarrow 3 \times (31 \times 39) \rightarrow 3 \times 1209 \rightarrow 3627$
$\{3\} \times \{3\}$ $\{3\}$

Multiplication of numbers whose last digits are same and first digits add upto 10

Here the rule is quite similar to squaring numbers between 50 to 59. In case of squaring numbers from 50 to 59 – we first squared the first number 5 and then added the last digit to get the left hand part of the answer; then suffixed the square of the last digit

Example 26:

(a) $37 \times 77 \rightarrow 2849 \rightarrow$ (28 is $3 \times 7 + 7$ and 49 is 7^2)
{1} × {5} {5}

(b) $89 \times 29 \rightarrow 2581 \rightarrow$ (25 is $8 \times 2 + 9$ and 81 is 9^2)
{8} × {2} {7}

(c) $912 \times 112 \rightarrow$ Here if we approximate these two numbers as 900x100, it yields 90000; hence it can be split as 090/000. With this logic –
$\therefore$ $912 \times 112 \rightarrow 102144 \rightarrow$ (102 is $9 \times 1 \times 10 + 12$ and 144 is 12^2)

(d) $822 \times 222 \rightarrow 182484 \rightarrow$ (182 is $8 \times 2 \times 10 + 22$ and 484 is 22^2)
{3}x {6} {9}

Mental Multiplication

The entire portion explained in the above seven pages deals with methods of mental multiplication only. However, most of them are special cases applicable to specific conditions.

As we have seen general mental multiplications of 2-digit and 3-digit multiplicands by single digit multiplier in the previous lesson, we shall see in this section general mental multiplication of 2-digit multiplicand by 2-digit multipliers. This can be tackled in the following ways -

a. Splitting the multiplicand or the multiplier in
   i. addition form i.e. splitting say 42 as 40 + 2 or
   ii. subtraction form i.e. splitting say 57 as 60 - 3
b. Factorising the multiplicand or multiplier suitably (if possible) i.e. splitting say 42 as 7 and 6 or 7, 3 and 2.

Example 27:

$$\begin{array}{rl} 37 & \\ \times\ 32 & (30 + 2) \\ \hline 1184 & (900 + 210 + 60 + 14) \end{array}$$

Here the multiplier 32 is split as 30 & 2 and the figures 900, 210, 60 and 14 shows that the multiplicand 37 is also split as 30 & 7. With practice the split and the intermediate multiplications will become natural, {DR check 1x5 = 5} Alternatively -

Example 27(a):

$$\begin{array}{rl} 37 & (40 - 2) \\ \times\ 32 & \\ \hline 1184 & (1280 - 96) \end{array}$$

Here the multiplicand is split as 40 & 3 and 32 x 40 is 1280 and instead of subtracting 96 (i.e. 32 x 3), subtract 100 and add 4.

Example 28:

$$\begin{array}{rl} 59 & \\ \times\ 81 & (80 + 1) \\ \hline 4779 & (4720 + 96) \end{array}$$

First multiply 80 x 59 as 4720 and add 59. Alternatively -

Example 28(a):

$$\begin{array}{rl} 59 & (60 - 1) \\ \times\ 81 & \\ \hline 4779 & (4860 - 1) \end{array}$$

81 x 60 is 4860 and subtract 100 and add 19.

In general in case of 2 by 2 multiplication if the units are small i.e. less than 5 then split in addition form i.e. 34 as 30 + 4 or 53 as 50 + 3, etc. If the units are larger than 5 than split in the subtraction form i.e. 67 as 70 -3 or 58 as 60 - 2, etc.

Mental Multiplication by Factorization:

This method bound to be easier because by factorizing a two-digit number we turn it two or more single digit numbers and just multiply the multiplicand with each single digit multiplier one after the other. In fact splitting the multiplier like 34 as 30 + 4 or 28 as 30 - 2 also equivalent to bringing the multiplier to single digits as the zero in the tens plays no major role in the process of multiplication. However, in splitting we have an additional addition or subtraction process is involved which is avoided in factorizing method. See examples below –

Example 29:

$$\begin{array}{r l} 52 & \\ \times\ 24 & (6 \times 4) \\ \hline 1248 & (52 \times 6) \times 4 \end{array}$$

It is alright to factorize 24 as 6 x 4; but I would prefer to factorize 24 as 2 x 2 x 2 x 3; the double 52 thrice (as explained in the beginning of the lesson - sec 3.1) to get mentally 416 and finally get 1248 by multiplying by 3.

Example 30:

$$\begin{array}{r l} 86 & \\ \times\ 28 & (7 \times 4) \text{ or } (2 \times 2 \times 7) \\ \hline 2408 & (52 \times 6) \times 4 \end{array}$$

Exercise: 1

a. 83 ×18	b. 72 ×17	c. 45 ×36	d. 27 ×14
e. 57 ×16	f. 85 ×42	g. 81 ×48	h. 48 × 37

You can solve multiplication sums in any way as long as you think creatively. However, you may try 2 by 2 or 3 by 3 or for that matter any digit-number by any-digit number using Vertically and Crosswise (VC) method which is explained in lesson 14 in elaborate detail.

□

12

Multiplication (Part-III)

Introduction

We are well acquainted of the formula – 'All from NINE' and the 'last from TEN'. We have shown this formula in earlier lesson of **'Subtraction – (Part-III)'** as well as in earlier lessons of this book. In the earlier lesson we have used for subtraction where the minuends are 10, 100, 1000, 10000, etc. It was also used for finding complement for 2 or more digit numbers;in case of converting vinculum numbers to non-vinculum, again this formula was used. In the earlier lesson we have also shown that Trachtenberg has used this formula slightly modified for multiplication by single digit numbers like 9, 8, 4, and 3.

We shall now see the easiest way to multiply numbers which are near to a base or multiple of base – using 'All from NINE ...' formula. For example we may find it difficult to multiply 988 x 987, because of the involvement of 7, 8s, and 9s. This lesson deals with methods to multiply both numbers which may be – below the base (both multiplicand and multiplier) or both above the base or one above and one below or near any intermediate base (i.e. sub-base).

Below Base

Example 1: Multiply 989 x 987

Procedure:

As said earlier both the multiplicand and multiplier are near its base i.e. 1000 and we first find its complements using 'All from NINE'

989 × 987

base 1000	number		complement
	989	–	011
	987	–	013

Step 1: The complement 011 and 013 are found using 'All from NINE'. As these numbers are less or deficient from it base 1000 (i.e. below base) the complements are connected by minus (–) sign.

Step 2: You may observe that if you cross subtract i.e. 989 – 013 or 987 – 011, you would get the same value i.e. 976 –

989 – 011

987 – 013

976 /

The above is true i.e. 989 – 013 = 987 – 011 as long as you work with a common base for both multiplicand and multiplier, in this case 1000. Now this common value is the left part of answer after multiplication [In the conventional multiplication we invariably multiply from right to left and the answer also emerges (digit by digit) from right to left – whereas we have half of the answer of the left part (976 in this case) and we are to only find the right half of the answer for which see step 3 below –

Step 3: Multiply the deficiencies (the complements i.e. 013 and 011) vertically and the outcome, 143 is the right part of answer.

989 – 011

987 – 013

976 / 143

∴ 989 × 987 = 976143

{8} × {6} {3}

Note: The DR checking is shown as usual in curly braces.

Example 2: Multiply 79 by 98

base 100

$$\begin{array}{r} 79 - 21 \\ \times \\ 98 - 02 \\ \hline 77 / 42 \\ \hline \end{array}$$

$\therefore 79 \times 98 = 7742$

{7} × {8} {2}

Explanation: The complements of 79 and 98 (found with – All from NINE) are 21 and 02 respectively. As these are deficient from the base (which is 100 in this case), the complements are connected with minus sign.

You would find that when you cross subtract (as shown by arrows) you would get the same result i.e. 79 – 02 = 98 – 21 = 77. This 77 is the left hand part of the answer. The right hand part of the answer can be found by simply multiplying the deficiencies i.e. 21 and 02 = 42.

$\therefore 79 \times 98 = 7742$

{7} × {8} {2}

Example 3:

(i) Multiply 88 by 96

$$\begin{array}{r} 88 - 12 \\ \times \\ 96 - 04 \\ \hline 84 / 48 \\ \hline \end{array}$$

$\therefore 88 \times 96 = 8448$

{7} × {6} {6}

(ii) Multiply 96 by 97

$$\begin{array}{r} 96 - 04 \\ \times \\ 97 - 03 \\ \hline 93 / 12 \\ \hline \end{array}$$

$\therefore 96 \times 97 = 9312$

{6} × {7} {6}

(iii) Multiply 99 × 97

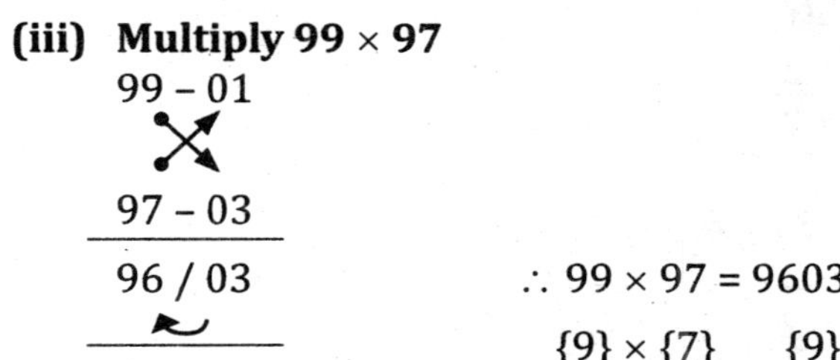

99 – 01

97 – 03

96 / 03

∴ 99 × 97 = 9603

{9} × {7} {9}

Note: In ex. 3(iii) above, note the 03 in the answer (i.e. the vertical product of deficiencies 01 & 03). As the working is with the base 100, two digits are needed on right hand part and hence 01 × 03 is taken as 03 and not merely 3.

Example 4: Multiply 88 by 89

88 – 12

89 – 11

77 / $_1$32 = 7832

∴ 88 × 89 = 7832

{7} × {8} {2}

Note: The deficiencies in ex. 4 above are 12 and 11 and their product yields to 132. The hundred of this 132 is carried to the left side as shown by (You may say that this note is sort of corollary of the note under ex. 3 (iii) above curved arrow.)

Even if only one of the numbers is near to base, we can use this method – see example 5 below –

Example 5: Multiply 568 by 998

568 – 432

998 – 002

566 / 864

∴ 568 × 998 = 566864

{1} × {8} {8}

This method woks very well for single digit numbers also

Example 6:

(a) Multiply 9 by 8

```
  9 – 1
  8 – 2
 -------
  7 / 2
 -------
```

(b) Multiply 8 by 8

```
  8 – 2
  8 – 2
 -------
  6 / 4
 -------
```

(c) Multiply 7 by 9

```
  7 – 3
  9 – 1
 -------
  6 / 3
 -------
```

In all the problems 1 to 6 above, the multiplicands as well as the multipliers were near a base but all of them were below the base i.e. they were deficient from its base; but cases where the multiplicands as well as the multipliers are excess of the base can also be envisaged as can be seen in examples 7 & 8 below -

4.2: Above Base:

Example 7: Multiply 103 by 104

```
  103 + 03
     ╳
  104 + 04
 ----------
  107 / 12
 ----------
```

$\therefore$ 103 × 104 = 10712
{4} × {5}   {2}

Explanation: The procedure is simple. Instead of deficiencies, we have excess over the base here and as such they are connected with '+' sign with multiplicand and multiplier. Also because of excess, they are cross-added (instead of cross-subtraction in ex. 1 to 6 above) to yield same left hand part of the answer i.e. 103 + 4 = 104 + 3 = 107. For right hand part as was done earlier we multiply the excess i.e. 03 × 04 = 12. Hence 103 × 104 = 10712.

Example 8:

(i) Multiply 12 by 13

$$\begin{array}{l} 12 + 2 \\ 13 + 3 \\ \hline 15 / 6 \\ \hline \end{array}$$

$\therefore$ 12 × 13 = 156
{3} × {4} {3}

(ii) Multiply 101 by 103

$$\begin{array}{l} 101 + 01 \\ 103 + 03 \\ \hline 104 / 03 \\ \hline \end{array}$$

$\therefore$ 101 × 103 = 10403 [**Note:** 03]
{2} × {4} {8}

(iii) Multiply 114 by 109

$$\begin{array}{l} 114 + 14 \\ 109 + 09 \\ \hline 123 / {}_{1}26 \\ \hline \end{array} = 12426$$

$\therefore$ 114 × 109 = 12426 [**Note:**$_1$26]
{6} × {1} {6}

One above & one below the base

Example 9: Multiply 122 by 99

$$\begin{array}{l} 122 + 22 \\ \times \\ 99 - 01 \\ \hline 121 / \overline{22} \\ \hline \end{array} = 12078$$

$\therefore$ 122 × 99 = 12078
{5} × {9} {9}

Explanation: Here the left hand part of the answer is found either cross-subtraction of 122 – 01 = 121 or by cross-addition of 99 + 22 = 121. However, for finding right hand part of the answer, we have to multiply algebraically the excess of the multiplicand and deficiency of the multiplier. Here 22 is excess or positive and 01 is deficient or negative. The vertical product will be negative and hence 22 x -1 is marked as $\overline{22}$ (i.e. with vinculum) in the right hand part of the answer.

So 122 x 99 = 121$\overline{22}$. Now from the lesson **'Subtraction 3'**, you already know how to deal with vinculum numbers. However this can be done as 12100 – 22 = 12078. [This subtraction can also be done mentally by applying **'All from NINE'** to –22 and reducing the 1 in hundred's place of $121\overline{22}$ to zero.

Example 10:

(a) Multiply 11 by 8

$$\begin{array}{l} 11 + 1 \\ \;\,8 - 2 \\ \hline 9 / \overline{2} \\ \hline \end{array} \qquad = 88 \qquad \therefore 11 \times 8 = 88$$

(b) Multiply 113 by 97

$$\begin{array}{l} 113 + 13 \\ \;\,97 - 03 \\ \hline 110 / \overline{39} \\ \hline \end{array} \qquad = 10961 \qquad \therefore 113 \times 97 = 10961$$

$$\{5\} \times \{7\} \quad \{8\}$$

(c) Multiply103 by 87

$$\begin{array}{l} 103 + 03 \\ \;\,87 - 13 \\ \hline 90 / \overline{39} \\ \hline \end{array} \qquad = 8961 \qquad \therefore 103 \times 87 = 8961$$

$$\{4\} \times \{6\} \quad \{6\}$$

(d) Multiply 10031 by 9997

$$\begin{array}{l} 10031 + 0031 \\ \;\,9997 - 0003 \\ \hline 10028 / \overline{0093} \\ \hline \end{array} \qquad = 100279907$$

$$\therefore 10031 \times 9997 = 100279907$$

$$\{5\} \times \{7\} \qquad \{8\}$$

Bases of different Powers

We may have numbers of different bases (difference in power like – multiplicand with base 10000 and multiplier of base 100) but each number being nearer to their respective bases. Such cases are dealt with as explained below –

Example 10: Multiply 9989 by 98

Procedure: In this problem the first number is near to base 10000 and the second nearer to base 100. The answer has to have four digits on the left part and two on the right part.

The deficiencies are 11 and 02 respectively from their respective bases. Here we only cross-subtract the deficiency of smaller number from the bigger number – but in the following way:

First take the bigger number as multiplicand and the smaller number as multiplier. Align the smaller number as left justified as shown below –

```
9989 – 11
98     – 02
-----------
9789 / 22
```

Now cross-subtract the deficiency of smaller number (here 98) from the digit just above the last digit of smaller number. In this case **02** is the deficiency of smaller number and the last digit of smaller number is 8. The digit just above this 8 is **9** (indicated by vertical small arrow). Subtract the **2** from this **9** to get **7**. So the left part of the answer is 9789 and the right part is found as usual by multiplying the deficiencies i.e. 11 and 02.

∴ **9989 × 98 = 978922**

{8} × {8}   {1}

It is worthwhile to note that the number of digits on the right hand part of the answer correspond to the base of smaller number (100 is base for smaller number, 98 in this case). The product of the deficiencies is also of 2 digits (i.e. 11 × 2) and hence 22 is fully accommodated on the right hand part of answer.

The logic of the above can be explained as below –

1. Take the larger number as it is i.e 9989
2. Multiply the smaller number i.e. 98 by 100 so that both numbers have equal digits (i.e. they have same base)
3. Now multiply 9989 and 9800 with a common base of 10000 as explained in ex. 1 to 5 above.

i.e.
```
9989 – 0011
9800 – 0200
-----------
9879 / 2200
```

4. Divide the answer 97892200 by 100 to nullify the effect of multiplying by 100 in step 2 above $9987 \times 98 = 978922$

Let us see two or more typical examples under this case –

Example 11: Multiply 10606 by 1004

$$\begin{array}{l} 10606 + 606 \\ \quad\uparrow \\ 1004 \quad + 004 \\ \hline 10646 /_{2} 424 \\ \hline \end{array} = 10648424 \qquad \therefore 10606 \times 1004 = 10648424$$

{4} × {5} {2}

Here we have excess over the base and hence the addition. Also the right hand part must correspond to the base of smaller number (smaller number 1004's base is 1000) and therefore the **2** of 2424 (the vertical multiplication of the excesses or the right hand part of the answer) is to be carried over to the left (shown by curved arrow) and added to 10646.

Alternatively – as was done in example 10 above bring both numbers to same base (by multiplying the smaller number by 10)

$$\begin{array}{l} 10606 + 0606 \\ \quad\uparrow \\ 10040 + 0040 \\ \hline 10646 /_{2} 4240 \\ \hline \end{array} = 106484240 \qquad \therefore \text{Dividing by 10}$$

= 10648424 (as before)

Example 12: Multiply 1132 by 97

1132 + 132

97 – 03

Here we first convert the smaller number to vinculum form i.e. 97 = 100 + 03. Now we proceed as below –

$$\begin{array}{l} 1\,1\,3\,2 + 1\,3\,2 \\ \quad\uparrow \\ 1\,0\,0 \quad + 0\,\bar{3} \\ \hline 1\,1\,0\,2 /_{\bar{3}}\, \bar{9}\bar{6} \\ 1\,1\,0\,\bar{1} / \bar{9}\bar{6} \\ \hline \end{array} = 109804 \qquad \therefore 1132 \times 97 = 109804$$

{7} × {7} {4}

Note: First we carried over $\bar{3}$ (in the right hand part of the answer) to left side (as the base for smaller number being 100 we cannot accommodate more than 2 digits and hence the carry over to left), and make 1102 of the left part to $110\bar{1}$. Now $\overline{196}$ in the right part is further complemented from 10000 to get 9804.

Example 13: Multiply 98 by 1017

$$1017 + 017$$
$$100 \quad + 0\bar{2}$$
$$1017 / \bar{3}\bar{4}$$
$$997 / \bar{3}\bar{4} \quad = 99666$$

$\therefore 98 \times 1017 = 99666$

$\{8\} \times \{9\} \qquad \{9\}$

Example 14: Multiply 102 by 10034

$$10034 + 34$$
$$102 \quad + 02$$
$$10234 / 68$$

$\therefore 102 \times 10034 = 1023468$

$\{3\} \times \{8\} \qquad \{6\}$

Example 15: Multiply 1007 by 95

$$1007 + 07$$
$$100 \quad + 0\bar{5}$$
$$1057 / \bar{3}\bar{5}$$
$$957 / \bar{3}\bar{5} \quad = 95665$$

$\therefore 1007 \times 95 = 95665$

$\{8\} \times \{5\} \qquad \{4\}$

At this stage all teachers/parents ought to understand that whatever is explained from examples 1 to 15 above are not magic but based on pure algebraic identity. Before we explain the algebra behind the procedures, let us see how the left hand part of the answer emerges in four different ways –

1. The difference between the sum of given numbers and the base will be left hand part of the answer.
   Ex: In $9 \times 7 \rightarrow 9+7-10 = 6$ is the LH part of $9 \times 7 = 63$.

2. The multiplicand minus the deficiency of the multiplier will be the LH part of the answer,
   Ex: In 9 × 7 → 9 is the multiplicand and the deficiency of multiplier i.e. 7 is 3. ∴ 9 – 3 = 6 is the LH part of 9×7=63.
3. The multiplier minus the deficiency of the multiplicand will be the LH part of the answer,
   Ex: In 9 × 7 → 7 is the multiplier and the deficiency of multiplicand i.e. 9 is 1. ∴ 7 – 1 = 6 is the LH part of 9×7=63
4. The difference between the base and the sum of deficiencies (of the multiplicand and the multiplier) also yields the LH part of the answer.
   Ex: In 9 × 7 → the base is 10 and the sum of deficiencies is 1+3=4. Hence 10 – 4 = 6,this is the LH part of multiplication in 9 × 7=63.

It is this fourth part that leads to the algebraic identity. i.e. $(x-a)(x-b) = x(x-a-b)+ab$; in case of 9 × 7 the deficiencies are 1 & 3 and 10(10-1-3)+ 1×3=63. Obviously X here is the base and a & b are deficiencies.

Exercises

Exercise 1: Multiply the following –

(a) 79 × 96 **(b)** 97 × 89 **(c)** 92 × 99
(d) 87 x 98 **(e)** 99 x 87 **(f)** 87 x 95

Exercise 2: Multiply the following –

1. 102 × 123 **2.** 15111 × 10003 **3.** 108 × 107
4. 1222 × 1003 **5.** 162 × 102 **6.** 1051 × 1007

Exercise 3: Multiply the following –

a. 568 × 998 **b.** 667 × 998 **c.** 768 × 997
d. 891 × 989 **e.** 8888 × 9996 **f.** 9876 × 9997
g. 90909 × 99994 **h.** 78989 × 99997
i. 883 × 998

Exercise 4: Multiply the following –

1. 96 × 102
2. 10003 × 9996
3. 108 × 92
4. 1222 × 999
5. 115 × 97
6. 103 × 87

Exercise 5: Multiply the following –

i. 97 × 993
ii. 92 × 989
iii. 9988 × 98
iv. 1122 × 104
v. 106 × 1012
vi. 9996 × 988
vii. 103 × 1015
viii. 10034 × 102

□

13

Multiplication (Part-IV)

Introduction

Numbers away from base

Suppose we wish to multiply 37 and 34. For this multiplication if we consider 10 as base then the excess over base are 27 and 24 respectively – which are not small figures to multiply mentally (for finding the RH part of the answer).

Example **Multiply 37 by 34**

With base 10

37 + 27

34 + 24

61 / → RH part is tedious to work mentally

Alternatively, if we choose 100 as base then the deficiencies are 63 and 66 respectively. Undoubtedly these two figures are also cumbrous to multiply and also the LH part yields **'negative'** result when cross- subtraction is done.

Example **Multiply 37 by 34**

With base 100

37 – 63

34 – 66

– 29 / → RH part is cumbrous to workout mentally

LH part is **'negative'**

In such cases we choose a working base **(WB)** nearer to the numbers to be multiplied, say 40 in this example, while the theoretical base **(TB)** will be 10. We proceed to find left hand (LH) part and right hand (RH) part as explained in earlier lesson and finally adjust only the LH part of the answer with the ratio of

$\frac{WB}{TB} = \frac{40}{10} = 4$ in this case.

Example 1: Multiply 37 by 34

$$WB = 40;\ TB = 10;\ \frac{WB}{TB} = 4$$

Explanation: Find the deficiencies as usual from the Working Base (WB) 40. Cross-subtract to get 31 as LH part and then vertically multiply to get 18 as RH part.

$$\begin{array}{l} 37 - 3 \\ 34 - 6 \\ \hline 31 \,/\, {}_{1}8 \\ \times 4 \\ \hline 124 \,/\, {}_{1}8 \\ \hline 125/8 \\ \hline \end{array}$$

Now because our WB is 40, which is 4 times the theoretical base (TB) 10, multiply the LH part 31 by 4 to get 124.

$$\therefore 37 \times 34 = 1258$$
$$\{1\} \times \{7\} \quad \{7\}$$

Since our TB is 10, we cannot accommodate more than one digit on the RH part of the answer and hence carry 1 of 18 to the LH side to get 125.

The final answer is 37 × 34 = 1258

Note: The DR check is shown as usual in curly braces.

We can do the same example considering WB as 30 (Ex.2)

Example 2: Multiply 37 by 34

$$WB = 30;\ TB = 10;\ \frac{WB}{TB} = 3$$

Here the LH of the answer is multiplied by 3 (as the ratio of WB/TB is 3). From RH part,2 of the 28 is carried to left side to get the same answer i.e. 1258.

$$\begin{array}{l} 37 + 7 \\ 34 + 4 \\ \hline 41 / {}_{2}8 \\ \times 3 \\ \hline 123/{}_{2}8 \\ \hline 1258 \\ \hline \end{array}$$

(same as before)

Example 3: Multiply 72 by 58

$$WB = 60;\ TB = 10;\ \frac{WB}{TB}$$

$$\begin{array}{l} 72 + 12 \\ 58 - \ \ 2 \\ \hline 70 / \ - \overline{\ } \\ \times 6 \\ \hline 420/ {}_{\bar{2}}\overline{4} \\ \hline 42\overline{2}\,\overline{4} \\ \hline \end{array} \quad = 4176$$

$\therefore$ **72 × 58 = 4176**

{9} × {4} {9}

Since WB is 6 times the TB, the LH part is multiplied by 6

Note: It will be interesting to know as to how this problem will work, if the theoretical base is 100 as against 10 and working base being the same i.e. 60 (see ex. 4 below) –

Example 4: Multiply 72 by 58

$$WB = 60;\ TB = 100;\ \frac{WB}{TB} = 0.6$$

Since WB is 0.6 times the TB, the LH part is multiplied by 0.6

$$\begin{array}{l} 72 + 12 \\ 58 - \ 2 \\ \hline 70 / \ \bar{2}\,\bar{4} \\ \times 0.6 \\ \hline 42/\bar{2}\,\bar{4} \\ 42\ \bar{2}\,\bar{4} \\ \hline \end{array} \qquad = 4176$$

Example 5: Multiply 478 by 512

$$\text{WB} = 500;\ \text{TB} = 100;\ \frac{WB}{TB} = 5$$

$$\begin{array}{l} 478 - 22 \\ 512 + 12 \\ \hline 490 / {}_{\bar{2}}\overline{64} \\ \times 5 \\ \hline 2450 / {}_{\bar{2}}\overline{64} \\ \\ 2452/{}_{\bar{2}}\overline{64} \\ \hline \end{array} \qquad = 244736 \qquad \therefore \mathbf{478 \times 512 = 244736}$$

$\{1\} \times \{8\} \qquad \{8\}$

The above problem can be tackled with 1000 as TB (see ex. 6 below) –

Example 6: Multiply 478 by 512

$$\text{WB} = 500;\ \text{TB} = 1000;\ \frac{WB}{TB} = 0.5$$

$$\begin{array}{l} 478 - 22 \\ 512 + 12 \\ \hline 490 / \overline{264} \\ \times 0.5 \\ \hline 245 / \overline{264} \\ \hline 245 / \overline{264} \\ \hline \end{array} \qquad = 244736$$

Example 7: Multiply 586 by 641

$$WB = 600;\ TB = 100;\ \frac{WB}{TB} = 6$$

$$\begin{array}{l} 586 - 14 \\ \underline{641 + 41} \\ 627 \,/\, {}_{\bar{5}}\overline{74} \\ \underline{\times 6} \\ 3762 \,/\, {}_{\bar{5}}\overline{74} \\ \hline 3757 / \overline{74} \end{array}$$

$= 375626 \;\therefore$ **586 × 641 = 375626**
{1} × {2} {2}

Multiplication with different bases

In **Multiplication-03,** this aspect was dealt from ex. 10 to 15. This is again dealt in a slightly different way. Readers may assimilate the difference with a careful study –

Example 8: Multiply 989 by 109

Here 989 is near base 1000 and 109 is near 100. We, hence multiply 109 by 9 to get 981; now both 989 and 981 are near 1000 and we can multiply as already explained in ex. 10 to 15 of lesson 12.

$$\begin{array}{l} 989 - 011 \\ \underline{981 - 019} \\ \underline{970 \,/\, 209} \end{array}$$

Now we have to re-adjust 970209 by dividing (the entire number) by 9 to get 107801. $\therefore$ **989 × 109 = 107801**
{8} × {1} {8}

Alternatively 109 in the above problem can be multiplied by 10 (see ex. 9 below) –

Example 9: Multiply 989 by 109

$$\begin{array}{ll} & 989 - 011 \\ 109\text{x}10 \rightarrow & \underline{1090 + 090} \\ & 1079 \,/\, \overline{990} \quad = 1078010 \end{array}$$

Dividing by 10 we get 107801 (same as before)

Example 10: Multiply 1006 by 98

$$\begin{array}{lr} & 1006 + 006 \\ 98\text{x}10 \rightarrow & 980 - 020 \\ \hline & 986 / \bar{1}\,\bar{2}\,0 \\ \hline \end{array} \rightarrow 985880 \div 10 = 98588$$

$\therefore$ **1006 × 98 = 98588**

{7} × {8} {2}

Example 11: Multiply 341 × 502

Here if we multiply – 341 by 3 and 502 by 2 we get 1023 and 1004 respectively; then 1023 and 1004 being near to 1000 – we multiply in the normal way –

$$\begin{array}{lcr} 341 \times 3 & \rightarrow & 1023 + 023 \\ 502 \times 2 & \rightarrow & 1004 + 004 \\ \hline & & 1027 / 092 \\ \hline \end{array}$$

To bring the multiplicand and multiplier near to base 1000 we multiplied by 3 and 2 respectively; hence we divide the above answer by

3x2 i.e. 6 → 1027092 ÷ 6 = 171182

$\therefore$ **341 × 502 = 171182**

{8} × {7} {2}

Multiplication of 3 or more numbers

Example 12: Multiply 7 × 9 × 8

All the numbers are near to base 10 –

Step 1: Write the numbers with their respective deficiency from 10

7 – 3
9 – 1
8 – 2

Step 2: Multiply all the deficiency algebraically

i.e. –3 × –1 × –2 = –6

$$\begin{array}{r} 7 - 3 \\ 9 - 1 \\ 8 - 2 \\ \hline / \bar{6} \\ \hline \end{array}$$

Step 3: Multiply deficiencies cyclically
i.e. –3x–1 + –1x–2 + –2x–3 = 11

7 – 3
9 – 1
8 – 2

$/ 11 / \bar{6}$

Step 4: Then from any one number subtract the deficiencies of other two numbers i.e.
7–1–2 or 9–3–2 or 8–3–1 = 4

7 – 3
9 – 1
8 – 2

$4 / {}_{1}1 / \bar{6}$

$5 / 1 / \bar{6}$ = 504

Explanation:

1. Find right most digit of the answer by multiplying the deficiencies i.e. If x, y, z are the numbers and a, b, c are deficiencies from base, then abc is the right most digit of the answer.
2. Then a x b + b x c + c x a will be middle part of the answer.
3. Then from any one number subtract sum of deficiencies of the other two numbers to get the left most digit of the answer –
   i.e. x–(b+c) = y–(c+a) = z–(a+b) = left most part

Example 13: 96 x 98 x 97

96 – 04 | 1. -04 × -02 × -03 = -24 = $\bar{2}\,\bar{4}$
98 – 02 | 2. 4 × 2 + 2 × 3 + 3 × 4 = 26
97 – 03 | 3. 96 – (2+3) = 98 – (4+3) = 97 – (4+2) = 91

$91 / 26 / \bar{2}\,\bar{4}$ → 912576

∴ **96 × 98 × 97 = 912576**
{6} × {8} × {7} {3}

Example 14: **111 × 102 × 103**

111 + 11 | 11x2x3 = 66

103 + 03 | 11x2 + 2x3 + 3x11 = 61

102 + 02 | 111 + (3+2) = 103 + (11+2) = 102 + (11+3) = 116

116 / 61 / 66 → 1166166

∴ 111 × 103 × 102 = 1166166

{3} × {4} × {3} {9}

Example 15: **992 × 995 × 998 × 1002**

992 – 008 | $\bar{8} \times \bar{5} \times \bar{2} \times 2 = \bar{1}\,\bar{6}\,0$

995 – 005 | $\bar{8} \times \bar{5} \times \bar{2} + \bar{8} \times \bar{5} \times 2 + \bar{8} \times \bar{2} \times 2 + \bar{5} \times \bar{2} \times 2 = 52$

998 – 002 | $\bar{8} \times \bar{5} \times \bar{2} + \bar{8} \times 2 + \bar{8} \times 2 + \bar{8} \times \bar{2} + \bar{5} \times 2 = 36$

1002 +002 | 992 – (5+2–2) = 995 – (8+2-2) = 998 – (8+5–2) = 987

987/036/052/$\bar{1}\,\bar{6}\,0$

∴ 992 × 995 × 998 × 1002 = 987036051840

{2} × {5} × {8} × {3} {6}

Exercises

Exercise 1:

a. 26 × 29 **b.** 71 × 79 **c.** 63 × 59

d. 378 × 412 **e.** 486 × 541 **f.** 52 × 48

Exercise 2:

1. 996 × 112 **2.** 302 × 503

Exercise 3:

i. 11 × 12 × 14 **ii.** 1001 × 1012 × 1008 × 1002

□

14

Multiplication (Part-V)

Introduction

VC-Method

Vertically and Crosswise (VC) method is the most generalized method of multiplying any number of any digits by another number which again could be of any number of digits; and the whole process of multiplication can be accomplished in a single line and that too mentally. This method can be applied to multiplication from right to left (as we usually do) or from left to right. However, we shall do the multiplication from right to left i.e. in the conventional way. Lets first start with 2–digit numbers –

2–Digit Numbers

Let the two digit multiplicand and multiplier be **ab** and **cd.** The steps involved in VC method are as follows –

(1) In the **first step** we multiply b & d directly i.e. vertically as do in normal multiplication.
i.e. b × d = bd

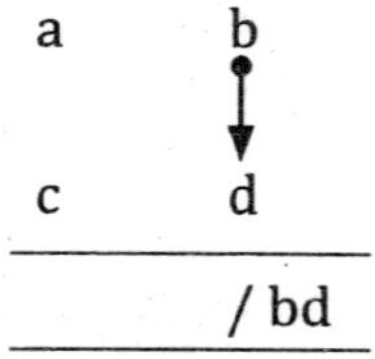

```
a      b
       │
       ▼
c      d
──────────
      / bd
──────────
```

(2) In the **second step** we multiply crosswise; axd and bxc and then add up to get (ad + bc)

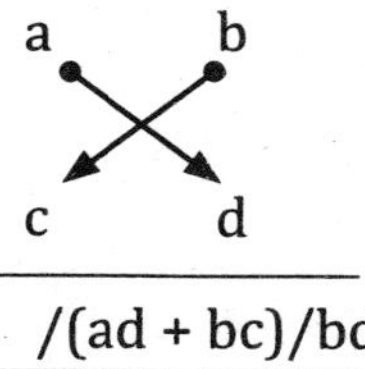

(3) In the **last step** we multiply again a × c directly i.e. a × c

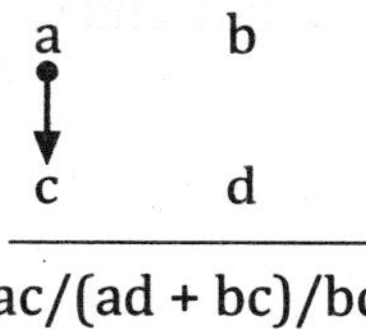

Thus we complete the entire multiplication in one line and can do this mentally.

Example 1: Multiply 76 × 37

Step 1: 7 × 6 = 42; put down 2 and carry 4

7 6
3 7

$/^{4}2$

Step 2: 7x7 + 6x3 = 67 + 4(carry) = 71; take 1 and carry 7

7 6
3 7

$/^{7}1/^{4}2$

Step 3: 7 × 3 = 21 + 7 (carry) = 28

7 6
3 7

$28/^{7}1/^{4}2$ $\quad \therefore$ 76 × 37 = 2812

{4} × {1} {4}

Note: DR check is shown in curly brackets

Example 2: Multiply 89 × 26

Step 1: 9 × 6 = 54; take 4 and carry 5

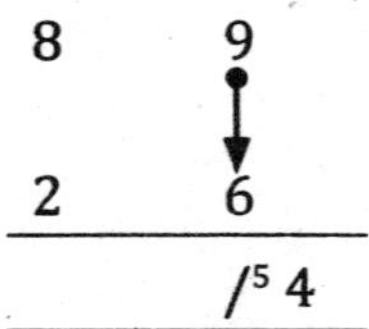

Step 2: 8x6 + 9x2 = 66+5(carry) = 71; take 1 and carry 7

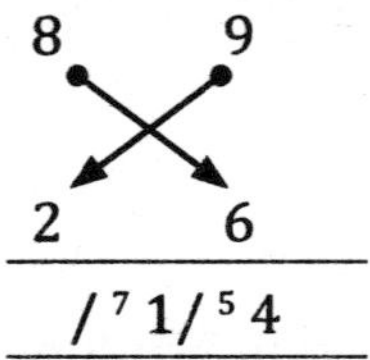

Step 3: 8 × 2 = 16 + 7 (carry) = 23

8 9

2 6

23/ ^{7}1 / ^{5}4 ∴ 89 × 26 = 2314

{8} × {8} {1}

Example 3: Multiply 58 × 27

Step 1: 8 × 7 = 56; take 6 and carry 5

Step 2: 5x7 + 8x2 = 51+5(carry) = 56; take 6 and carry 5

Step 3: 5 × 2 = 10 + carry 5

5 8

2 7

15/ ^{5}6/ ^{5}6 ∴ 58 × 27 = 1566

{4} × {9} {9}

3-Digit Numbers

Let the three-digit numbers be **abc** and **def**. The steps involved in **VC** method are as follows –

Step 1: In the first step we multiply c &f directly i.e. vertically as do in normal multiplication

i.e. c × f = cf

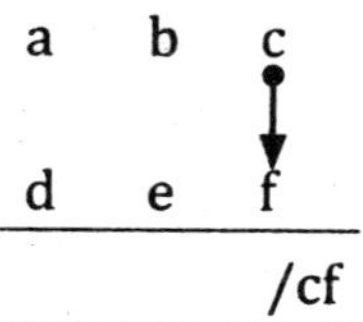

Step 2: Crosswise on the right side i.e. b × f + c × e

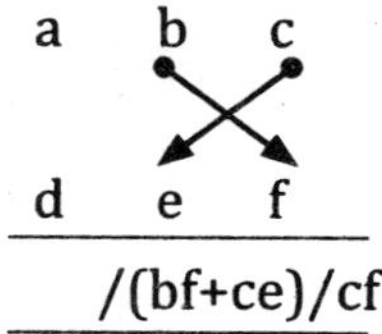

Step 3: crosswise i.e. a × f + vertically i.e.
b × e + crosswise i.e. c × d
i.e. af + be + cd

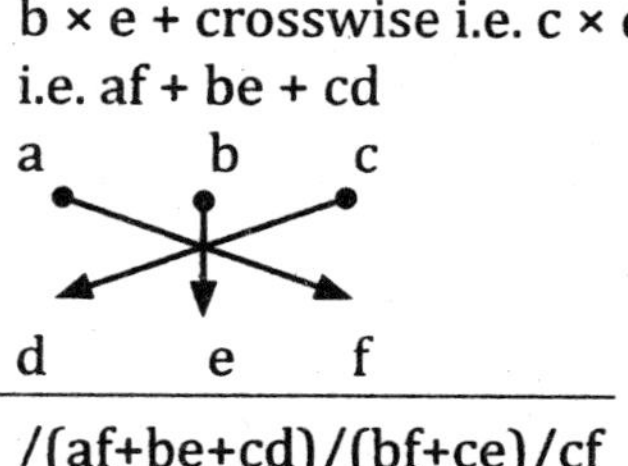

Step 4: Crosswise on the left side i.e. a × e + b × d i.e ae + bd

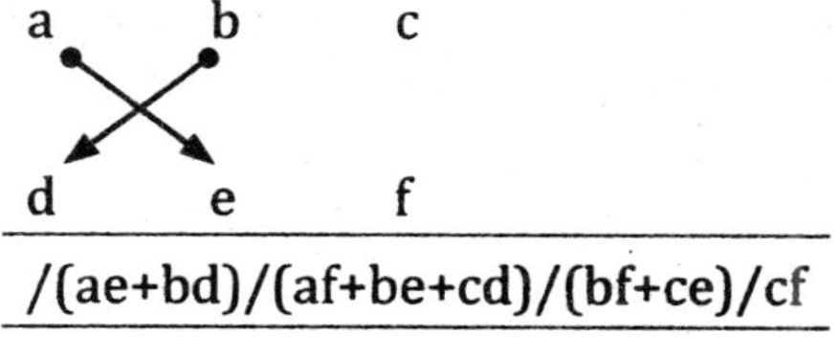

Step 5:vertically on the left i.e. a × d

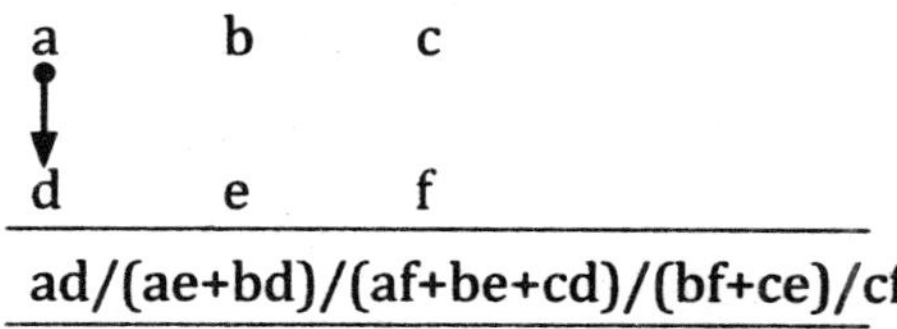

The above five steps are illustrated in ex. 4 below –

Example 4: Multiply 372 by 879

Step 1: vertically $2 \times 9 = 18$; take 8 and carry 1

3 7 2

8 7 9

$^{1}8$

Step 2: crosswise on the right side i.e. $7 \times 9 + 2 \times 7 = 77 + 1$ (carry in step 1) $= 78$; take 8 and carry 7

3 7 2

8 7 9

$^{7}8\ ^{1}8$

Step 3: crosswise, vertically and crosswise i.e. $3 \times 9 + 7 \times 7 + 2 \times 8 = 92 + 7$ (carry in step 2) $= 99$; take 9 and carry 9

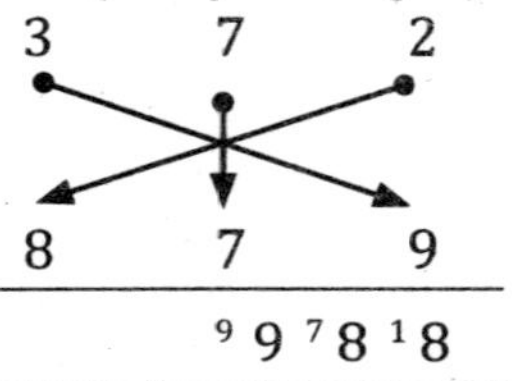

Step 4: crosswise on the left side i.e. $3 \times 7 + 7 \times 8 = 77 + 9$ (carry from step 3) $= 86$; take 6 and carry 8

3 7 2

8 7 9

$^{8}6\ ^{9}9\ ^{7}8\ ^{1}8$

Step 5: vertically on the left $3 \times 8 = 24 + 8$ (carry in step 4) $= 32$

3 7 2

8 7 9

$32\ ^{8}6\ ^{9}9\ ^{7}8\ ^{1}8 \quad \therefore 372 \times 879 = 326988$

$\{3\} \times \{6\} \quad \{9\}$

Example 5: Multiply 909 by 97

Note: First we add a leading zero to the multiplier to match the digits in the multiplicand

9	0	9
0	9	7

$8\ {}^{8}8\ {}^{7}1\ {}^{8}7\ {}^{6}3$

Step 1: 9 × 7 =63; take 3 and carry 6

Step 2: 0 × 7 + 9 × 9 = 81 + 6 (carry in step 1) = 87; take 7 and carry 8

Step 3: 9 × 7 + 0 × 9 + 9 × 0 = 63 + 8 (carry in step 2) = 71; take 1 and carry 7

Step 4: 9 × 9 + 0 × 0 = 81 + 7 (carry in step 3) = 88; take 8 carry 8

Step 5: 9 × 0 = 0 + 8 (carry from step 4) = 8

∴ 909 × 97 = 88173

{9} × {7} {9}

Note: You may find a different approach for shorter multiplier (known as shifting multiplication) see ex. 8 below.

4-Digit Numbers

Step 1: vertically on the right → d × h and

Step 2: crosswise on right → c × h + d × g

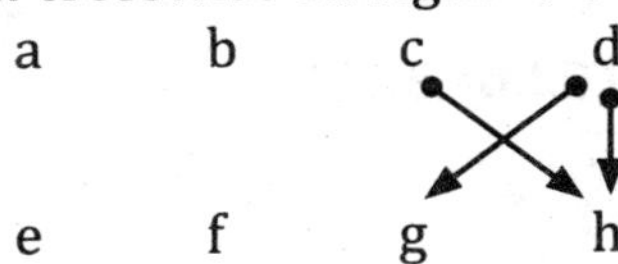

Step 3: crosswise, vertically, and crosswise on the right i.e. bh + cg + df

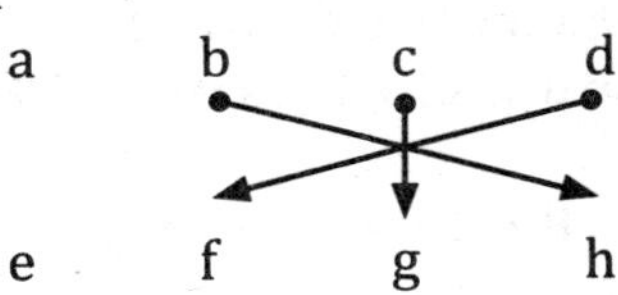

Step 4: crosswise using all digits

i.e. a × h + b × g + c × f + d × e

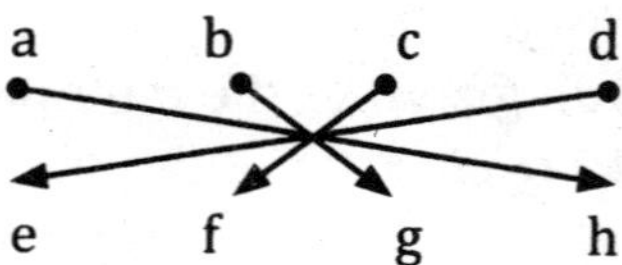

Step 5: same as step 3 but on the left side

i.e. a × g + b × f + c × e

a b c d

e f g h

Step 6: same as step 2 but on the left side

i.e. a × f + b × e and

Step 7: vertically on the left i.e. a × e

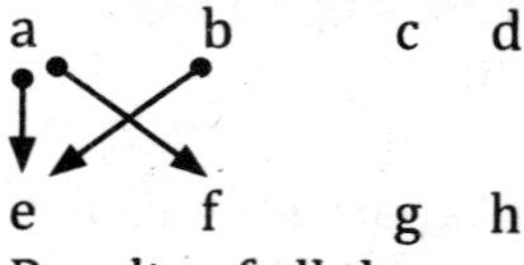

Results of all the seven steps are shown below –

a	b	c	d
e	f	g	h

ae/(af+be)/(ag+bf+ce)/(ah+bg+cf+de)/(bh+cg+df)/(ch+dg)/dh

Example 6: Multiply 3152 by 3871

$$\begin{array}{r} 3\ 1\ 5\ 2 \\ 3\ 8\ 7\ 1 \\ \hline 12\ {}^{3}2\ {}^{5}0\ {}^{6}1\ {}^{5}3\ {}^{1}9\ 2 \\ \hline \end{array}$$

Step 1: 2 × 1 = 2; take 2

Step 2: 5 × 1 + 2 × 7 = 19; take 9 and carry 1

Step 3: 1 × 1 + 5 × 7 + 2 × 8 = 52 + 1 (carry) = 53; take 3 and carry 5

Step 4: 3 × 1 + 1 × 7 + 5 × 8 + 2 × 3 = 56 + 5 (carry) =61; take 1 and carry 6

Step 5: 3 × 7 + 1 × 8 + 5 × 3 = 44 + 6 (carry) = 50; take 0 and carry 5

Step 6: 3 × 8 + 1 × 3 = 27 + 5 (carry) = 32; take 2 and carry 3

Step 7: 3 × 3 = 9 + 3 (carry) = 12

Example 7: Multiply 9326 by 37

Note: ***First add two leading zeros to multiplier.***

$$\begin{array}{r} 9\ 3\ 2\ 6 \\ 0\ 0\ 3\ 7 \\ \hline 0\ 3\ {}^{3}4\ {}^{7}5\ {}^{3}0\ {}^{3}6\ {}^{4}2 \\ \hline \end{array}$$

Step 1: 6 × 7 = 42; take 2 and carry 4

Step 2: 2 × 7 + 6 × 3 = 32 + 4 (carry) = 36; take 6 carry 3

Step 3: 3 × 7 + 2 × 3 + 6 × 0 = 27 + 3 (carry) = 30; take 0 and carry 3

Step 4: 9 × 7 + 3 × 3 + 2 × 0 + 6 × 0 = 72 + 3 (carry) = 75; take 5 and carry 7

Step 5: 9 × 3 + 3 × 0 + 2 × 0= 27 + 7 (carry) = 34; take 4 and carry 3

Step 6: 9 × 0 + 3 × 0 = 0 + 3 (carry) = 3

Step 7: 9 × 0 = 0

∴ **3152 × 3871 = 12201392**

{2} × {1} {2}

9326 × 37 = 345062

{2} × {1} {2}

Note: If we carefully observe from **Step 3** above, we realise that the two digit multiplier is shifted towards left step by step. Let us do the sum again by actually shifting the multiplier.

Example 8: Multiply 9326 × 37

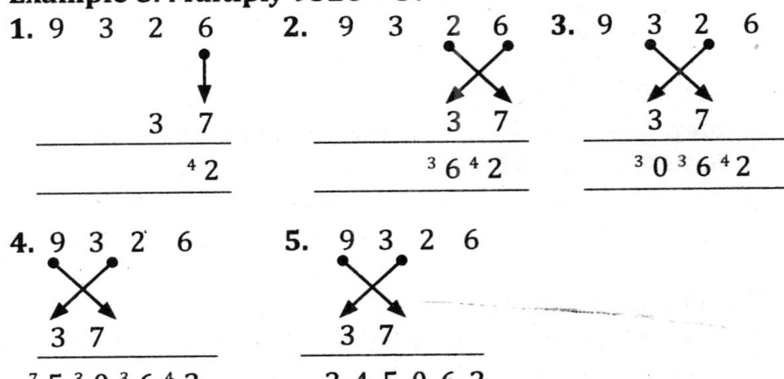

Note:

1. From the above one can see that normally a 4 digit by 4 digit multiplication is done on 7 steps. Example 8 above seems to have been done in 5 steps. Kindly observe the fallacy.
2. Also the number of steps in any n-digit by n-digit multiplication is predetermined by the formula → No. of steps = 2n – 1. And a general formula for multiplying m-digit by n-digit is → No. of steps = m+n-1

Example 9: Multiply 84621 by 321

$$\begin{array}{r} 8\ 4\ 6\ 2\ 1 \\ 3\ 2\ 1 \\ \hline {}^{1}3\ 4\ 1 \\ \hline \end{array}$$

Step 1: 1 × 1 = 1; take 1
Step 2: 2 × 1 + 1 × 2 = 4
Step 3: 6 × 1 + 2 × 2 + 1 × 3 = 13; take 3 carry 1

$$\begin{array}{r} 8\ 4\ 6\ 2\ 1 \\ 3\ 2\ 1 \\ \hline {}^{2}3\ {}^{1}3\ 4\ 1 \\ \hline \end{array}$$

Step 4: 4 × 1 + 6 × 2 + 2 × 3 + 1(carry) = 23; take 3 carry 2

$$\begin{array}{r} 8\ 4\ 6\ 2\ 1 \\ 3\ 2\ 1 \\ \hline 27\ {}^{3}1{}^{3}6{}^{2}3{}^{1}3\ 4\ 1 \\ \hline \end{array}$$

Step 5: 8 × 1 + 4 × 2 + 6 × 3 + 2(carry) = 36; take 6 carry 3
Step 6: 8 × 2 + 4 × 3 + 3(carry) = 31; take 1 carry 3
Step 7: 8 × 3 + 3 (carry) = 27

∴ 84621 × 321 = 27163341
{3} × {6} {9}

VC-Method using Vinculum

We can use vinculum numbers in the VC method – which makes the larger digits like 7, 8, 9 to smaller digits.

Example 10: Multiply 19 by 24

$$
\begin{array}{r}
19 \rightarrow 2\,\bar{1} \\
24 \rightarrow 2\,4 \\
\hline
4\,6\,\bar{4} \\
\hline
= 456
\end{array}
\qquad \therefore\ 19 \times 24 = 456
$$

$$\{1\} \times \{6\} = \{6\}$$

Step 1: $\bar{1} \times 4 = \bar{4}$; take $\bar{4}$

Step 2: $2 \times 4 + \bar{1} \times 2 = 8 - 2 = 6$; take 6

Step 3: $2 \times 2 = 4$

Example 11: Multiply 29 by 24

$$
\begin{array}{r}
29 \rightarrow 3\,\bar{1} \\
24 \rightarrow 2\,4 \\
\hline
7\,^{1}0\,\bar{4} \\
\hline
= 696
\end{array}
\qquad \therefore\ 29 \times 24 = 696
$$

$$\{2\} \times \{6\} \quad \{3\}$$

Step 1: $\bar{1} \times 4 = \bar{4}$; take $\bar{4}$

Step 2: $3 \times 4 + \bar{1} \times 2 = 12 - 2 = 10$; take 0 and carry 1

Step 3: $3 \times 2 + 1$ (carry) $= 7$

Example 12: Multiply 39 by 58

$$
\begin{array}{r}
39 \rightarrow 4\,\bar{1} \\
58 \rightarrow 6\,\bar{2} \\
\hline
23\,^{\bar{1}}\bar{4}\;\;2 \\
\hline
= 2262
\end{array}
\qquad \therefore\ 39 \times 58 = 2262
$$

$$\{3\} \times \{4\} \quad \{3\}$$

Step 1: $\bar{1} \times \bar{2} = 2$; take 2

Step 2: $4 \times \bar{2} + \bar{\ } \times 6 = \overline{14}$; take $\bar{4}$ and carry $\bar{1}$

Step 3: $6 \times 4 + \bar{1}$ (carry) $= 24 - 1 = 23$

3 & 4 Digit Numbers as 2-digits

Example 13: Multiply 113 by 112

Note: This can be treated as 3 digit number as explained in sec 5.2 or alternatively it can be split as 11/3 and 11/2 respectively and then treat this 2-digit numbers as shown in sec 5.1

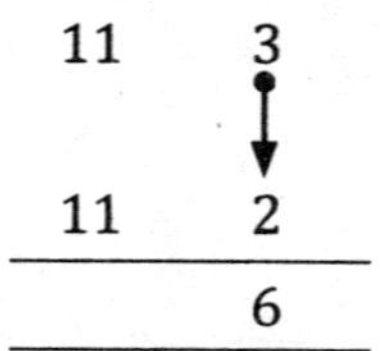

Step 1: 3 × 2 = 6; take 6

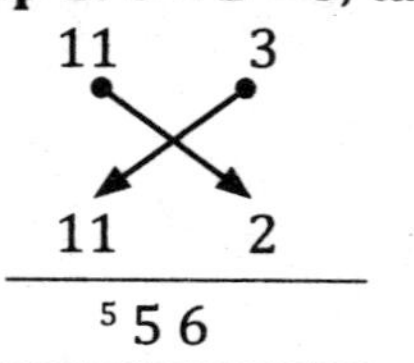

Step 2: 11 × 2 + 11 × 3 = 55; take 5 and carry 5

11 3

↓

11 2

126 ^{5}5 6

∴ 113 × 112 = 12656

{5} × {4} {2}

Step 3: 11 × 11 = 121 + 5 carry = 126

Note: After splitting if we have single digit on the right hand part of split, then we can accommodate only single digit in step 1 & step 2 (observe this in the above example)

Example 14: Multiply 1102 by 1211

Note: This can be split as 11/02 and 12/11 respectively and then treated as 2-digit multiplication

11 02

↓

12 11

/22

Step 1: 02 × 11 = 22; take 22

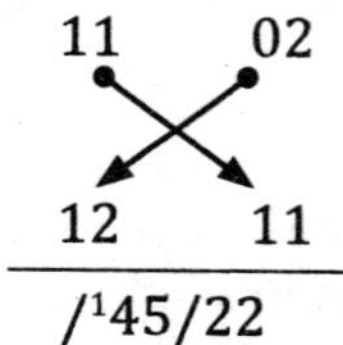

Step 2: 11 × 11 + 02 × 12 = 145; take 45 and carry 1

```
11      02
 |
 ↓
12      11
---------------
133/¹45/22
---------------
```

∴ 1102 × 1211 = 1334522
{4} × {5} {2}

Step 3: 11 × 12 + 1 (carry) = 133

Note: After splitting we have 2-digit on the right side and hence we have accommodated 2-digits in step 1 and step 2 (please observe this point in above example)

Example 15: Multiply 311 by 1101

```
03 11
11 01
---------------
34¹2411
---------------
```

∴ 311 × 1101 = 342411
{5} × {3} {6}

Step 1: 11 × 01 = 11; take 11

Step 2: 03 × 01 + 11 × 11 = 124; take 24 and carry 1

Step 3: 03 × 11 + 1 = 34

Multiplication & Addition/Subtraction

Multiplication, addition and/or subtraction can be done simultaneously by vertically and crosswise method. See example 16 below –

Example 16: Evaluate (33 × 46) + (26 × 29) – (51 × 13)

Procedure:

```
          33        26        51
               +         –
          46        29        13
---------------------------------------------
(3x4 + 2x2 – 5x1)/[(3x6+3x4) +
                    (2x9+6x2) – (5x1+1x1)]/
                                (3x6 + 6x9 – 1x3)
11          /         44        /69
---------------------------------------------
```

$11/_{4}4/_{6}9 = 1609$

∴ (33 × 46) + (26 × 29) – (51 × 13) = 1609
{6 × 1} + {8 × 2} – {6 × 4} {7}

Exercises

Ex. 1: Multiply (mentally)

1. 55 × 59 **2.** 35 × 67 **3.** 51 × 54
4. 34 × 66 **5.** 22 × 52 **6.** 33 × 34
7. 34 × 19 **8.** 48 × 72 **9.** 45 × 81
10. 54 × 81 **11.** 31 × 36 **12.** 22 × 53
13. 31 × 72 **14.** 23 × 43 **15.** 21 × 47
16. 61 × 31 **17.** 23 × 41 **18.** 33 × 84
19. 33 × 69 **20.** 28 × 22

Ex. 2: Multiply the following by moving multipliers

1. 321 × 21 **2.** 421 × 23 **3.** 1212 × 21
4. 1313 × 31 **5.** 34526 × 14

Ex. 3: Multiply treating the numbers as two digits

1. 112 × 203 **2.** 123 × 131 **3.** 1121 × 1131
4. 712 × 112 **5.** 703 × 211

Ex. 4: Multiply the following 3 & 4 digits as 2-digits

1. 222 × 321 **2.** 765 × 321 **3.** 357 × 223
4. 3201 × 4302 **5.** 5113 × 5331 **6.** 2131 × 3022
7. 567 × 82 **8.** 243 × 216
9. 243 × 216 **10.** 113 × 1011

Ex. 5: Multiply using vinculum

1. 19 × 34 **2.** 59 × 23 **3.** 28 × 31
4. 19 × 49 **5.** 38 × 39 **6.** 292 × 398

(**Hint:** In this last problem use vinculum for 9 in the multiplicand and for 98 in the multiplier)

Ex. 6:Do the combined calculations by VC method.

1. (36 × 49) + (62 × 42)
2. (34 × 44) + (53 × 63)
3. (4343 × 32) – (56 × 44)
4. (444 × 32) – (617 × 8)

Hint for problem 3 & 4 above: Add leading zeros to make all the numbers of equal digits.

□

15

Squaring (Part-I)

Introduction

We have already seen how to multiply numbers which are near base – may be above the base or may be below the base. Please brush up ex. 1 to 8 of lesson 12 –**Multiplication-03.**

Squaring Numbers near base:

Based on the multiplication learnt in earlier lesson – we can easily square the numbers that are nearer to base.

Example 1: Square 96

i.e. 96 × 96 or 96^2

Now both numbers are deficient by 04 from its base 100

96 – 04
96 – 04
______
92 /
______

Step 1: cross-subtract the deficiency from multiplicand/ multiplier i.e. 96–04 = 92 and we all know that this is left part of answer

Step 2: the right part is the vertical multiplication of deficiencies i.e. $(04)^2$.

96 – 04
96 – 04
______
92 / 16 $\therefore 96^2 = 9216$
______

{6^2} {9}

Example 2: Square 106

$$\begin{array}{l} 106 + 06 \\ 106 + 06 \\ \hline 112 / 36 \\ \hline \end{array} \qquad \therefore 106^2 = 11236$$

$\{7^2\}$ $\{4\}$

In examples 1 and 2 above, the two steps can be simplified as first reduce deficiency (or add the excess – as the case may be) from the number to be squared and get this as left part of the answer and then simply annex the square of the deficiency (or excess). So,

$$96^2 = (96 - 04)/04^2 = 9216$$
$$106^2 = (106 + 06)/06^2 = 11236$$

Example 3: Square 1008

$$1008^2 = (1008 + 008)/008^2 = 1016064$$

$\{9^2\}$ $\{9\}$

Note: In example 3 above, we first added 8 (the excess) to 1008, to get 1016 and then suffixed 8^2. But as our number to be squared is near to base 1000, we suffixed 8^2 or $(008)^2$ as as064 to satisfy 3-digits on the right side of the answer.

Also one may note that squaring of numbers nearer to base or otherwise is nothing but simple algebraic manipulation. For e.g. $a^2 = a^2 - b^2 + b^2$

$$= (a + b)(a - b) + b^2$$
$$\therefore 96^2 = (96 + 4)(96 - 4) + 4^2$$
$$= 100 \times 92 + 16 = 9216$$

Similarly

Example 4: Square 27

(i) $27^2 = (27 + 3)(27 - 3) + 3^2$
$= 30 \times 24 + 9 = 729$

(ii) $63^2 = (63 + 3)(63 - 3) + 3^2$
$= 66 \times 60 + 9 = 3969$

(iii) $18^2 = (18 + 2)(18 - 2) + 2^2$
$= 324$

Exercise

Ex 1: Square the following numbers

1. 89	**2.** 93	**3.** 108	**4.** 113
5. 88	**6.** 33	**7.** 48	**8.** 102
9. 37	**10.** 77		

Duplex

Introduction

We know that when the multiplicand and the multiplier are the same then the resulting process is squaring. In VC-Method we know how to multiply **ab** x **cd** But VC-Method gives an easier procedure for squaring. This will be done with a term known as **duplex** or **D**. Lets observe the following procedure closely –

2.1: a b

↓

a b

/ b^2

Step 1: Vertically on the right; i.e. b × b = b^2

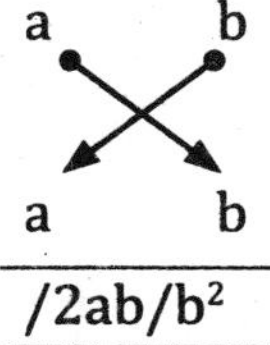

/2ab/b^2

Step 2: Crosswise i.e. a × b + b × a = 2ab

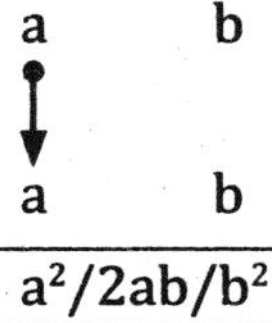

a^2/2ab/b^2

Step 3: vertically on the left; i.e. c × c = c^2

Note: From the above we try to explain **'Duplex'** or **'D'** as below –

(1) For a single digit **D** is the square of the digit – i.e. D(a) or D(x) or D(4) is a^2 or x^2 or 4^2 = 16

(2) For 2 digit number **D** is twice their product i.e. D(ab) or D(23) is 2ab or 2x2x3 = 12

2.2: To know **duplex** or **D** for 3-digits we have to square a 3-digit number:

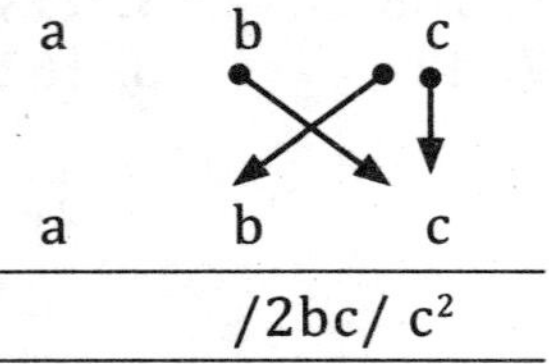

Step 1: vertically on the right i.e. c × c

Step 2: crosswise on the right i.e. b × c + c × b = 2bc

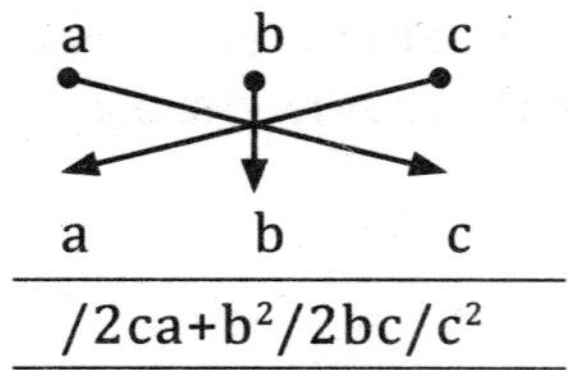

Step 3: crosswise, vertically, & crosswise i.e.

$$a \times c + b \times b + c \times a = 2ca + b^2$$

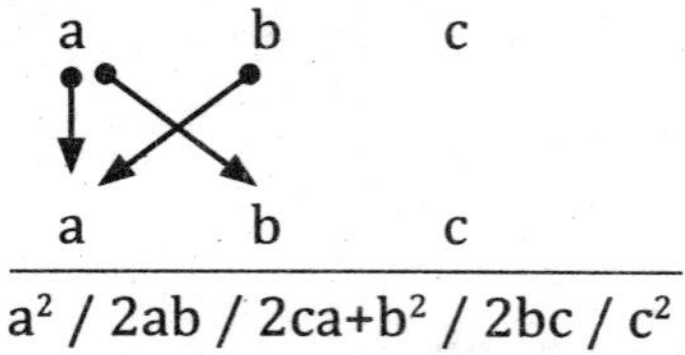

So finally $a^2/2ab/(2ca+b^2)/2bc/c^2$

Step 4: crosswise on the left i.e. 2ab

Step 5: vertically on the left i.e. a^2

In the above, ***duplex*** of single digit, 2-digits and 3-digits are involved at different steps of multiplication.

D(a)	- a^2 already explained in (1) above
D(ab)	- 2ab already explained in (2) above
D(abc)	- $2ac+b^2$ i.e. twice the product of end numbers + square of middle numbers
D(bc)	- 2bc already explained in (2) above
D(c)	- c^2 already explained in (1) above

2.3: On the same logic the **D**(abcd) i.e. duplex of 4-digits will be 2ad + 2bc i.e. twice the product of end digits and twice the product of middle digits or twice the product of outer pairs and twice the product of inner pairs.

2.4: Similarly **D**(abcde) i.e. duplex of 5-digits will be 2ae + 2bd + c^2. To understand and apply this, let's do problems with numerals –

Example 1:

$67^2 \rightarrow$ This involves D(6)/D(67)/D(7)

$D(6) \rightarrow 6^2 = 36$

$D(67) \rightarrow 2\times6\times7 = 84$

$D(7) \rightarrow 7^2 = 49$

Explanation

$D(1) \rightarrow 1^2 \rightarrow 1$

$D(14) \rightarrow 2\times1\times4 \rightarrow 8$

$D(143) \rightarrow 2\times1\times3 + 4^2 \rightarrow 22 \rightarrow_2 2$

$D(1435) \rightarrow 2\times1\times5 + 2\times4\times3 \rightarrow 10 + 24 \rightarrow 34 \rightarrow_3 4$

$D(435) \rightarrow 2\times4\times5 + 3^2 \rightarrow 40 + 9 \rightarrow 49 \rightarrow_4 9$

$D(35) \rightarrow 2\times3\times5 \rightarrow 30 \rightarrow_3 0$

$D(5) \rightarrow 5^2 \rightarrow 25 \rightarrow_2 5$

Example 6:

$14351^2 \rightarrow$ D(1)/D(14)/D(143)/D(1435)/D(14351)/D(4351)/D(351)/D(51)/D(1)

$14351^2 \rightarrow 1/8/_2 2/_3 4/_5 1/_3 8/_3 1/_1 0/1 \rightarrow 205951201\ \{5^2\} \rightarrow \{7\}$

Explanation

$D(1) \rightarrow 1^2 \rightarrow 1$

$D(14) \rightarrow 2\times1\times4 \rightarrow 8$

$D(143) \rightarrow 2\times1\times3 + 4^2 \rightarrow 22 \rightarrow_2 2$

$D(1435) \rightarrow 2\times1\times5 + 2\times4\times3 \rightarrow 10 + 24 \rightarrow 34 \rightarrow_3 4$

$D(14351) \rightarrow 2\times1\times1 + 2\times4\times5 + 3^2 \rightarrow 2 + 40 + 9 \rightarrow 51 \rightarrow_5 1$

$D(4351) \rightarrow 2\times4\times1 + 2\times3\times5 \rightarrow 8 + 30 \rightarrow 38 \rightarrow_3 8$

$D(351) \rightarrow 2\times3\times1 + 5^2 \rightarrow 6 + 25 \rightarrow 31 \rightarrow_3 1$

$D(51) \rightarrow 2\times5\times1 \rightarrow 10 \rightarrow_1 0$

$D(1) \rightarrow 1^2 \rightarrow 1$

Note: As explained in VC-Method, the number of ***duplexes*** involved are twice the number of digits minus one.

Algebraic Squaring

The duplex can very conveniently be used for algebraic squaring. See examples 7 to 11 below –

Example 7:

$(a + 3)^2 \rightarrow D(a) + D(a,3) + D(3);$

$D(a) \rightarrow a^2;\ D(a,3) \rightarrow 2 \times a \times 3 = 6a;\ D(3) \rightarrow 9^2$

$\rightarrow a^2 + 6a + 9$

Example 8:

$(3a - 2b)^2 \rightarrow D(3a) + D(3a, -2b) + D(-2b)$

$D(3a) \rightarrow 9a^2;\ D(3a, -2b) \rightarrow 2 \times 3a \times -2b$

$\rightarrow -12ab;\ D(-2b) \rightarrow 4b^2 \rightarrow 9a^2 - 12ab + 4b^2$

Example 9:

$(2x + 7y)^2 \rightarrow D(2x) + D(2x, 7y) + D(7y)$

$\rightarrow 4x^2 + 28xy + 49y^2$

Example 10:

$(2a+b+3) \rightarrow D(2a) + D(2a,b) + D(2a,b,3) + D(b,3) + D(3)$

$\rightarrow 4a^2 + 4ab + 12a + b^2 + 6b + 9$

$\rightarrow 4a^2 + b^2 + 12a + 6b + 9$

Example 11:

$(x - 2y + z) \rightarrow D(x) + D(x, -2y) + D(x, -2y, z) + D(-2y, z) + D(z)$

$\rightarrow x^2 - 4xy + 2xz + 4y^2 - 4yz + z^2$

$\rightarrow x^2 + 4y^2 + z^2 - 4xy - 4yz + 2xz$

Exercises

Ex 1: Square the following using duplex principle –

1. 31 **2.** 56 **3.** 203 **4.** 116

5. 341 **6.** 4332 **7.** 3103 **8.** 4144

9. 217 **10.** 513 **11.** 43 **12.** 191

Ex 2: Square the following

1. $(3x + 4)$ **2.** $(2x - 1)$ **3.** $(x + 7)$ **4.** $(x - 8y)$

5. $(2a + b)$ **6.** $(3x - 5y)$ **7.** $(5 - y)$ **8.** $(x - 3y)$

9. $(3a + b + 7)$ **10.** $(6a - b + 2c + 3)$

□

16

Squaring (Part-II)

Introduction

In this chapter we would cover squaring of numbers ending 25, Duplex using splitting, squaring numbers away from base, sums of squares and difference of squares (along with use of vinculums).

Squaring Numbers ending 25

In case a number ends in 25, the following method of squaring would be easy and fast. There could be two cases –

Case 1: Three digit number ending in 25 i.e. x25, then

$$(x25)^2 = x(x2 + 3)/\ 25^2$$

Example 1:

$(125)^2 = 1(12 + 3)/\ 25^2 \rightarrow 15/625 \rightarrow 15625$; [here x = 1 and x2 = 12]

$\{8^2\}$ $\{1\}$

Example 2:

$(425)^2 = 4(42 + 3)/\ 25^2 \rightarrow 180/625 \rightarrow 180625$; [here x = 4 and x2 = 42]

$\{2^2\}$ $\{4\}$

Example 3:

$(625)^2 = 6(62 + 3)/25^2 \rightarrow 390/625 \rightarrow 390625$; [here x = 6 and x2 = 62]

$\{4^2\}$ $\{7\}$

Case 2: Four digit number ending in 25 i.e. ab25

$$(ab25)^2 = ab(ab2 + 3)/\ 25^2$$

Example 4:

$(1125)^2 = 11(112+3)/25^2 = 1265625$; [here ab = 11 and ab2 = 112]

$\{9^2\}$ $\{9\}$

Example 5:

$(1325)^2 = 13(132+3)/25^2 = 1755625$; [here ab = 13 and ab2 = 132]

$\{2^2\}$ $\{4\}$

Duplex using splitting

Say we have to square 325. This 325 can be split as 32/5 or 3/25, then duplex can be employed.

Example 6:

(i) $(325)^2 \rightarrow D(32)/\ D(32{,}5)/\ D(5)$

$\rightarrow 1024/\ _{32}0/\ _{2}5 \rightarrow 105625$

$\{1^2\}$ $\{1\}$

(ii) $(325)^2 \rightarrow D(3)/\ D(3,\ 25)/\ D(25)$

$\rightarrow 9/\ _{1}50/\ _{6}25 = 105625$

Note: From the above two examples, it is obvious that number of digits during ***duplex*** operation depends upon the number of digits in the original on RHS after we have marked the split. That is we had single digit on RHS when the number was split as 32/5 {example 6(i)} and 2-digits on RHS as 3/25 {example 6(ii)}. Consequently in ***duplex*** operations we had single and double digits respectively between strokes.

(iii) If we apply duplexon 3-digits -

$(325)^2 \rightarrow D(3)/D(32)/D(325)/D(25)/D(5)$

$\rightarrow 9/\ _{1}2/\ _{3}4/\ _{2}0/\ _{2}5$

(iv) If we follow the procedure shown in sec 3.1 above

$(325)^2 \rightarrow 3(32+3)/25^2 \rightarrow 105625$ [Here × = 3 and × 2 = 32]

All the four methods yield same result.

Squaring Numbers near base

This has already been explained in sec 1.1 of Lesson 15.

However, the same is repeated once again –

(i) Near base 100

$94^2 \rightarrow (94 - 06)/06^2 = 8836$

(ii) Near base 1000

$1009^2 \rightarrow (1009 + 009)/(009)^2 = 1018081$

In the above cases the numbers to be squared were very near to base. But in case the numbers which require Working Base (WB) and Theoretical Base (TB) i.e. the number is near some sub-base, then the method explained in lesson 13 of ***'Multiplication-2'*** can be employed. See example 7, 8 and 9 below –

Squaring Numbers away from base

Example 7:

$(249)^2 \rightarrow$

1. TB = 1000; WB = 250; WB/TB = ¼;
2. Deficit from WB = -001;
3. LH part = (249 – 001) × ¼ = 62
4. RH part $(-001)^2$ = 001 (base being 1000)

$\therefore (249)^2 = 62001$

$\{6^2\}$ $\{9\}$

Example 8:

$(261)^2 \rightarrow$

1. TB = 1000; WB = 250; WB/TB = ¼;
2. Excess from WB =+011;
3. LH part = (261 + 011) × ¼ = 68
4. RH part $(011)^2$ = 121 (base being 1000)

$\therefore (261)^2 = 68121$

$\{9^2\}$ $\{9\}$

Example 9:

$(266)^2 \rightarrow$

1. TB = 1000; WB = 250; WB/TB = ¼;
2. Excess from WB = +016;
3. LH part = (266 + 016) × ¼ = 70½
4. RH part $(+016)^2$ = 256 + ½ 1000 = 256 + 500 = 756 (base being 1000)

$\therefore (266)^2 = 70756$

$\{5^2\}$ $\{7\}$

3.5: Sum of Squares

The sum of squares can be found by adding the respective **duplexes.**

Example 10:

$34^2 + 23^2$

$34^2 \rightarrow D(3) / D(34) / D(4) \rightarrow 9 / 24 / 16$

+

$23^2 \rightarrow D(2) / D(23) / D(3) \rightarrow \underline{4 / 12 / 09}$

$\rightarrow 13/{}_{3}6/{}_{2}5 \rightarrow 1685$

$\therefore 34^2 + 23^2 = 1685$

$\{7^2\} + \{5^2\} \quad \{2\}$

Example 11:

$210^2 + 104^2$

$210^2 \rightarrow 4 / 4 / 1 / 0 / 0$

+

$104^2 \rightarrow 1 / 0 / 8 / 0 /{}_{1}6$

$\overline{\underline{5 / 4 / 9 / 1 / 6}}$

$\therefore 210^2 + 104^2 = 54916$

$\{3^2\} + \{5^2\} \quad \{7\}$

3.6: Difference of Squares

Example 12:

On the above logic we can find difference of squares –

$78^2 - 35^2$

$78^2 \rightarrow 49 / 112 / 64$

–

$35^2 \rightarrow \overline{\underline{09 / 30 / 25}}$

$40 /{}_{8}2 /{}_{3}9 \rightarrow 4859$

$\therefore 78^2 - 35^2 = 4859$

$\{6^2\} - \{8^2\} \quad \{8\}$

Example 13:

$61^2 - 43^2$

$61^2 \rightarrow 36 / 12 / 01$

$-$

$43^2 \rightarrow \underline{16 / 24 / 09}$

$20 / {}_1\bar{2} / {}_0\bar{8} \rightarrow 19\,\bar{2}\,\bar{8} \rightarrow 1872$

$\therefore 61^2 - 43^2 = 1872$

$\{7^2\} - \{7^2\} \quad \{9\}$

Note: It may be remembered that while subtracting the duplex, use vinculum (if required) and then convert the final value to non-vinculum. It would have been clear from example 13 above.

Exercises

Ex. 1: Find the squares of –

1. 23 **2.** 252 **3.** 499 **4.** 502

Ex. 2: Find the squares of –

1. 325 **2.** 725 **3.** 1025 **4.** 1425

Ex. 3:

1. $65^2 + 37^2$ **2.** $37^2 + 23^2$ **3.** $63^2 - 34^2$

4. $34^2 - 29^2$ **5.** $313^2 + 428^2$ **6.** $428^2 - 313^2$

7. $3131^2 + 2233^2$ **8.** $1343^2 - 1002^2$

□

17

Squaring (Part-III)

Special Methods for squaring 2-digit Numbers

Introduction

In the earlier lesson **'Multiplication'** we have seen squaring numbers from 50 to 59. Similarly we shall see the rules for squaring numbers from 10 to 19, 20 to 29, 30 to 39, etc.

Squaring 2-digit numbers from 10 to 19

Steps:

1. Square the unit digit.
2. Multiply the units digit by 2 and add the carry (if any) from step 1
3. Square ten's digit and add carry from step 2.

Example 1:

$16^2 \rightarrow$ Step 1: Square of unit digit 6 is 36; take 6 carry 3
Step 2: $2 \times 6 + 3$ (carry) = 15; take 5 carry 1
Step 3: $1^2 + 1$ (carry) = 2
$\therefore 16^2 = 256$
{7^2} {4}

Example 2:

$19^2 \rightarrow$ Step 1: Square of 9 is 81; take 1 carry 8
Step 2: $2 \times 9 + 8$ (carry) = 26; take 6 carry 2
Step 3: $1^2 + 2$ (carry) = 3
$\therefore 19^2 = 361$
{1^2} {1}

Squaring 2-digit numbers from 20 to 29

Steps

1. Square the unit digit.
2. Multiply the units digit by 4 and add the carry (if any) from step 1
3. Square ten's digit and add carry from step 2.

Example 3:

$23^2 \rightarrow$ Step 1: Square of 3 is 9; take 9 carry 0

Step 2: $4 \times 3 \rightarrow 12$; take 2 carry 1

Step 3: $2^2 + 1$ (carry) = 5

$\therefore 23^2 = 529$

$\{5^2\}$ $\{7\}$

Example 4:

$28^2 \rightarrow$ Step 1: Square of 8 is 64; take 4 carry 6

Step 2: $4 \times 8 \rightarrow 32 + 6$ (carry) $\rightarrow 38$; take 8 carry 3

Step 3: $2^2 + 3$ (carry) = 7

$\therefore 28^2 = 784$

$\{1^2\}$ $\{1\}$

Squaring 2-digit numbers from 30 to 39

Steps

1. Square the unit digit.
2. Multiply the units digit by 6 and add the carry (if any) from step 1
3. Square ten's digit and add carry from step 2.

Example 5:

$34^2 \rightarrow$ Step 1: Square of 4 is 16; take 6 carry 1

Step 2: $6 \times 4 \rightarrow 24 + 1$ (carry) $\rightarrow 25$; take 5 carry 2

Step 3: $3^2 + 2$ (carry) = 11

$\therefore 34^2 = 1156$

$\{7^2\}$ $\{4\}$

Example 6:

$37^2 \rightarrow$ Step 1: Square of 7 is 49; take 9 carry 4

Step 2: $6 \text{ x } 7 \rightarrow 42 + 4$ (carry) $\rightarrow 46$; take 6 carry 4

Step 3: $3^2 + 4$ (carry) = 13

$\therefore 37^2 = 1369$
{1^2} {1}

Squaring 2-digit numbers from 40 to 49

Steps

1. Square the unit digit.
2. Multiply the units digit by 8 and add the carry (if any) from step 1
3. Square ten's digit and add carry from step 2.

Example 7:

$43^2 \rightarrow$ Step 1: Square of 3 is 09; take 9 carry 0
Step 2: $8 \times 3 \rightarrow 24 + 0$ (carry) $\rightarrow 24$; take 4 carry 2
Step 3: $4^2 + 2$ (carry) $= 18$
$\therefore 43^2 = 1849$
{7^2} {4}

Example 8:

$48^2 \rightarrow$ Step 1: Square of 8 is 64; take 4 carry 6
Step 2: $8 \times 8 \rightarrow 64 + 6$ (carry) $\rightarrow 70$; take 0 carry 7
Step 3: $4^2 + 7$ (carry) $= 23$
$\therefore 48^2 = 2304$
{3^2} {9}

Squaring 2-digit numbers from 50 to 59

Steps

1. Square the unit digit.
2. Multiply the units digit by 10 and add the carry (if any) from step 1
3. The ten digit's square and add carry from step 2.

Example 9:

$54^2 \rightarrow$ Step 1: Square of 4 is 16; take 6 carry 1
Step 2: $10 \times 4 \rightarrow 40 + 1$ (carry) $\rightarrow 41$; take 1 carry 4
Step 3: $5^2 + 4$ (carry) $= 29$
$\therefore 54^2 = 2916$
{9^2} {9}

Note: Note the difference between the above procedure and the procedure explained in sec 3.7 of chapter 3 of the book 'Do You Know Multiplication?'

Example 10:

57^2 → Step 1: Square of 7 is 49; take 9 carry 4

Step 2: 10 × 7 → 70 + 4 (carry) → 74; take 4 carry 7

Step 3: 5^2 + 7 (carry) = 32

∴ 57^2 = 3249

{3^2} {9}

Squaring 2-digit numbers from 60 to 69

Steps

1. Square the unit digit.
2. Multiply the units digit by 12 and add the carry (if any) from step 1
3. Square Ten's digit and add carry from step 2.

Example 11:

63^2 → Step 1: Square of 3 is 09; take 9 carry 0

Step 2: 12 × 3 → 36 + 0 (carry) → 36; take 6 carry 3

Step 3: 6^2 + 3 (carry) = 39

∴ 63^2 = 3969

{9^2} {9}

Example 12:

69^2 → Step 1: Square of 9 is 81; take 1 carry 8

Step 2: 12 × 9→108 + 8 (carry)→116; take 6 carry11

Step 3: 6^2 + 11 (carry) = 47

∴ 69^2 = 4761

{6^2} {9}

Squaring 2-digit numbers from 70 to 79

Steps

1. Square the unit digit.
2. Multiply the units digit by 14 and add the carry (if any) from step 1
3. Square ten's digit and add carry from step 2.

Example 13:

$74^2 \rightarrow$ Step 1: Square of 4 is 16; take 6 carry 1

Step 2: $14 \times 4 \rightarrow 56 + 1$ (carry) $\rightarrow 57$; take 7 carry 5

Step 3: $7^2 + 5$ (carry) $= 54$

$\therefore 74^2 = 5476$

$\{2^2\}$ $\{4\}$

Example 14:

$77^2 \rightarrow$ Step 1: Square of 7 is 49; take 9 carry 4

Step 2: $14 \times 7 \rightarrow 98 + 4$ (carry) $\rightarrow 102$; take 2 carry 10

Step 3: $7^2 + 10$ (carry) $= 59$

$\therefore 77^2 = 5929$

$\{5^2\}$ $\{7\}$

Squaring 2-digit numbers from 80 to 89

Steps

1. Square the unit digit.
2. Multiply the units digit by 16 and add the carry (if any) from step 1
3. Square ten's digit and add carry from step 2.

Example 15:

$82^2 \rightarrow$ Step 1: Square of 2 is 04; take 4 carry 0

Step 2: $16 \times 2 \rightarrow 32 + 0$ (carry) $\rightarrow 32$; take 2 carry 3

Step 3: $8^2 + 3$ (carry) $= 67$

$\therefore 82^2 = 6724$

$\{1^2\}$ $\{1\}$

Example 16:

$87^2 \rightarrow$ Step 1: Square of 7 is 49; take 9 carry 4

Step 2: $16 \times 7 \rightarrow 112 + 4$ (carry) $\rightarrow 116$; take 6 carry 11

Step 3: $8^2 + 11$ (carry) $= 75$

$\therefore 87^2 = 7569$

$\{6^2\}$ $\{9\}$

Squaring 2-digit numbers from 90 to 99

Steps

1. Square the unit digit.

2. Multiply the units digit by 18 and add the carry (if any) from step 1
3. Square ten's digit and add carry from step 2.

Example 17:

$93^2 \rightarrow$ Step 1: Square of 3 is 09; take 9 carry 0
Step 2: $18 \times 3 \rightarrow 54 + 0$ (carry) $\rightarrow 54$; take 4 carry 5
Step 3: $9^2 + 5$ (carry) $= 86$
$\therefore 93^2 = 8649$
{3^2} {9}

Example 18:

$98^2 \rightarrow$ Step 1: Square of 8 is 64; take 4 carry 6
Step 2: $18 \times 8 \rightarrow 144 + 6$ (carry) $\rightarrow 150$; take 0 carry 15
Step 3: $9^2 + 15$ (carry) $= 96$
$\therefore 98^2 = 9604$
{8^2} {1}

Note: Examples 16, 17, 18 can be tackled as explained in sec 1.1 of chapter 1

Corollary of procedures explained above

Squaring 2-digit numbers ending in 1

Steps: 1. Subtract 1 from the number
2. Square the difference
3. Add the difference twice to its square
4. Add 1

Example 19:

$11^2 \rightarrow$ Step 1: $11 - 1 = 10$
Step 2: $10^2 = 100$
Step 3: $100 + 10 + 10 = 120$
Step 4: $120 + 1 = 121$

Example 20:

$71^2 \rightarrow$ Step 1: $71 - 1 = 70$
Step 2: $70^2 = 4900$
Step 3: $4900 + 70 + 70 = 5040$
Step 4: $5040 + 1 = 5041$

Squaring 2-digit numbers ending in 2

Steps:

1. Last digit will be 4
2. Multiply Ten's digit by 4 (keep carry)
3. Square the ten's digit and add carry in step 2 above

Example 21: $32^2 \rightarrow$

Step 1: last digit 4
Step 2: $3 \times 4 = 12$; take 2 carry 1
Step 3: $3^2 + 1$ (carry) = 10
$\therefore 32^2 = 1024$
{5^2} {7}

Example 22: $82^2 \rightarrow$

Step 1: last digit 4
Step 2: $8 \times 4 = 32$; take 2 carry 3
Step 3: $8^2 + 3$ (carry) = 67
$\therefore 82^2 = 6724$
{1^2} {1}

Squaring 2-digit numbers ending in 3

Steps:

1. Last digit will be 9
2. Multiply ten's digit by 6 (keep carry)
3. Square the ten's digit and add carry in step 2 above

Example 23: $23^2 \rightarrow$

Step 1: Last digit 9
Step 2: $6 \times 2 = 12$; take 2 carry 1
Step 3: $2^2 + 1$ (carry) = 5
$\therefore 23^2 = 529$
{5^2} {7}

Example 24: $93^2 \rightarrow$

Step 1: Last digit 9
Step 2: $6 \times 9 = 54$; take 4 carry 5
Step 3: $9^2 + 5$ (carry) = 86
$\therefore 93^2 = 8649$
{3^2} {9}

Squaring 2-digit numbers ending in 4

Steps:

1. Square the 4 → 16; take 6 carry 1
2. Multiply ten's digit by 8, add carry in step 1 above (keep carry)
3. Square the ten's digit and add carry in step 2 above

Example 25:

24^2→ Step 1: 4^2→ 16; take 6 carry 1

Step 2: 2 × 8 + 1 (carry) = 17; take 7 carry 1

Step 3: 2^2 + 1 (carry) = 5

∴ 24^2 = 576

{6^2} {9}

Example 26:

84^2→ Step 1: 4^2→ 16; take 6 carry 1

Step 2: 8 × 8 + 1 (carry) = 65; take 5 carry 6

Step 3: 8^2 + 6 (carry) = 70

∴ 84^2 = 7056

{3^2} {9}

Squaring 2-digit numbers ending in 6

Steps:

1. Square unit digit; keep carry
2. Multiply ten's digit by 2 and add carry from step 1; keep carry
3. Multiply ten's digit by the next consecutive digit and add carry

Example 27:

26^2→ Step 1: 6^2→ 36; take 6 carry 3

Step 2: 2 × 2 + 3 (carry) → 7; take 7 carry 0

Step 3: 2 × 3 + 0 (carry) ® 6

∴ 26^2 = 676

{8^2} {1}

Example 28:

$76^2 \rightarrow$ Step 1: $6^2 \rightarrow 36$; take 6 carry 3

Step 2: $2 \times 7 + 3$ (carry) $\rightarrow 17$; take 7 carry 1

Step 3: $7 \times 8 + 1$ (carry) $\rightarrow 57$

$\therefore 76^2 = 5776$

$\{4^2\}$ $\{7\}$

Squaring 2-digit numbers ending in 7

Steps:

1. Square unit digit; keep carry
2. Multiply ten's digit by 4 and add carry from step 1; keep carry
3. Multiply ten's digit by the next consecutive digit and add carry

Example 29:

$37^2 \rightarrow$ Step 1: $7^2 \rightarrow 49$; take 9 carry 4

Step 2: $4 \times 3 + 4$ (carry) $= 16$; take 6 carry 1

Step 3: $3 \times 4 + 1$ (carry) $= 13$

$\therefore 37^2 = 1369$

$\{1^2\}$ $\{1\}$

Example 30:

$87^2 \rightarrow$ Step 1: $7^2 \rightarrow 49$; take 9 carry 4

Step 2: $4 \times 8 + 4$ (carry) $= 36$; take 6 carry 3

Step 3: $8 \times 9 + 3$ (carry) $= 75$

$\therefore 87^2 = 7569$

$\{6^2\}$ $\{9\}$

Squaring 2-digit numbers ending in 8

Steps:

1. Square unit digit; keep carry
2. Multiply ten's digit by 6 and add carry from step 1; keep carry
3. Multiply ten's digit by the next consecutive digit and add carry

Example 31:

28^2→ Step 1: 8^2→ 64; take 4 carry 6

Step 2: 6 × 2 + 6 (carry) = 18; take 8 carry 1

Step 3: 2 × 3 + 1 (carry) = 7

∴ 28^2 = 784

{1^2} {1}

Example 32:

78^2→ Step 1: 8^2→ 64; take 4 carry 6

Step 2: 6 × 7 + 6 (carry) = 48; take 8 carry 4

Step 3: 7 × 8 + 4 (carry) = 60

∴ 78^2 = 6084

{6^2} {9}

Squaring 2-digit numbers ending in 9

Steps:

1. Square unit digit; keep carry
2. Multiply ten's digit by 8 and add carry from step 1; keep carry
3. Multiply ten's digit by the next consecutive digit and add carry

Example 33:

39^2→ Step 1: 9^2→ 81; take 1 carry 8

Step 2: 8 × 3 + 8 (carry) = 32; take 2 carry 3

Step 3: 3 × 4 + 3 (carry) = 15

∴ 39^2 = 1521

{3^2} {9}

Example 34:

79^2→ Step 1: 9^2→ 81; take 1 carry 8

Step 2: 8 × 7 + 8 (carry) = 64; take 4 carry 6

Step 3: 7 × 8 + 6 (carry) = 62

∴ 79^2 = 6241

{7^2} {4}

□

18

Squaring (Part-IV)

Special Methods for squaring 3-digit Numbers

Introduction

In the earlier lesson we have seen special methods for squaring 2 digit numbers. This lesson is continuation of the earlier part-1 of lesson 17.

Squaring Numbers in 100s

Steps:

1. The units and tens place of the answer is the square of the units and tens place of the given number; keep carry
2. The first three digits of the square is the given number plus tens and units place of the given number plus carry (if any in step 1 above)

Example 1: $107^2 \rightarrow$

Step 1: $07^2 \rightarrow 49$; take 49 carry 0
Step 2: 107 + 07 + 0 (carry) = 114
$\therefore$ **107^2 = 11449**
{8^2} {1}

Example 2: $134^2 \rightarrow$

Step 1: $34^2 \rightarrow 1156$; take 56 carry 11
Step 2: 134 + 34 + 11 (carry) = 179
$\therefore$ **134^2 = 17956**
{8^2} {1}

Example 3: $196^2 \rightarrow$

Step 1: $96^2 \rightarrow 9216$; take 16 carry 92
Step 2: 196 +96 + 92 (carry) = 384
$\therefore$ **196^2 = 38416**
{7^2} {4}

Squaring Numbers in 200s

For numbers 200 to 209 (the working is done from left to right)

Steps:
1. Left most digit is $2^2 \rightarrow 4$
2. The next two digits are 4 times the last digit
3. Square the last digit

Example 4: $203^2 \rightarrow$

Step 1: 4 _ _ _ _

Step 2: $4 \times 3 = 12$; 412 _ _

Step 3: $3^2 = 9$; 41209

$\therefore \mathbf{203^2 = 41209}$

$\{5^2\}$ $\{7\}$

For numbers from 210 to 299 (the working is done from right to left)

Steps:
1. Square the last two digits; keep the carry
2. 4 times the last two digits + carry
3. Square the first digit + carry

Example 5:

$214^2 \rightarrow$ Step 1: $14^2 \rightarrow 196$; take 96 carry 1

Step 2: $14 \times 4 + 1 = 57$

Step 3: $2^2 \rightarrow 4$

$\therefore \mathbf{214^2 = 45796}$

$\{7^2\}$ $\{4\}$

Example 6:

$263^2 \rightarrow$ Step 1: $63^2 \rightarrow 3969$; take 69 carry 39

Step 2: $63 \times 4 + 39 = 291$; take 91 carry 2

Step 3: $2^2 + 2 = 6$

$\therefore \mathbf{263^2 = 69169}$

$\{2^2\}$ $\{4\}$

Squaring Numbers in 300s

For numbers 300 to 309 (the working is done from left to right)

Steps:
1. Left most digit is $3^2 \rightarrow 9$
2. The next two digits are 6 times the last digit
3. Square the last digit

Example 7: 307^2→ Step 1: 3^2→ 9
Step 2: 6 × 07 → 42
Step 3: 7^2→ 49
∴ **307^2 = 94249**
{1^2} {1}

For numbers 310 to 399 (the working is done from right to left)

Steps:
1. Square the last two digits; keep the carry
2. 6 times the last two digits + carry
3. Square the first digit + carry

Example 8:

321^2→ Step 1: 21^2→ 441; take 41 carry 4
Step 2: 6 × 21 + 4 (carry) = 130; take 30 carry 1
Step 3: 3^2 + 1 (carry) = 10
∴ **321^2 = 103041**
{6^2} {9}

Example 9:

367^2→ Step 1: 67^2→ 4489; take 89 carry 44
Step 2: 6 × 67 + 44 (carry) = 446; take 46 carry 4
Step 3: 3^2 + 4 (carry) = 13
∴ **367^2 = 134689**
{7^2} {4}

Squaring Numbers in 400s

For numbers 400 to 409 (the working is done from left to right)

Steps:
1. First two digits is 4^2→ 16
2. The next two digits are 8 times the last digit
3. Square the last digit

Example 10: 407^2→ Step 1: 4^2→ 16
Step 2: 8 × 7 = 56
Step 3: 7^2→ 49
∴ **407^2 = 165649**
{2^2} {4}

For numbers 410 to 499 (the working is done from right to left)

Steps:
1. Square the last two digits; keep the carry
2. 8 times the last two digits + carry
3. Square the first digit + carry

Example 11:

$424^2 \rightarrow$ Step 1: $24^2 \rightarrow 576$; take 76 carry 5

Step 2: $8 \times 24 + 5$ (carry) = 197; take 97 carry 1

Step 3: $4^2 + 1$ (carry) = 17

$\therefore$ **$424^2 = 179776$**

$\{1^2\}$ $\{1\}$

Example 12:

$483^2 \rightarrow$ Step 1: $83^2 \rightarrow 6889$; take 89 carry 68

Step 2: $8 \times 83 + 68$ (carry) = 732; take 32 carry 7

Step 3: $4^2 \rightarrow 16 + 7$ (carry) = 23

$\therefore$ **$483^2 = 233289$**

$\{6^2\}$ $\{9\}$

Squaring Numbers in 500s

For numbers 500 to 509 (the working is done from left to right)

Steps:
1. First two digits is $5^2 \rightarrow 25$
2. The next two digits are 10 times the last digit
3. Square the last digit

Example 13: $507^2 \rightarrow$ Step 1: $5^2 \rightarrow 25$

Step 2: $10 \times 07 \rightarrow 70$

Step 3: $7^2 \rightarrow 49$

$\therefore$ **$507^2 = 257049$**

$\{3^2\}$ $\{9\}$

For numbers 510 to 599 (the working is done from right to left)

Steps:
1. Square the last two digits; keep the carry
2. 10 times the last two digits + carry
3. Square the first digit + carry

Example 14:

542^2 → Step 1: 42^2→ 1764; take 64 carry 17

Step 2: 10×42 + 17 (carry)→ 437; take 37 and carry 4

Step 3: 5^2→ 25 + 4 (carry) → 29

∴ **542^2 = 293764**

{2^2} {4}

Example 15:

586^2→ Step 1: 86^2→ 7396; take 96 carry 73

Step 2: 10 × 86 + 73 (carry) = 933; take 33 carry 9

Step 3: 25 + 9 (carry) → 34

∴ **586^2 = 343396**

{1^2} {1}

Squaring Numbers in 600s

For numbers 600 to 609 (the working is done from left to right)

Steps:
1. First two digits is 6^2→ 36
2. The next two digits are 12 times the last digit
3. Square the last digit

Example 16: 603^2→ Step 1: 6^2→ 36

Step 2: 12 × 03 → 36

Step 3: 03^2→ 09

∴ **603^2 = 363609**

{9^2} {9}

For numbers 610 to 699 (the working is done from right to left)

Steps:
1. Square the last two digits; keep the carry
2. 12 times the last two digits + carry
3. Square the first digit + carry

Example 17:

633^2→ Step 1: 33^2→ 1089; take 89 carry 10

Step 2: 12 × 33 + 10 (carry) = 406; take 06 carry 4

Step 3: 6^2→ 36 + 4 (carry) = 40

∴ **633^2 = 400689**

{3^2} {9}

Example 18:

678²→ Step 1: $78^2 \rightarrow$ 6084; take 84 carry 60

Step 2: 12 × 78 + 60 (carry) = 996; take 96 carry 9

Step 3: $6^2 \rightarrow$ 36 + 9 (carry) = 45

∴ **678^2 = 459684**

{3^2} {9}

Squaring Numbers in 700s

For numbers 700 to 707(the working is done from left to right)

Steps: 1. First two digits is $7^2 \rightarrow$ 49

2. The next two digits are 14 times the last digit

3. Square the last digit

Example 19: $706^2 \rightarrow$ Step 1: $7^2 \rightarrow$ 49

Step 2: 14 × 6 → 84

Step 3: $6^2 \rightarrow$ 36

∴ **706^2 = 498436**

{4^2} {7}

For numbers 708 to 799 (the working is done from right to left)

Steps: 1. Square the last two digits; keep the carry

2. 14 times the last two digits + carry

3. Square the first digit + carry

Example 20:

$709^2 \rightarrow$ Step 1: $9^2 \rightarrow$ 81

Step 2: 14 × 09 = 126; take 26 carry 1

Step 3: $7^2 \rightarrow$ 49 + 1 (carry) = 50

∴ **709^2 =502681**

{7^2} {4}

Example 21:

$774^2 \rightarrow$ Step 1:$74^2 \rightarrow$ 5476; take 76 carry 54

Step 2: 14 × 74 + 54 (carry) = 1090; take 90 carry 10

Step 3: $7^2 \rightarrow$ 49 + 10 = 59

∴ **774^2 = 599076**

{9^2} {9}

Squaring Numbers in 800s

For numbers 800 to 806 (the working is done from left to right)

Steps: 1. First two digits is $8^2 \rightarrow 64$

2. The next two digits are 16 times the last digit

3. Square the last digit

Example 22: $803^2 \rightarrow$ Step 1: $8^2 \rightarrow 64$

Step 2: $16 \times 3 = 48$

Step 3: $3^2 \rightarrow 09$

$\therefore$ **$803^2 = 644809$**

{2^2} {4}

For numbers 807 to 899 (the working is done from right to left)

Steps: 1. Square the last two digits; keep the carry

2. 16 times the last two digits + carry

3. Square the first digit + carry

Example 23:

$823^2 \rightarrow$ Step 1: $23^2 \rightarrow 529$; take 29 carry 5

Step 2: $16 \times 23 + 5$ (carry) = 373; take 73 carry 3

Step 3: $8^2 \rightarrow 64 + 3 = 67$

$\therefore$ **$823^2 = 677329$**

{4^2} {7}

Example 24:

$835^2 \rightarrow$ Step 1: $35^2 \rightarrow 1225$; take 25 carry 12

Step 2: $16 \times 35 + 12$ (carry) = 572; take 72 carry 5

Step 3: $8^2 \rightarrow 64 + 5$ (carry) = 69

$\therefore$ **$835^2 = 697225$**

{7^2} {4}

Squaring Numbers in 900s

For numbers 900 to 905 (the working is done from left to right)

Steps: 1. First two digits is $9^2 \rightarrow 81$

2. The next two digits are 18 times the last digit

3. Square the last digit

Example 25: 904^2→ Step 1: 9^2→ 81

Step 2: 18 × 4 = 72

Step 3: 4^2→ 16

∴ **904^2 = 817216**

{4^2} {7}

For numbers 906 to 999 (the working is done from right to left)

Steps:
1. Square the last two digits; keep the carry
2. 18 times the last two digits + carry
3. Square the first digit + carry

Example 26:

927^2→ Step 1: 27^2→ 729; take 29 carry 7

Step 2: 18 × 27 + 7 (carry) = 493; take 93 carry 4

Step 3: 9^2→ 81 + 4 (carry) = 85

∴ **927^2 = 859329**

{9^2} {9}

Example 27:

977^2→ Step 1: 77^2→ 5929: take 29 carry 59

Step 2: 18 × 77 + 59 (carry) → 1445; take 45 carry 14

Step 3: 9^2→ 81 + 14 (carry) = 95

∴ **977^2 = 954529**

{5^2} {7}

□

19

Square Rooting

Preface

Finding square root is not an easy task and many students avoid problems on square root. Of course, now-a-days a calculator is used and some students may use logarithmic tables. Use of logarithmic table also requires skill and expertise. Knowing how to find square roots for those numbers which are perfect square will be of immense help to know the basics of Mathematics. Till the legal usage of calculators allowed and achieving expertise in using logarithmic tables acquired, a simple procedure for finding square roots is explained in this **'Square Rooting'.** Teachers/parents should teach their students/wards at least the process of finding square root of perfect squares from the procedure explained in this lesson. The procedure for finding square root with decimal value is also dealt with.

Author

To find Square-Root of perfect Squares

Introduction

In the **'Squaring?'** (Lesson 15 – part-II) we had explained about finding squares of numbers using **DUPLEX.** Using the principles of **duplex** we can also find square root of a number and this method is much easier than the conventional method taught to us in schools. However, first it would be appropriate to know certain basics about square root. As the value of square root can be either positive or negative the term is used as plural word i.e. square roots; however we prefer to use the singular form i.e. square root.

Square root – Basics

(a) Before resorting to square root, arrange the number (for which the square root is to be found) in groups of two digits from the right to left (as we do normally in our known method of finding square root). If a single digit is left out at the left end, than that single digit will be treated as a group in itself.

(b) The number of groups in the given number (including the one represented by a single digit) and the number of digits in the square root will be the same.

(c) If the given number, whose square root is to be found has n digits the root will contain $n/2$ or $(n+1)/2$ digits depending upon whether n is even or odd respectively. Thus 441 as well as 3025 will be of two groups and will have two digits in their square roots.

(d) Conversely, if root contains N digits, its square will have $2N$ or $2N - 1$ digits.

(e) In case of decimals (if the given decimal is a perfect square) then it will have double the digits as its square root. Thus if there are m digits in the given decimal number, then the square root will have $m/2$ digits (again in case of perfect square only).

Let us now see the procedure for finding square root by using **duplex**.

Example 1: Find $\sqrt{450241}$

Steps:

1. First mark the number into groups of 2-digits from right.
   i.e. 450241 → 45/02/41
2. Find the nearest square that can be accoınmodated in the left most group. The left most group is 45 in this case and the nearest square that can be accommodated within this 45 is 6^2 i.e. 36
3. Now make a tabular form as below -

	Divisor ↓				
Reminder line →			96	10	
Given Number →		45	02	41	
	12				
Answer line→		6	71.00		

   Take 6 of the 6^2 in the answer row and double to get 12 and put it in the divisor column as shown above.
4. The remainder of 36 from 45 is 9. Take this 9 to the remainder line as shown above. This 9 along with the next digit in the given number i.e. 0 becomes the next dividend i.e. 90
5. Divide 90 by the divisor i.e. 12. 90 ÷ 12 →Q7 & R6; take quotient 7 to answer line and remainder 6 to remainder line as shown above.
6. The new number on which further working is to be done is 62; form this subtract the duplex of the quotient in step 5 above i.e. D(7). So the new dividend is 62 – D(7) = 62 – 49 = 13.
7. Divide 13 by divisor 12. 13 ÷ 12 → Q1 & R1; take the quotient 1 to the answer line and remainder 1 to remainder line as shown above.
8. The new number on which working is to be done is remainder 1 in step 7 and the next digit in the given number i.e. 4. So 14 is the next number. From this 14 remove the duplex of quotients arrived in step 5 &7 i.e. D(71). So the new dividend is 14 – D(71) = 14 – 14 = 0.
9. Divide 0 by 12; Q0 &R0; place a decimal point [as per square root basics (c) above – we have three groups in the given number and hence the decimal point after third

digit in the answer] and take 0 in the answer line and 0 in the remainder line.

10. The new number on which working is to be done is reminder 0 and the last digit in the given number 1; i.e. 01. From this 01 subtract the duplex of the quotients in step 5, 7 and 9 i.e. D(710); 01 – D(710) = 01 – 1 = 0. So the new dividend is 0 and 0 ÷ 12 = 0.
11. Hence 450241 is a perfect square and its square root is 671.

12. $\sqrt{\mathbf{450241}}$ **= 671** [a perfect square]
{7} ⇐ {5^2} {please note the reverse arrow in **DR** check}

Example 2: Find $\sqrt{\mathbf{447561}}$

Steps:

1. Mark in groups of 2 digits from right i.e. 44/75/61
2. 6^2 = 36 is the nearest to 44 in the left most group; take 6 in the answer line and double of 6 i.e. 12 is the divisor.
3. Now make a tabular form as below -

	Divisor ↓			
Reminder line →			8 15	11 8
Given Number →		44	7 5	6 1
	12			
Answer line →		6	6 9 . 0 0	

4. The remainder of 36 from 44 is 8. Take this 8 to the remainder line as shown above. This 8 along with the next digit in the given number i.e. 7 becomes the next dividend i.e. 87
5. Divide 87 by the divisor i.e. 12.
87 ÷ 12 → Q7 & R3; however a quotient of 6 and reminder of 15 is taken instead of 7 and 3 to avoid negative values in further steps; take quotient 6 to answer line and remainder 15 to remainder line as shown above.
6. 155 – D(6) = 155 – 36 = 119 ÷ 12 = Q9 & R11
7. 116 – D(69) = 116 – 108 = 8 ÷ 12 = Q0 & R8
8. 81- D(690) = 81 – 81 = Q0 & R0

9. $\therefore \sqrt{\mathbf{447561}}$ = **669**[a perfect square]
{9} ⇐ {3^2}

Example 3: Find $\sqrt{\mathbf{119716}}$

1. 11/97/16
2. Within 11 we have 3^2; so the divisor is 6
3. 11 – 9 = 2

	Divisor			
Reminder line →	↓		2 5	5 3
Given Number →		11	9 7	1 6
	6			
Answer line→		3	4 6 . 0 0	

4. 29 ÷6 → Q4 & R5
5. 57 – D(4) → 41 ÷ 6 → Q6 & R5
6. 51 – D(46) → 3 ÷ 6 → Q0 & R3
7. 36 – D(460) → 36 – 36 = 0; 0 ÷ 6 → Q0 & R0

$\therefore \sqrt{\mathbf{119716}}$ = **346** [a perfect square]
{7} ⇐ {4^2}

Example 4: Find $\sqrt{\mathbf{738915489}}$

1. 7/38/91/54/89
2. Within 7 we have 2^2; so the divisor is 4
3. 7 – 4 = 3

	Divisor					
Reminder line →	↓		3 5	5 13	6 7	4 0
Given Number →		7	3 8	9 1	8 4	8 9
	4					
Answer line→		2	7 1	8 3 . 0 0	0 0	

4. 33 ÷ 4 → Q7 & R5 {a lesser quotient}
5. 58 – D(7) → 58 – 49 → 9 ÷ 4 → Q1 & R5 {a lesser quotient}
6. 59 – D(71) → 59 – 14 → 45 ÷ 4 → Q8 & R13 {a lesser quotient}
7. 131 – D(718) → 131 – 113 → 18 ÷ 4 → Q3 & R 6 {a lesser quotient}

8. 65 – D(7183) → 65 – 58 → 7 ÷ 4 → Q0& R7 {a lesser quotient}
9. 74 – D(71830)→ 74 – 70 → 4 ÷ 4 → Q0 & R4 {a lesser quotient}
10. 48 – D(718300) → 48 – 48 → 0 ÷ 4 → Q0 & R0
11. 09 – D(7183000) → 09 – 09 → 0 End of operation

$\therefore \sqrt{\mathbf{738915489}}$ = **27183** [a perfect square]

{9} ⇐ $\{3^2\}$

Example 5: Find $\sqrt{\mathbf{25745476}}$

1. 25/74/54/76
2. 5^2→ 25; divisor is 10; 25 – 25 = 0 ÷ 10 → Q0 & R0
3. 07 ÷ 10 → Q0 & R7
4. 74 – D(0) → 74 ÷ 10 → Q7 & R4
5. 45 – D(07) → 45 – 0 → 45 ÷ 10 → Q4 & R5
6. 54 – D(074) → 54 – 49 → 5 ÷ 10 → Q0 & R5

	Divisor				
Reminder line →	↓		0 7	4 5	5 1
Given Number →		25	7 4	5 4	7 6
	10				
Answer line→		5	0 7 4 . . 0 0		

7. 57 – D(0740) → 57 – 56 → 1 ÷ 10 → Q0 & R1
8. 16 – D(07400) → 16 – 16 → 0 ÷ 10 → Q0 & R0

$\therefore \sqrt{\mathbf{25745476}}$ = **5074** [a perfect square]

{4} ⇐ $\{7^2\}$

Example 6: Find $\sqrt{\mathbf{2.0736}}$

1. 02/.07/36
2. Within 02 only square of 1 can be accommodated and hence divisor is 2
3. 02 – 1 → 1 ÷ 2 → Q0 & R1

	Divisor			
Reminder line →	↓		1 2	3
Given Number →		02	. 0 7	3 6
	2			
Answer line→		1	4 4 0 0	

4. 10 ÷ 2 → Q4 & R2 {a lesser quotient}
5. 27 – D(4) → 27 – 16 → 11 ÷ 2 → Q4 & R3 {a lesser quotient}
6. 33 – D(44) → 33 – 32 → 1 ÷ 2 → Q0 & R1
7. 16 – D(440) → 16 – 16 → 0 ÷ 2 → Q0 & R0

$\therefore \sqrt{\mathbf{2.0736}} = \mathbf{1.44}$

{9} ⇐ {9^2}

1.3: Example 7 below shows how to find square root for an imperfect square with decimal result

Example 7: Find $\sqrt{1882}$

Note: The procedure is same as explained in ex. 1 to 6 above. Only that, after the decimal (which is after second digit in the square root) we will not get zeros as we had in above problems.

1. 18/82
2. Within 18 we will have 4^2; so divisor is 4 × 2 = 8
3. So 18 – 4^2 = 2
4. The new gross dividend is 28; 28 ÷ 8 = Q3 & R4

	Divisor					
Reminder line →	↓		2 4	8 . .	. .	.
Given Number →		18	8 2.	0 0	0 0	0 0
	10					
Answer line→		4	3. 3 8 ...			

5. 42 – D(3) → 42 – 9 → 33 ÷ 8 → Q3 & R9 {a lesser quotient}
6. Place a decimal and new gross dividend is 90
7. 90 – D(33) → 90 – 18 → 72 ÷ 8 → Q8 & R8 {a lesser quotient}
8. 80 – D(338) → 80 – 57 → 23 and so on.

$\therefore \sqrt{\mathbf{1882}} = \mathbf{43.38}$ ...

□

Miscellaneous Topic on Higher Powers

Introduction

The binomial form various powers are as below –

$(x + y)$	$x + y$
$(x + y)^2$	$x^2 + 2xy + y^2$
$(x + y)^3$	$x^3 + 3x^2y + 3xy^2 + y^3$
$(x + y)^4$	$x^4 + 4x^3y + 6x^2y^2 + 4xy^3 + y^4$

From the above binomial expansion we can form the Pascal triangle as below –

1	1st order
1 2 1	2nd order
1 3 3 1	3rd order
1 4 6 4 1	4th order
1 5 10 10 8 1	5th order
1 6 15 20 15 6 1	6th order
1 7 21 35 35 21 7 1	and so on ...

From the above if we are to find 5th order binomial expansion of $(x + y)$, then it can be readily written down as $a^5 + 5a^4b + 10a^3b^2 + 10a^2b^3 + 5ab^4 + b^5$

Third Power

In the earlier book **'Squaring'** we have shown how to square numbers using duplex and few other methods. Here with the help of binomial expansion let us first see how to cube a number.

Here we use the 3rd order expansion i.e. $x^3 + 3x^2y + 3xy^2 + y^3$ ... ... (1)

Now the expression (1) above can be split as below –

$x^3 + x^2y + xy^2 + y^3$ ... ... (2)

and $2x^2y + 2xy^2$ ... ... (3)

The addition of (2) & (3) above yields (1). Now the expression (2) above reveals that if we move from left to right each successive element is in the ratio **y/x** and in the same expression if we move from right to left each element is in the ratio **x/y**. In expression (3) above, the elements are twice the elements of middle two of expression (2) above. With this as basis, let us find out say 23^3.

Example 1: Find 23^3

Here let us assume that x is 2 and y is 3 and y/x is 3/2

$\therefore 23^3 \rightarrow$	2^3	$2^2 \times 3$	2×3^2	3^3		
	8	12	18	27	... ...	(1)
		2×12	2×18		... ...	(2)
Adding (1) & (2)	8	36	54	27		

or $8 /_{3} 6 /_{5} 4 /_{2} 7$ = 12167

$\therefore 23^3 = 12167$

$\{5^3\}$ $\{8\}$

Example 2: Find 123^3

Let a = 12; b = 3; a/b = 12/3 = 4; moving from right to left

$432 \times 4 \leftarrow$	$108 \times 4 \leftarrow$	27×4	$\leftarrow 27$	
1728	432	108	27	... ... (1)
	x2	x2		
+	864	216		... ...(2)
1728	1296	324	27	... (1) + (2)

or $1728/_{129} 6/_{32} 4/_{2} 7$ = 1860867

$\therefore 123^3 = 1860867$

$\{6^3\}$ $\{9\}$

Cubing near a base

Cubing can be done differently when the numbers are near base

Example 3: Find 104^3

Base = 100

$104^3 \rightarrow$

(i) 1st excess on base $\rightarrow$ 104 – 100 = 04

(ii) Number + twice excess = 104 + 2 × 04 = 112

(iii) 2nd excess = 112 – 100 = 12

(iv) 1st excess × 2nd excess = 4 × 12 = 48

(v) cube of 1st excess $\rightarrow 4^3 = 64$

$\therefore 104^3 = 112/48/64$

$\{5^3\}$ $\{8\}$

Example 4: Find 97^3

Base = 100

$97^3 \rightarrow$

(i) 1st deficit $\rightarrow$ 97 –100 = –03

(ii) Number + twice deficit = 97 + (2 × –03) = 91

(iii) 2nd deficit = 91 –100 = –09

(iv) 1st deficit × 2nd deficit = –03 × –09 = 27

(v) Cube of 1st deficit = $(-03)^3 = -27 = \overline{27}$

$\therefore 97^3 = 91/27/\overline{27} = 912673$

$\{7^3\}$ $\{1\}$

Fourth Power

From Pascal's Triangle explained in sec 2.0 above the fourth order binomial expansion will be –

$(a+b)^4 \rightarrow a^4 + 4a^3b + 6a^2b^2 + 4ab^3 + b^4$ ……… (1)

This can be split as –

$a^4 + a^3b + a^2b^2 + ab^3 + b^4$ ……… (2)

$3a^3b + 5a^2b^2 + 3ab^3$ ……… (3)

$a^4 + 4a^3b + 6a^2b^2 + 4ab^3 + b^4$ ……… (1)

As in the case of 3rd power – expression (2) above reveals that if we move from left to right each successive elements is in the ratio **b/a** and if we move from right to left it is in the ratio of **a/b**. And in expression (3) the elements are multiples of 2nd, 3rd, and 4th elements of expression (2).

Example 5: Find 21^4

Here if a = 2 and b= 1, then a/b =2; so we shall proceed from right to left.

				1^4
			2	←x2
		4	←x2	
	8	←x2		
16	←x2			
16	8	4	2	1
	x3	x5	x3	
+	24	20	6	
16/	32/	24/	8/	1

or $16\,/_3\,2\,/_2\,4/8/1$ = 194481

∴ 21^4 = 194481

{3^4} {9}

Example 6: Find 12^4

In this case if a = 1 and b =2, then b/a = 2 and we can proceed from left to right as shown below -

1^4				
x2 →	2			
	x2 →	4		
		x2 →	8	
			×2 →	16
1	2	4	8	16
	×3	×5	×3	
+	6	20	24	
1	8	24	32	16

or $1\,/\,8\,/_2\,4\,/_3\,2\,/_1\,6$ = 20736

∴ 12^4 = 20736

{3^4} {9}

Example 7: Find 93^4

93^4 can be found from right to left with a/b = 3

3^8	3^7	3^6	3^5	3^4
	←×3	←×3	←×3	←×3
6561	2187	729	243	81
	×3	×5	×3	
+	6561	3645	729	
6561	8748	4374	972	81

or $6561\,/_{874}\,8/_{437}\,4/_{97}\,2\,/_{8}\,1 = 74805201$

$\therefore 93^4 = 74805201$
$\{3^4\}$ $\{9\}$

Example 8: Find 39^4

If we are to find 39^4 we can use the same ratio, but we have to proceed from left to right.

81/ 972/ 4374/ 8748/ 6561

or $81/_{97}\,2/_{437}\,4/_{874}\,8/_{656}\,1 = 2313441$

$\therefore 39^4 = 2313441$
$\{3^4\}$ $\{9\}$

□

20

Cube Rooting

Preface

In the earlier lesson **'Square-Rooting'** we have seen how to find square root for numbers which are perfect square as well as for numbers which are not perfect square. But in case of finding cube roots only for those numbers which are perfect cubes is explained. Otherwise finding cube root for numbers, which are not perfect, cubes use of logarithmic tables are the best known method. Two different methods are explained; one based on the basic cubes and digital root while the second method is based on the algebraic principle – similar to the one employed for finding square roots.

To find Cube Root-I

Introduction

This method applies to those numbers which are perfect cubes. For this we first understand the basics of cubes and cube roots.

Observe the following table –

Table 1.0

Number	cube	Digital Root
1	1	1
2	8	8
3	27	9
4	64	1
5	125	8
6	216	9
7	343	1
8	512	8
9	729	9
10	1000	1

Important observations from the above –

1. A number to be a perfect cube its digital root (or digit sum) has to be 1, 8, or 9.
2. If the number is ending in three zeros, the cube root will end in a single zero.
3. If the digit at unit place of cube is 1, 4, 5, 6, 9, or 0, then the cube root will also have 1, 4, 5, 6, 9, or 0 at its unit place respectively.
4. For other digits in unit place of cube i.e. 2, 3, 7, and 8, its complement from 10 will be at unit place of cube root.

Method of finding Cube Root

(For perfect cube)

The following steps are involved in finding cube root of a given number. Let us find cube roots of the following cubes –

Example 1:

1. 32768 **2.** 103823 **3.** 125000
4. 3375 **5.** 97336 **6.** 10648

Step 1: Mark in group of three digits from right to left as shown below –

Table 1.1.1

SN	Example	Groups
1	32768	32/768
2	103823	103/823
3	125000	125/000
4	3375	3/375
5	97336	97/336
6	10648	10/648

Step 2: Using the tips (3) and (4) above we proceed to find the unit digits of cube root for each of the given number –

Table 1.1.2

SN	Given No.	Unit digit of given no.	Unit digit of cube root
1	32/768	8	2
2	103/823	3	7
3	125/000	0	0
4	3/375	5	5
5	97/336	6	6
6	10/648	8	2

Step 3: We are sure of the unit's place of the cube root (last column of the above table. To find the ten's place we have to work out the nearest (lower side) or equal of perfect cube of the left group –

Table 1.1.3

SN	Given No.	Left Group	Nearest cube root
1	32/768	32	3
2	103/823	103	4
3	125/000	125	5
4	3/375	3	1
5	97/336	97	4
6	10/648	10	2

So the final cube root of the given 6 numbers are –

Table1.1.4

SN	Example	Cube root
1	32768	32
2	103823	47
3	125000	50
4	3375	15
5	97336	46
6	10648	22

The table below shows the digital root check for all the 6 examples–

Table 1.1.5

SN	Given Number	Cube root	DR of cube root	Checking	DR of Given Number
1	32768	32	5	$5^3 = 8$	8
2	103823	47	2	$2^3 = 8$	8
3	125000	50	5	$5^3 = 8$	8
4	3375	15	6	$6^3 = 9$	9
5	97336	46	1	$1^3 = 1$	1
6	10648	22	4	$4^3 = 1$	1

To find Cube Root-II

Introduction

Cube root can be found using algebraic principle – similar to square root. [Ex. 1 to 7 of the lesson **'Square Rooting'**]. For this, suppose a number **cba** can be represented as 100**c** + 10**b** + **a**.

$\therefore (100c + 10b + a)^3$

$=10^6c^3+300000bc^2+30000ac^2+30000b^2c+1000b^3+6000abc+300a^2b+300a^2c+30ab^2+a^3$ ... ... (A)

Removing the powers of ten and putting the result from the end w.r.t. place value we observe the following –

1. the unit's place is determined by a^3

2. the ten's place is determined by $3ab^2$
3. the hundred's place is determined by $3a^2b+3a^2c$
4. the thousand's place is determined by b^3+6abc
5. the ten thousand's is determined by $3ac^2+3b^2c$
6. the lakh's place is determined by $3bc^2$
7. the millionth's place is determined by c^3

Note: The correctness of the above observations can be confirmed with the number of ZEROES in the various coefficients in the algebraic expression (A) above.

Procedure

The procedure is similar to the procedure adopted for extraction of square root. The two differences are – first the divisor in this context will not be double the first digit of the root but three times the square there of; and second duplex of the respective quotients are not considered for subtraction from the gross dividend.

1. From the second gross dividend no subtraction is done and directly divided by the divisor.
2. From the third gross dividend $3ab^2$ is subtracted (instead of DUPLEX of second quotient), where 'a' is first quotient and 'b' is the second one and then divided by the divisor.
3. From the fourth gross dividend $6abc+b^3$ is subtracted (instead of DUPLEX of second and third quotient) where a, b, and c are 1st, 2nd, and 3rd quotients respectively and then divided by divisor.
4. In this way from each gross dividend the subtractions are $3a^2c+3b^2c$; then $3bc^2$ and finally c^3, where a, b, and c are first, second and third quotients respectively and after subtraction the net dividend is divided by the divisor which is 3 times the square of first quotient.

Example 1: Find the cube root of 13824.

Steps:

1. Make group of 3 digits from right → 13|824
2. 8 is the nearest cube for 13 i.e. 2^3. ∴ The first quotient is 2 and divisor is $3\times2^2 = 12$

	Divisor		
Reminder line →	↓		5 10 6
Given Number →		1 3	8 2 4
	12		
Answer line→		2	4. 0 0

3. $13 - 2^3 = 5$. ∴ R = 5
4. So the first gross dividend is 58 and without subtraction 58 ÷ 12→Q4 & R10
5. The second gross dividend is 102. Subtract $3ab^2$, where a = 2, and b = 4. ∴ Subtract $3 \times 2 \times 4^2 = 96$. ∴ The second working dividend is 102 – 96 = 6 and 6 ÷ 12 = Q0 & R6.
6. The third gross dividend is 64; subtract $6abc + b^3$, where a=2, b=4 and c=0. ∴ $64 - 4^3 = 0$. ∴ 0 ÷ 12 = Q0 & R0.

∴ **24** is an exact cube of **13824**.

Example 2: Find the cube root of 1728

Steps:

1. Mark group → 1|728

	Divisor		
Reminder line →	↓	0	0 1 0
Given Number →		1	7 2 8
	3		
Answer line→		1	2. 0 0

2. Nearest cube of 1 is 1; ∴ Divisor is 3×1^2
3. ∴ Q= 0 & R = 0
4. First gross dividend is 07; subtract nothing and divide by divisor i.e. 07 ÷ 3 = Q2 & R1
5. Second gross dividend is 12; subtract $3ab^2$ where a = 1 and b = 2. ∴ $12 - 3\times1\times2^2 = 0$; ∴ Q0 & R0
6. The third gross dividend is 08; subtract $6abc + b^3 = 8 - 8 = 0$

∴ **12** is an exact cube of **1728**.

□

21

Division

Preface

In division also we have innumerable methods; in conventional method wherein the method is based on thorough knowledge of tables and also involves subtraction; whereas most of the Vedic methods do not involve multiplication tables. It does not also involve subtraction of multiple of the divisor to arrive at the intermediate remainder. Division with 2 digit numbers and also 3 digit numbers near base are very easy and almost a fun to do regularly. A bit of practice makes the entire procedure very simple and some of the smaller divisions can be accomplished by mental calculations.

Division (Part-I)

Division By 9

Introduction

The number 9 is very special and it is easy to divide by 9. Division by 9 can be accomplished by 2 distinct ways viz. Simple method and Method of cumulating.

Simple Method

This simple method is applicable directly as explained in examples below to divisor 9 only and not to other divisors like 8 or 7. However, the underlying principle being division with complements, the same can be extended to 8 and 7 also.

Example 1: Divide 2312 by 9

Here dividend is 2312; divisor is 9

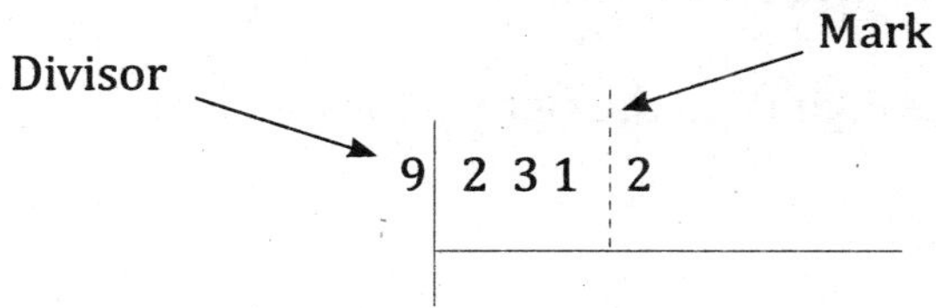

Procedure

Arrange the sum as shown above i.e.

1. First mark a line from right equivalent to number of digits in the divisor. Here we have one digit in the divisor and hence mark after one digit from right on the dividend as shown above by dotted line. **Note:** The left side of the mark i.e. dotted line, is quotient part and the right side is the remainder part

```
9 | 2 3 1 : 2
  | ↓ 2 5 : 6
  |__________________
  | ↗ ↗ ↗
  2 5 6 8
```

2. Now the left most digit, 2 is brought down.

3. Then the 2 is taken up on the blank space as shown by the symbol and added to the 3 in 2312 and the result 5 is put down.
4. 5 is taken up and added to 1 and the result 6 is taken down.
5. As we have reached the mark the quotient part of the answer is 256
6. Then 6 is taken up crossing the mark and added to the 2 (after the mark) and this 8 is the remainder of the final division.

∴ 2312÷ 9 = Q-256 & R-8

We know that division is the reverse process of multiplication; hence the above result can be expressed as **quotient × divisor + remainder = dividend**. i.e. **256 × 9 + 8 = 2312**

{4} × {9} + {8} = {8} → DR check

Example 2: Divide 1234 by 9

Steps:

Mark one digit from the right in the dividend 1234.

```
9 | 1 2 3 : 4
  | ↓ 1 3 : 6
  |---------------
  |  ↗ ↗ :↗
    1 3 6  10
```

Adopting the same procedure and steps 1 to 5 from the example 1 above we get Quotient as 136 and R as 10. But the remainder has one 9 and add 1 to quotient 136 i.e. 136 + 1 = 137 and R now works out to 1.

∴ 1234 ÷ 9 = Q-137 & R-1 or **137 × 9 + 1 = 1234**

{2} × {9} + {1} = {1} → DR check

Example 3: Divide 311101 by 9

```
9 | 3  1  1  1  0 : 1
  | ↓  3  4  5  6 : 6
  |    ↗  ↗  ↗  ↗ :
--|------------------
  | 3  4  5  6  6 : 7
```

∴ 311101 ÷ 9 = Q-34566 & R-7 or **34566 × 9 + 7 = 311101**

{6} × {9} + {7} = {7}

Exercise:

(a)	713	**(b)**	212	**(c)**	444	**(d)**	3102
(e)	56	**(f)**	11202	**(g)**	234	**(h)**	31
(i)	46	**(j)**	3011	**(k)**	53	**(l)**	2002
(m)	203010	**(n)**	114	**(o)**	70		

Example 4: Divide 3272 by 9

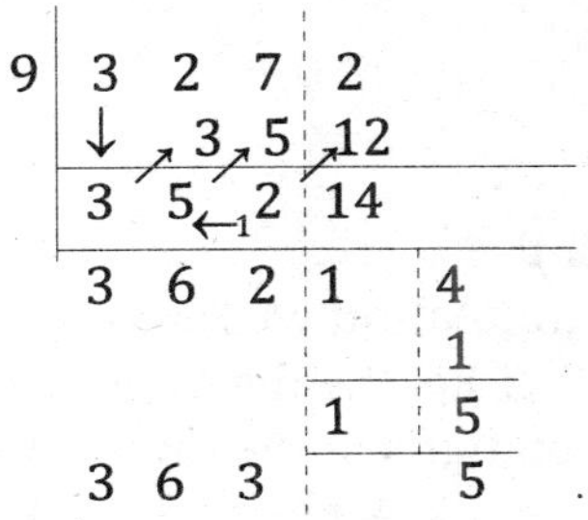

```
9 | 3   2   7 : 2
  | ↓  ↗3 ↗5 :↗12
  |-----------------------
  | 3   5 ←1 2 : 14
  |-----------------------
    3   6   2 : 1   : 4
              :     : 1
              :-----------
              : 1   : 5
              :-----------
    3   6   3 :       5
```

∴ 3272 ÷ 9 = Q-363 & R-5

Steps:

1. Bring down 3 of the dividend
2. Take this 3 diagonally up below 2 and add 2 & 3 and bring down the 5
3. Take 5 diagonally up below 7 and add 7 & 5 and bring down the 12
4. From the 12 retain 2 as the unit place of quotient and carry back the 1 to left and make the current quotient as 362.
5. However take the entire 12 diagonally up below 2 in the remainder part and add 2 & 12 to get 14 as remainder.
6. As the remainder cannot be more than 9 divide the remainder by 9 as usual i.e. mark one digit from right, etc. With 14 divided by 9 we get one more quotient and this quotient added to the one we got in step 4 above; thus the final quotient is 363 and the remainder is 5.

Exercise: Divide the following by 9

1.	443322	**2.**	6153	**3.**	75057	**4.**	3171
5.	12345	**6.**	555	**7.**	2938	**8.**	8252
9.	5747	**10.**	661	**11.**	4741	**12.**	1918161

Method of Accumulation

This method is similar to simple method, and applicable to division by 9, 99, 999, etc also. **This method of accumulation cannot be applied for other divisors like 8, 6, 7, etc.**

Suppose 31 is to be divided by 9. In the simple method we lay the sum as below –

```
9 | 3 ⁝ 1
  | ↓ ⁝ 3
  |---------
  | 3 ⁝ 4
```

$\therefore$ **31 ÷ 9 = Q-3 & R-4**

In method of accumulation we first mark with a line in 31 as was done earlier. i.e. 3 ⁝1 i.e. the digits on RHS of the mark correspond to the number of digits in the divisor i.e. one.

So 3 ⁝1 → 3 ⁝3 + 1 = 4. i.e. instead of bringing down the 3 and then taking up diagonally to add to 1 , it is straight away added with next digit. The procedure will be more clear from 11212 ÷9 –

Example 5: Divide 11212 by 9

Steps:

1. mark a line from right leaving a single digit – 1 1 2 1 ⁝ 2
2. Now 1, 1+1=2, 2+2=4, 4+1=5 ⁝5+2=7
3. So Q = 1 2 4 5 and R = 7

Example 6: Divide 132 by 9

Ans: 132 → 13 ⁝ 2 → 1, 1+3=4 ⁝ 4+2=6

$\therefore$ **132 ÷ 9 = Q-1 4 & R-6**

Example 7: Divide 314 by 9

Ans: 31 4 → 31 ⁝ 4 → 3, 3+1=4 ⁝ 4+4=8

$\therefore$ **314 ÷ 9 = Q is 34 & R is 8**

Note: The examples in sec 1.4 above, the remainders were less than 9, unlike example 4 above. So a second division was not needed. However, when remainder exceeds the divisor we may have to resort a different mode of calculation (in this accumulation method) which are explained in examples 9, 10, and 11 below.

Example 8: Divide 612 by 9

Ans: 612 → 61 ⁝ 2 → 6, 6+1=7 ⁝ 7+2=9

∴ **Q is 67 & R is 9.** But R has to be less than 9

∴ **Q (= 67 + 1) = 68 and R (= 9 – 9) =0**

Note: In the above accumulation if the Q digit contains 2-digits (at any intermediate accumulation) write them in accordion style and then collapse it as in the following examples –

Example 9: Divide 748 by 9

Ans: 748 → 74 ⁝ 8 → 7, 7+4=11 ⁝ 11+8=19

The above is written as $7/_1 1/_1 9$. Here we first carry over the subscripted numbers to the left and simultaneously add the numbers in the right most segment i.e. $/_1 9$.

So, $7/_1 1 ⁝ _{1+} 9 \rightarrow 82_1 ⁝ 9 \rightarrow 82_{1+} ⁝ 0 \rightarrow 831$; ∴ **748 ÷ 9** → Q-83 & R-1

If we add the 1 & 9 in the right most segment we get 10. This again being more than nine carry 1 to left as well as add 1 & 0 to get the final quotient as 83 and final remainder as 1.

Note: If you refer back, you would realize that writing the outcome in accordion style was first introduced in example 16 under sec 6.6 of Chapter 6 of the book **'Multiplication'** There the result of (33x46 + 26x29 – 51x13) was written as $11/_4 4/_6 9$.

And while collapsing the above we have only carried over the subscripted numbers 6 & 4 to its left place and thus we got

$$11/_4 4/_6 9 \rightarrow 11/_{4+1} 0/9 \rightarrow 1609$$

But in case of collapsing accordion style of writing results in accumulation method of division above, there is an additional feature in the right most part (which is the remainder part). Here subscripted digit which is not only to be carried over to left but should also be added within the group. Observe again the following two examples carefully to understand this –

Example 10: Divide 68729 by 9

Ans: 68729→6872 ⁝ 9→ 6, 6+8=14, 14+7=21,
21+2=23 ⁝ 23+9=32

or $6/\ _{1}4/\ _{2}1/\ _{2}3 \vdots\ _{3+}2 \rightarrow 7\,6\,3\,6\,5$

$\therefore$ **68729 ÷ 9 = Q is 7636 & R is 5**

Example 11: Divide 190091 by 9

Ans: 190091 → 19009 ⋮ 1

→ 1, 1+9=10, 10+0=10, 10+0=10, 10+9=19 ⋮ 19+1=20

or $1/\ _{1}0/\ _{1}0/\ _{1}0/\ _{1}9 \vdots\ _{2+}0$

2 1 1 2 1 ⋮ 2

Accumulation Method for Divisors 99, 999, etc.

We have seen accumulation method for dividing by divisor 9 and the same can be extended to divisors 99, 999, etc as shown in following examples –

Example 12: Divide 347 by 99

Ans: The procedure is similar to the one explained for divisor 9 except that the mark is after two digit from right (for remainder part) as the divisor 99 has two digits and also in the quotient part group of two digits from the mark should be dealt with at every stage of division. If any such group contains single digit (the left most group may contain single digit) then add a leading zero and make the number of digits in quotient part even.

So, 347 → 03 47; note the mark and the leading zero.

03 47 → 03 03+47=50

$\therefore$ **347 ÷ 99 = Q is 3 & R is 50**

Example 13: Divide 7603 by 99

Ans: 7603 → 76 ⋮ 03 → 76 76+03=79

$\therefore$ **7603 ÷ 99 →Q is 76 and R is 79**

Example 14: Divide 21673 by 99

Ans: 21673 → 02 16 73 → 2, 2+16=18 18+73=91

$\therefore$**21673 ÷ 99 = Q is** 218 & R is 91

Example 15: Divide 63381 by 99

Ans: 63381 → 06 33 81 → 6, 6+33=39 39+81=120

or $6/39 \vdots\ _{1+}20 \rightarrow 640\ 21$

$\therefore$ **63381 ÷ 99 = Q is 640 & R is 21**

Example 16: Divide 633891 by 99

Ans: 633891 → 63,38 ⋮ 91 → 63, 63+38=101 ⋮ 101+91=192

or 63/ ⋮ $_{1}$01 ⋮ $_{1+}$92 → 6402 ⋮ 93

∴ **633891 ÷ 99 = Q is 6402& R is 93**

Division by 999 & 9999

Example 17: Divide 213134 by 999

Ans: 213134 → 213 ⋮ 134 → 213 ⋮ 213+134=347

∴ **213134 ÷ 999 = Q is 213 & R is 347**

Example 18: Divide 62183 by 9999

Ans: 62183 → 6 ⋮ 2183 → 6 ⋮ 6+2183=2189

∴ **62183 ÷ 9999 = Q is 6 & R is 2189**

Example 19: Divide 619990 by 9999

Ans: 619990 → 61 ⋮ 9990→ 61 ⋮ 61+9990=10051

or 61 ⋮ $_{1+}$0051 → 62 |0052

∴ **619990 ÷ 9999 = Q is 62 & R is 52**

Exercise

Ex 1: Divide by 9

1.	31	**2.**	53	**3.**	70	**4.**	46
5.	56	**6.**	212	**7.**	114	**8.**	234
9.	444	**10.**	713	**11.**	555	**12.**	661
13.	655	**14.**	166	**15.**	777	**16.**	3102
17.	6153	**18.**	3272	**19.**	8252	**20.**	4471
21.	5747	**22.**	2938	**23.**	3172	**24.**	2311
25.	6153	**26.**	7232	**27.**	2852	**28.**	4714
29.	7457	**30.**	3928	**31.**	2121	**32.**	11202
33.	11111	**34.**	20002	**35.**	75057	**36.**	12345
37.	311101	**38.**	442323	**39.**	203010	**40.**	1918161

1.7.2: Divide the above (from 6 to 40) by 99

1.7.3: Divide the above (from 16 to 40) by 999

1.7.4: Divide the above (from 32 to 40) by 9999

1.7.5: Divide the above (from 37 to 40) by 99999

□

22

Division (Part-II)

Division By 9 (Complement Method)

Introduction

Two methods of division with divisor as 9 were seen in the earlier lesson. One was simple method and the other was accumulation method. Readers may remember that the simple method explained for 9 can be easily adopted for 99, 999, etc also. Please see ex. below

E.g. Divide 63381 by 99 by simple method - Ex.15 of lesson 21 is repeated

99	06 33		81
01	06		39
	06 39	1	20
			01
		1	21
	0640		21

$\therefore$ **63381 ÷ 99**
= Q is 640 & R is 21

You may try all problems which are solved by the accumulation method in the earlier lesson by simple method also.

In this lesson we are going to introduce a complement method of division with the same divisor 9, 99, 999, etc. and later in the next lesson we will show how the complement method of division can be used for other divisors like, 8, 7 etc.

Complements

Complements are nothing but difference between the given number and its nearest base. For single digit numbers the base is 10, for 2-digit numbers 100, for 3-digit numbers 1000 and so on.

As we are continuing to show examples with divisor 9, 99, etc – complement of 9 is 1 (since the nearest base being 10); for 99 also complement is 1 or 01 (since the nearest base being 100); and so on.

Complement Method

Example 1: Divide 1231 by 9

Steps:

1. Mark the line for separating Q part and R part as done earlier.
   i.e.

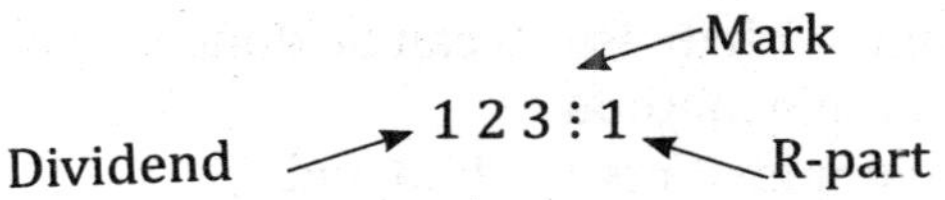

   Mark → 1 2 3 : 1 ← R-part
   Dividend → 1 2 3 : 1

2. Now write the complement of the divisor 9, as shown below –

9	1 2 3	1
1	↓ 1 3	6
	1 3 6	7

3. Take the first digit of the dividend 1, down; this is the first Q-digit.
4. Multiply the first Q-digit and the complement of divisor i.e. 1x1, and write below 2 (the second digit of dividend); add 2 &1 to get 3 and this is the 2nd Q-digit.
5. Multiply the 2nd Q-digit and complement of the divisor i.e. 3x1; write below 3 and add to get 6. This is the 3rd and last Q-digit.
6. Multiply the 3rd Q-digit and complement i.e. 6x1; write below 1 in the R-part and add to get 7.

$\therefore$ **1231 ÷ 9 → Q is 136 & R is 7**

The subtle change between simple method and complement method will be more obvious when we use divisor 8 or 7. However, you may try all the problems solved in *Division* **1** by accumulation method by complement method also.

Example 2: Divide 398 by 9

Ans: 398 → 39 : 8 →

9	3	9		8
1		3		12
	3	$_1 2$	2	0
				2
			2	2
	4	4		2

$\therefore$ **398 ÷ 9** → Q is 44 & R is 2

As said earlier the impact of complement method will be more obvious when we deal with divisors 8 or 7 in lesson23.

So division with divisor 9 can be done in three ways i.e.

1. by simple method
2. by complements method and
3. by accumulation method.

□

23

Division (Part-III)

Divisors other than 9 (Complement Method)

Introduction

We have seen about complement method in lesson22 with divisor 9; we also made it clear that its impact will be known from divisors 8 or 7. In fact the simple method shown for 9 has the underlying principle of complement method only, but as the complement of 9 being 1 multiplying each quotient by 1 does not give a direct impact.

Division with divisor 7 or 8

Here we cannot use the simple method or the accumulation method used for divisors 9, 99, 999, etc. explained in **Division 01** earlier. However, method of complement can be used for easy and quick division as explained in lesson **Division 02**.

Example 1: Divide 206 by 7

Ans: As usual mark after one digit from the right in the dividend as the divisor is a single digit number. So 206 → 20:6. Division by 7 with its complement 3 is arranged as shown below–

```
7 | 2  0 :  6
3 | ↓  6 :  18
  |----------------
  | 2  6 : 2 : 4
  |    ↑      6
  |    └─ 2 : 1 : 0
  |----------------
  | 2  8          3
  |    ↑        
  |    └──── 1 :  3
  |----------------
  | 2  9          3
```

∴ 206 ÷ 7 → Q is 29 & R is 3

Steps:

1. Bring down the 2 of the dividend as 1st quotient
2. Multiply 1st quotient and the complement 3 of the divisor i.e. 2x3 and take this 6 diagonally up (below 0 of the dividend) and add to 0 to get 6 as the 2nd quotient (and last).
3. Multiply 2nd quotient and the complement 3 of the divisor i.e. 6x3 and take 18 diagonally up (below 6 in the remainder part) and add 6 to get 24 – which is the remainder.
4. As the remainder is more than 7 take this 24 as new dividend and divide by 7 as was explained in steps 1 to 3. i.e. mark one digit from right i.e. 2 :4.
5. Bring down the 2 of the new dividend as additional quotient
6. Add this additional quotient 2 to the already arrived quotient i.e. 26 to get the new quotient as 28 and also multiply new additional quotient 2 and the complement 3 of the divisor i.e. 2x3 and take diagonally up (below 4 of the new dividend) and add 4 to get 10 – which is new remainder.
7. This new remainder is also above 7 and divide 10 (taking again as new dividend) by 7 as explained in steps 1 to 3 or 5 & 6 to get another additional quotient i.e. 1 and final remainder as 3. Adding this additional quotient to the one we arrived at step 6 above we get the final quotient as 29 and final remainder as 3.

Alternatively at step 3 above we had quotient of 26 and remainder of 24. We know from basic Arithmetic that 24 contains 3x7=21 and hence add 3 to quotient 26 i.e. 26+3=29 and subtract 3x7=21 from the remainder i.e. 24–21=3. This is shown below –

Divisor	Quotient part	Remainder part
7	2 0	6
3	6	18
	2 6	24
	+3	-21
	2 9	3

Example 2: Divide 390 by 8

Ans: Steps—

1. Mark one digit from right in the dividend.
2. Take the complement of divisor 8 and write below the divisor as shown below –

$390 \rightarrow 39 : 0$

8	3	9	0	
$\bar{2}$		6	3	0
	3 $_{\leftarrow 1}$	5	3	0
	4	5	3	0
		↑		6
		└	3	6
	4	8		6

$\therefore$ **390 ÷ 8 → Q is 48 & R is 6**

3. Take down the first digit 3 below as 1st quotient. Multiply 1st quotient and the complement 2, to get 3×2=6.
4. Take the 6 diagonally up below 9; add 9&6 to get 15 (this is the second and last quotient); retain 5 and carry the left side 1 to further left and add to 3; with this step we get the adjusted quotient is 45.
5. Multiply 2nd quotient and the complement 2 of the divisor, to get 15×2=30 as the remainder.
6. This 30 is the remainder, but this being more than 8 (the divisor), take 30 as new dividend and divide by 8 as explained in steps 2, 3 and 4 above. i.e. take the 3 below as the 3rd quotient (which is to be added to the adjusted quotient 45, to get final quotient as 45+3=48; multiply the 3rd quotient and complement of divisor to get 3x2=6 and when this is taken diagonally up and added to 0 we get the final remainder as 6.

$\therefore$ **390 ÷ 8 → Q is 48 & R is 6**

Alternatively at step 5 we know that the remainder 30 contains three 8s and hence add 3 to adjusted quotient 45 to get the final quotient as 48 and subtract 3×8=24 from the remainder 30 to get final remainder as 6. (see below for details)

```
8 | 3   9 : 0
- |
2 |     6 : 30
  |------------
  | 3 ←1 5 : 30
  | 4    5 : 30
  |     +3 : −24
  |------------
  | 4    8 :  6
```

Example 3: Divide 3045 by 88

Ans: Steps—

1. mark two digits from right as divisor 88 has two digits i.e. 30 ⁝ 45
2. Complement of 88 is 12
3. So

```
88 | 3  0 : 4  5
-- |
12 | ↓  3 : 6
   |        3  6
   |--------------
   | 3  3 : 13 ,1 1
   | 3  3 : 1 4 1
   |          1 2
   |     1    5 3
   |--------------
   | 3  4     5 3
```

∴ **3045 ÷ 88 → Q is 34 & R is 53**

4. Take the first digit of dividend 3 below and this is the 1st quotient.
5. Multiply 1st quotient and complement 12 of the divisor to get 3×12=36. Take 36 diagonally up (partly in quotient part and partly in remainder part) as shown above. Add 0&3 and bring it down as 2nd& last quotient.
6. Multiply 2nd quotient and the complement 12, of the divisor i.e. 3×12 =36 and take 36 diagonally up (entirely in remainder part) as shown above.
7. Add the digits in remainder part column-wise and after adjustments get the remainder as 141.

8. 141 being more than the divisor 88, divide 141 by 88 using complement 12 as shown above. This division gives an additional quotient of 1 and final remainder of 53. Adding this additional quotient to 33 we get final Q as 34 and R as 53.

Example 4: Divide 21456 by 878

Ans: Steps—

1. Mark three digits from right as the divisor has 3 digits. i.e. 21 456
2. Complement of 878 is 122
3. So -

```
878 | 2 1 : 4 5 6
122 | 1 2 : 4 4
    |     : 3 6 6
    |-------------------
    | 2 3 : 1 1₁ 5₁ 2
    | 2 3 : 1 2 6 2*
    |       : 1 2 2
    |     ---------------
    |     1 : 3 8 4
    |-------------------
    | 2 4   : 3 8 4
```

$\therefore$ **21456 ÷ 878 → Q is 24 & R is 384**

4. The four arrows above gives clear idea about the procedure. *the remainder 1262 is more than the divisor. So divide the remainder as if it is a new dividend i.e. as shown above.
5. Alternatively simply add 1 to 23, the existing quotient and subtract 878 from 1262, the existing remainder, to get 384 and thus getting the final Q as 23+1=24 and final R as 1262-878=384 same as above.

Exercises

Ex 1: Divide the following numbers by 8

1. 101 2. 1101 3. 2121
4. 11111 5. 132

Ex 2: Divide the following with respective numbers

1. 121 ÷ 88 2. 211 ÷ 76 3. 132 ÷ 83

4.	333÷98	**5.**	1225 ÷ 887	**6.**	1513 ÷ 867
7.	2222 ÷ 779	**8.**	3001 ÷ 765	**9.**	13103 ÷8907
10.	12321÷ 7999	**11.**	21012 ÷ 7789	**12.**	44344 ÷8888

Ex 3: Divide the following as shown –

1.	1108 ÷ 79	**2.**	1121123 ÷ 8989	**3.**	1012 ÷ 898
4.	1021 ÷ 88	**5.**	1122 ÷ 88	**6.**	1001 ÷ 79
7.	1111 ÷ 97	**8.**	10011 ÷ 888	**9.**	11243 ÷ 887
10.	21212 ÷ 899	**11.**	30125 ÷ 988	**12.**	201020 ÷ 8899

□

24

Division (Part-IV)

Division – Multiples Method

Introduction

In the earlier lesson, all the examples (1 to 4) used the complement method. It was easy to use complement because the divisors were quite nearer to base and hence the consequent complements were small. [We also know that if the divisor is small then its complement from the base will be larger and cannot be used as working divisor easily.] If the divisor is small and the complement is larger, then adopt the multiple methods as shown in this lesson.

Multiples Method

Example 1: Divide 2328 by 31

Ans: Steps—

1. Mark from right two digits as usual as divisor 31 has two digits.
2. The complement of 31 is 69 and to have 69 as working divisor will be not convenient since multiplication of quotients' and complement cannot be accomplished mentally.
3. So the divisor 31 is multiplied by 3 to get 93 and complement of 93 is 07 (note the zero)
4.

Divisor				
31 × 3	2	3	2	8
93		1	4	
07			2	8
	2	4	8	$_{1}6$
		+1	-9	3
	2	5*		3
		× 3		
	7	5		3

∴ 2328 ÷ 31 = Q is 75 and R is 3

5. Here multiple of 31 i.e. 93 is taken as temporary divisor and its complement 07 is taken as working divisor. With 07 we get Q as 24 and R as 96. The remainder 96 contains one temporary divisor i.e. 93. So add one to Q i.e. 24+1=25 and subtract 93 from remainder 96.
6. *As the divisor was multiplied by 3 the quotient is also multiplied by 3.

Example 2: Divide 21128 by 29

Ans:

1. 21128 → 211 28
2. Complement of 29 is 71, which is too big. So multiply 29 by 3 to get temporary multiplier as 87 and its complement is 100-87=13.
3. 13 will be used as working divisor.
4. We first get Q as 240 and R as 248.
5. This 248 is again divided by using complement 13 to get additional Q as 2 and R as 74.
6. The gross quotient now is 240+2= 242 and remainder is 76 which cannot be further divided by 87.

Divisor	Quotient part	Remainder part
29 × 3	2 1 1	2 8
87	2 6	
13	3	9
		13 0
	2 3 $_1$0	2 4 8
	2 4 0	2 6
		2 7 4
	2 4 2	7 4
	× 3	
	7 2 6	7 4
	+ 2	- 5 8
	7 2 8	16

∴ 21128 ÷ 29 → Q is 728 & R is 16

7. Now the quotient 242 is multiplied by 3 (as the original divisor was multiplied by 3) to get the adjusted quotient as 726. But the remainder is still more than the original

divisor 29; it contains two 29s. So add 2 to 726 and subtract 2×29=58 from 74 to get a final reminder as 16.

Example 3: Divide 4128 by 63

Ans:

1. Complement of 63 is 37; 37 is not easy to handle mentally.
2. Multiply 63 by 16 to get 1008. Complement of 1008 is -008 (negative because it is above the base)
3. The mark from the right is based on the number of digits on the working divisor. Here the working divisor has 3 digits i.e. 008. $\therefore 4128 \rightarrow 4 \vdots 128$
4. So

63x 16	4	1	2	8
1008		0	0	$\overline{32}$
-008	4	1	2	$\overline{24}$
	x16	1	0	$\overline{4}$
	64		9	6
	+1	-	6	3
	65		33	

$\therefore$ **4128 ÷ 63 → Q is 65 & R is 33**

Note: In the above, the divisor 63 is not near base so it is first multiplied by 16 to get 1008. This is near base 1000, but as it is above the base its complement is taken as –008.

This leads to a new method, when the first digit of the divisor is unity i.e. **'Change Sign'** method, which is discussed in the next lesson.

□

25

Division (Part-V)

Division – Change Sign Method

Introduction

The complement method is preferred when divisors are large i.e. very near to base or powers of 10. In case the divisors are intermediate, then 'multiples' method can be adopted. In case divisors are small and its first digit (from left) is unity, then **'Change Sign'** method.

In example 3 of lesson24, the divisor 63 is not near base so it was first multiplied by 16 to get 1008. This is near base 1000, but as it is above the base its complement is taken as –008.

These led to a new method i.e. when the first digit of the divisor is unity, 'Change Sign' of the complement and then divide with this complement as usual.

Change Sign Method

Example 1: Divide 311 by 12

Ans: Steps—

1. Drop the unity (extreme left digit) of the divisor and change the sign of the remaining digit(s) to negate the value.
2. The mark on the dividend from right is based on the number digits after the unity is dropped. Here it is –2 i.e. one digit. So 31 1→ 31 ⁝ 1
3. So

$$
\begin{array}{r|rr:r}
12 & 3 & 1 & 1 \\
\bar{2} & & \bar{6} & \\
 & & & 10 \\
\hline
 & 3 & \bar{5} & 11 \\
 & 2 & 5 & 11
\end{array}
$$

$\therefore$ **311 ÷ 12 → Q is 25 & R is 11**

Example 2: Divide 1761 by 131

Ans:

$$
\begin{array}{r|rr:rr}
131 & 1 & 7 & 6 & 1 \\
\overline{31} & & \bar{3} & \bar{3} & \\
 & & & \overline{12} & \bar{4} \\
\hline
 & 1 & 4 & \bar{7} & \bar{3}^{*} \\
 & -1 & & +131 & \\
\hline
 & 13 & & & 58
\end{array}
$$

$\therefore$ **1761 ÷ 131 → Q is 13 & R is 58**

*Initially the remainder is −73. To make this positive take away 1 from the quotient 14 and we know that this one quotient is equivalent to 131 and hence add 131 to remainder −73 to get a +ve remainder of 58. $\therefore$ **1761 ÷ 131 → Q is 13 & R is 58**

Example 3: Divide 31468 by 1132

Ans:

$$
\begin{array}{r|rr:rrr}
1132 & 3 & 1 & 4 & 6 & 8 \\
\mathbf{\overline{132}} & & \bar{3} & \bar{9} & \bar{6} & \\
 & & & 2 & 6 & 4 \\
\hline
 & 3 & \bar{2} & \bar{3} & 6 & {}_{1}2 \\
 & 28 & & \bar{3} & 7 & 2^{*} \\
 & 28 & & -2 & 2 & 8^{*} \\
 & -1 & & +1132 & & \\
\hline
 & 27 & & & 904 &
\end{array}
$$

$\therefore$ **31468 ÷ 1132 → Q is 27 & R is 904**

* $3\,\overline{7}2 \rightarrow -228$ i.e. converting vinculum to non-vinculum

Example 4: Divide 5143 by 150

Ans:

Divisor		
150	5 1	4 3
$\overline{5}0$	25	0
		120 0
	5 $_2\overline{4}$	124 3
	3 $\overline{4}$	1 2 : 4 3
	2 6	$\overline{5}$: 0
		15 0
	0 7←1 $\overline{3}$	19 3
	+1	-150
	3 4	43

∴ 5143 ÷ 150→ Q is 34 & R is 43

Multiple & Change Sign Method

Example 5: Divide 2328 by 31(this example is already solved by multiple method in the previous lesson – ex. 1)

Ans: Here we shall use both multiple method and CS (Change Sign) method. Earlier we multiplied 31 by 3 to get 93 and we took 07 its complement as working divisor. Here we multiply divisor 31 by 4 yielding 124 and dropping unity we use –24 as working divisor.

Divisor		
31 × 4	2 3	2 8
124	4	$\overline{8}$
$\overline{24}$		2 4
	2 $\overline{1}$	4$_1$2*
	1 9	-2 8
	× 4	
	76	-28
	-1	+ 31
	75	3

∴ 2328 ÷ 31 → Q is 75 & R is 3

*** The remainder 4 which is negative in tens place and 12 is positive. The 1 in the tens place of 12 will be carried over to left**

and thus the 4 in tens place becomes 3 again negative i.e. -30 and the retained 2 in units place is positive. After adjusting the net remainder is -28. To make this remainder positive take away one quotient from 76 (which equals to 31) and add 31 to remainder to get +3 as the final remainder. $\therefore$ **2328 ÷ 31 → Q is 75 & R is 3**

Example 6: Divide 21128 by 29 (this example is already solved by multiple method in the previous lesson – ex.2)

Ans: Earlier we multiplied 29 by 3 and used the temporary divisor 29×3=87 and complement (of 87) 13 as the working divisor. Here we shall use both Multiple and CS method. First we multiply 29 by 4 to get temporary divisor as 116 and its complement -16 as the working divisor.

29 × 4	2	1	1	2	8
116		$\bar{3}$	$\bar{2}$		
$\bar{1}\bar{6}$			3	2	
				$\bar{3}$	$\bar{2}$
	2	$\bar{2}$	2	1	6
	1	8	2		
		×	4		
	728			16	

$\therefore$ **21128 ÷ 29 → Q is 728 & R is 16**

Example 7: Divide 311 by 12

Ans:

12	3	1	1
$\bar{2}$		6	
			10
	3	5	11
	2	$\bar{5}$	11

$\therefore$ **311 ÷ 12 → Q is 25 & R is 11**

Note: In case, the left most digit of the divisor is not equal to unity, the CS method will not work. For example in 4139 ÷ 829 – you cannot divide by -29. In such cases the following way can be adopted.

1. The larger digits of the divisor i.e. 8 and 9 of the divisor 829, can be converted to equivalent vinculums. So 829

can be replaced by 1 $\bar{2}\,\bar{3}$ 1; now the left most digit (after converting to vinculum) being unity, **CS** method can be employed. See example 8 below

Example 8:

Divisor		
8 2 9	4	1 3 9
1 $\bar{2}$ 3 $\bar{1}$		8 $\overline{12}$ 4
2 $\bar{3}$ 1	4	9 $\bar{8}$ 3

or **Q is 4 and R is 823**

2. If the divisor is smaller, then it can be multiplied (or larger number can be divided) by suitable number to make the left most digit as unity and then **CS** method can be adopted. See examples 9, 10, and 11

Example 9: Divide 3117 by 184

Ans:

Divisor		
1 8 4	3 1	1 7
2 $\bar{2}$ 4	3	$\bar{6}$
÷ 2		4 $\bar{8}$
1 $\bar{1}$ 2	3 4	$\bar{1}$ $\bar{1}$
1 $\bar{2}$	÷ 2	
	1 7	- 11
	- 1	+184
	16	173

∴ 3117 ÷ 184→ Q is 16 & R is 173

Example 10: Divide 5416 by 484

Ans:

Divisor		
4 8 4	5 4	1 6
÷4	$\overline{10}$	$\bar{5}$
1 2 1		12 6
$\bar{2}$ $\bar{1}$		
	5 $\bar{6}$	8 $_1$2
	4 4	9 2
	÷ 4	
	11	92

∴ 5416 ÷484→ Q is 11 & R is 92

Example 11: Divide 1732 by 42

Ans:

4 2	1	7	3	2
÷3		$\bar{4}$		
1 4			$\overline{12}$	
$\bar{4}$				36
	1	3	$\bar{9}$	3 8
	1	2	1	3 8
			÷ 3	
	40 1/3			3 8
			40	38 + (1/3) 42
			40	38 + 14 = 52
			+1	- 42
			41	10

∴ **1732 ÷ 42 → Q is 41 & R is 10**

Exercises

Ex 1: Divide the following numbers – which are just above the base by divisors (using CS method) indicated in each sum:

1. 1377÷123 **2.** 1481 ÷ 131 **3.** 121 ÷ 13
4. 256 ÷ 121 **5.** 1366 ÷132 **6.** 13545 ÷ 1212
7. 1781 ÷ 161 **8.** 321987 ÷ 1003

Ex 2: Divide the following based on multiple method –

1. 121 ÷44 Hint 2×44, then complement of 88
2. 2222 ÷59 Hint 2×59, etc
3. 1225 ÷ 36 Hint 3×36, etc
4. 2584 ÷ 492 Hint492 ÷4, etc
5. 79999 ÷ 444 Hint 444 ÷ 4, etc.

□

26

Division (Part-VI)

Division – VC Product Method

Introduction

The VC or Vertically and Crosswise method was explained in **'Multiplication'** In this lesson we shall see how this method can be used in division.

Using Flag digit

In the earlier chapter all the divisions were with complements and the complement is multiplied by the quotient digits. In fact the complement is designated as working divisor, but this working is multiplication, as no direct division is involved in the division methods so far we have learnt. But in VC method,the right most digit(s) of the divisor is taken **Flag** or **Index** digit and the remaining digit(s) towards left is taken as working divisor. In this method actual division is done using tables as we normally do. The number of digits in the flag decides the **mark** which we had shown in the earlier chapters. All these will be clear from the following examples.

Example 1: Divide 41703 by 71

Ans:

Steps: 1. From the divisor 71, write 1 slightly raised and this 1 is the **Flag** or **Index** –

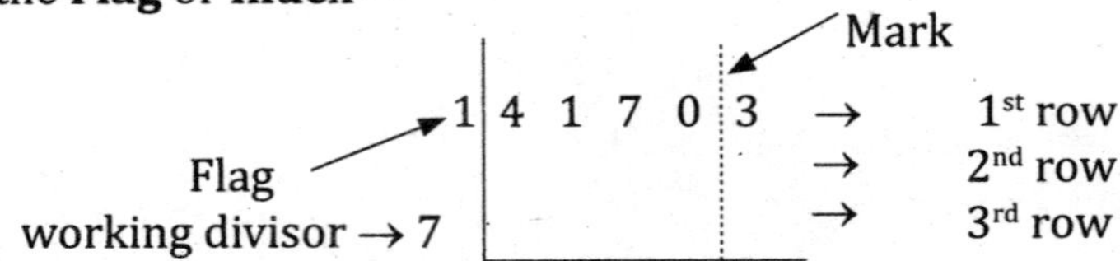

2. The vertical line in the dividend (shown by dotted line) is marked from right side of the dividend based on the number of digits in flag or index (whereas in the earlier lessons this mark was made based on the number digits in the entire divisor).
3. Now we start dividing with working divisor 7. Since 4 cannot be divided by 7, take 41 of the dividend and divide it by 7 to get q=5 & r=6

	4 1 7 0	3
1	4 1 7 0	3
	6 6	3
7		
	5 8 7	26

$\therefore$ 41703 $\div$ 71 $\rightarrow$ Q= 587 & R=26

4. Place this first q-digit i.e. 5 in the 4th row (below 1 of 41) and r6 between 1 & 7 of the dividend in the second row.
5. Take 67 as dividend; subtract product of flag digit (which is 1 in this case) and the 1st quotient (which is 5) i.e. 67 – (1×5) = 62; divide this 62 by working divisor 7 to get q=8 & r=6; take 8 as the 2nd quotient in 4th row and r6 between 7 & 0 of the dividend as shown above.
6. Now take 60; subtract product of flag and 2nd q-digit, i.e. 60 – (1×8) = 52; divide 52 by 7 to get 3rd q-digit as 7 and r3; place 7 in the 4th row and r3 in between 0 & 3 of the dividend but after the mark
7. Take 33 and subtract 1×7 to get 33 – (1×7)=26. As we have dealt with all digits of dividend and also crossed the mark, 26 is the final reminder. $\therefore$ 41703 $\div$ 71 $\rightarrow$ Q= 587 & R=26

Example 2: Divide 58911 by 73

Ans: 358911

3	5 8 9 1	1
	2 5	2
7		
	8 0 7	0

Steps: (a) 58÷7 =q 8 & r 2

(b) 29 – (3x8) = 5÷7 = q 0 & r 5

(c) 51 – (3x0) = 51÷7 = q 7 & r 2

(d) 21 – (3x7) = 0; division ended

Note: *If the flag digit happens to be lager than 5, we can use vinculum. Suppose the divisor is 39, then as per procedure explained* *above, 9 would be flag or index digit and 3 would be working divisor. But 9 of 39 being larger we can write down 39 as 4 $\bar{1}$ and now the flag or index will be $\bar{1}$ (which is easy to handle) and working divisor 4. (see ex. 3 below) –*

Example 3: Divide 34567 by 39

Ans: Steps—

(a) 34 ÷ 4 = q 8 & r 27

(b) 25 – (1×8) = 33÷4= q 8 & r 1

(c) 16 – (1×8) = 24÷4= q 6 & r 0

(d) 07 – (1×6) = 13

$\bar{1}$	3	4	5	6	7
			2	1	0
4					
		8	8	6	13

$\therefore 34567 \div 39 \rightarrow$ Q-886 & R-13

Note: The method does not show the VC method blatantly as the flag or index digit being single digit and all the multiplications after the 1st quotient is arrived at are vertically multiplication only and no crosswise multiplication is involved. However, application of VC method will be more obvious in the next chapter where we will deal with more than one flag digit.

Exercises

1. Divide the following with respective divisors using single digit flag–try other methods like multiple or CS method wherever possible –

1. 97 ÷ 28 (try with flag 8 and also with vinculum for 8 also)
2. 50607 ÷ 123 **3.** 17496 ÷ 72 **4.** 503 ÷ 72
5. 19902 ÷ 62 **6.** 44749 ÷ 73
7. 1936 ÷ 88 (use vinculum for 8) **8.** 4032 ÷ 82
9. 4154 ÷ 92 **10.** 23824÷ 51 **11.** 92054 ÷ 63
12. 142857 ÷ 61 **13.** 12233 ÷ 53 **14.** 9018 ÷ 71
15. 23568÷ 112* **16.** 14018 ÷ 64 **17.** 40000000÷ 61
18. 4712 ÷ 45 **19.** 2222 ÷ 76** **20.** 651258 ÷ 82
21. 301291 ÷ 56** **22.** 8901 ÷ 72 **23.** 547171 ÷ 73
24. 360293 ÷ 46**

* verify by change sign method also.

**use vinculum for 6

□

27

Division (Part-VII)

Division – VC Product Method (with flag more than one digit)

Introduction

We have seen division with a single **flag-digit.** But if the divisor is like 511 or 819 we can use 11 or 19 (or $2\bar{1}$ – in vinculum form) respectively as flag digits and the remaining 5 or 8 respectively as working divisor. The division with larger divisor and with more than one flag digit is dealt in this lesson.

[**Note:** Small 'q' and small 'r' is used for intermediate quotient and remainders, while Q and R is used for the final quotient and remainders respectively.]

Example 1: Divide 7039 by 813

Ans: Here we break the divisor 813 into two parts viz. 13 as the index or flag digits and 8 as the working divisor. Since we have 2 digits in the flag, we have to leave 2 digits from right of the dividend to mark line –

13	7 0	3 9
		6
8		
	0 8	535

Steps:

1. 70 ÷ 8 = q-8 & r-6
2. Now we have 639 after the mark. As 639 is less than 813 no further division is needed. However to adjust the flag digit, we have to do the following operation –

Remainder digits after the mark (i.e. 639 in this case) minus 10 times the cross product of flag digits and quotient digits before mark minus product of last flag digit and last quotient digit i.e.

$$639 - 10\begin{vmatrix}1 & 3\\0 & 8\end{vmatrix} - \begin{vmatrix}3\\8\end{vmatrix}$$

$$= 639 - 10\times8 - 3\times8 = 639 - 80 - 24 = 535$$

∴ 7039 ÷ 813 = Q-8 & R-535

Note: Concept of VC method would now be clear as we have 2 flag-digits. This would be further clear from example 2 below –

Example 2: Divide 2250255 by 721

Ans:

21	2	2	5	0	2	5	5
			1	2	1	0	
7							
		3	1	2	1	14	

Steps:

1. 22 ÷ 7 → q-3 & r-1
2. 15 – 2×3 [the product of first flag digit (from left) and the first q-digit);
   9 ÷ 7 → q-1 & r-2
3. $20 - \begin{vmatrix}2 & 1\\3 & 1\end{vmatrix}$ (the cross-product of the flag digits and the → 20 – 5 = 15 ÷ 7 → q-2 & r-1 (2 quotients)
4. $12 - \begin{vmatrix}2 & 1\\1 & 2\end{vmatrix}$ → 12 – 5 = 7 ÷ 7 → q-1 & r-0 (q-part is over)
5. $055 - 10\begin{vmatrix}2 & 1\\2 & 1\end{vmatrix} - \begin{vmatrix}1\\1\end{vmatrix}$ → 55 – 40 – 1 → 14

∴ 2250255÷721 = Q-3121& R-14

Example 3: Divide 1251413 by 519

Ans:

19	1	2	5	1	4	1	3
5							

Here the flag digit 9 can be converted to vinculum i.e. 19 can be replaced by with $2\bar{1}$ –

$$\begin{array}{r|ccccc:cc} 2\,\bar{1} & 1 & 2 & 5 & 1 & 4 & 1 & 3 \\ & & & 2 & 1 & 0 & 1 & \\ \underline{5} & & & & & & & \\ \hline & & 2 & 4 & 1 & 1 & \multicolumn{2}{c}{104} \end{array}$$

Steps:1. $12 \div 5 \rightarrow$ q-2 & r-2

2. $25 - \begin{vmatrix} 2 \\ 2 \end{vmatrix} \rightarrow 25 - 4 = 21 \div 5 \rightarrow$ q-4 & r-1

3. $11 - \begin{vmatrix} 2\bar{1} \\ 24 \end{vmatrix} \rightarrow 11 - 6 = 5 \div 5 \rightarrow$ q-1 & r-0

4. $04 - \begin{vmatrix} 2\bar{1} \\ 41 \end{vmatrix} \rightarrow 04 - (-2) = 6 \div 5 \rightarrow$ q-1 & r-1

5. $113 - 10 \begin{vmatrix} 2\,\bar{1} \\ 1\,1 \end{vmatrix} - \begin{vmatrix} \bar{1} \\ 1 \end{vmatrix} \rightarrow 113 - 10 + 1 = 104$

$\therefore$ 1251413÷519 = Q-2411& R-104

Example 4: Divide 20006 by 623

Ans:

$$\begin{array}{r|ccc:cc} 2\,3 & 2 & 0 & 0 & 0 & 6 \\ & & & 2 & 2 & \\ 6 & & & & & \\ \hline & & 3 & 2 & \multicolumn{2}{c}{70} \end{array}$$

Steps:

1. $20 \div 6 \rightarrow$ q-3 & r-2
2. $20 - \begin{vmatrix} 2 \\ 3 \end{vmatrix} \rightarrow 20 - 6 = 14 \div 6 \rightarrow$ q-2 & r-2
3. $206 - 10 \begin{vmatrix} 2\,3 \\ 3\,2 \end{vmatrix} - \begin{vmatrix} 3 \\ 2 \end{vmatrix} \rightarrow 206 - 130 - 6 = 70$

$\therefore$ 20006 ÷ 623 = Q-32 & R-70

Example 5: Divide 6789 by 1089

Ans: Here the 8 & 9 in the divisor can be converted to vinculum and thus 1089 can be changed to $11\overline{11}$. Thus $\overline{11}$ is taken as flag-digits and 11 is taken as working divisor.

$$\begin{array}{r|cc:cc} \overline{11} & 6 & 7 & 8 & 9 \\ & & & 1 & \\ \underline{11} & & & & \\ \hline & & 6 & \multicolumn{2}{c}{255} \end{array}$$

Steps:

1. $67 \div 11 \rightarrow$ q-6 & r-1
2. $189 - 10 \begin{vmatrix} \bar{1}\ \bar{1} \\ 0\ 6 \end{vmatrix} - \begin{vmatrix} \bar{1} \\ 6 \end{vmatrix} \rightarrow 189 + 60 + 6 = 255$

$\therefore$ **6789÷1089 = Q-6& R-255**

Example 6: Divide 7777 by 493

Ans: Here 9 in the divisor can be changed to vinculum and 493 becomes $5\bar{1}3$. Now 5 will be the working divisor and $\bar{1}$ 3 are the flag-digits.

$\bar{1}$ 3	7 7	7 7
	2	3
5		
	1 5	382

Steps:

1. $7 \div 5 \rightarrow$ q-1 & r-2
2. $27 - \begin{vmatrix} 1 \\ 1 \end{vmatrix} \rightarrow 27 - (-1) = 28 \div 5 \rightarrow$ q-5 & r-3
3. $377 - 10 \begin{vmatrix} \bar{1}\ 3 \\ 1\ 5 \end{vmatrix} - \begin{vmatrix} 3 \\ 5 \end{vmatrix} \rightarrow 377 + 20 - 15 = 382$

$\therefore$ **7777÷493 = Q-15& R-382**

Exercises

Ex 1: Divide the following

1. $167 \div 88^*$ **2.** $111010 \div 725$ **3.** $17078 \div 812$

4. $30345 \div 721$ **5.** $23654 \div 713$ **6.** $253545 \div 821$

7. $13531 \div 629^*$ **8.** $7676 \div 588^*$ **9.** $65432 \div 421$

10. $47831 \div 1198^*$

* Vinculum may be used suitably.

□

28

Division (Part-VIII)

Division – By all Methods
(with remainders in decimal form)

Introduction

In all the earlier lessons division by various methods like – simple method, accumulation method, complement method, Change Sign method, multiple method and division with flag digit(s) were seen. But all the earlier examples had its remainder in integer form; but we should be able to express the remainders in decimal form also. So we shall solve all the earlier examples (wherever the remainder is non-zero) and understand the procedure for decimalising the remainder.

Example 1: Divide 2311 by 9(ex. 1 of lesson 21)

Ans:

9	2	3	1	1	0	0
		2	5	6	7	7
	2	5	6 •	7	7	7

$\therefore$ **2311 ÷ 9 → 256.777...**

Example 2: Divide 311001 by 9 (ex. 3 of lesson 21)

Ans:

9	3	1	1	0	0	1	0	0
		3	4	5	5	5	6	6
	3	4	5	5	5 •	6	6	6

$\therefore$ **311001÷ 9 → 34555.666...**

Note: Two specific observations is made from the above two examples –

1. The decimal point is where we mark the line from right (for separating quotient part and remainder part)
2. The last digit we get after the decimal point will recur i.e. 7 in the ex. 1 above and 6 in the ex. 2 above recurs. But this is applicable to all divisions by 9 only. However, see ex. 3 below -

Example 3: Divide 1234 by 9 (ex. 2 of lesson 21)

Ans:

```
9 | 1  2  3 | 4
1 |    1  3 | 6
  |---------|-----
  | 1  3  6 | 10*
  |      +1 | -9
  |---------|-----
  |  1 3 7  | 1
```

*Here the remainder is 10 which contains one 9. So adjust the quotient 136 to 137 and final reminder will be 1 and this 1 will recur.

$$\therefore \mathbf{1234 \div 9 \rightarrow 137.111...}$$

Example 4: Divide 3272 by 9

Ans:

```
9 | 3  2  7  | 2
1 |    3  5  | 12
--|----------|--------
  | 3  5 ,2  | 1 | 4
  |      1   |   | 1
  |          |--------
  |          | 1 | 5
--|----------|--------
  |  3  6  3 |  • 5 5 5
```

$$\therefore \mathbf{3272 \div 9 \rightarrow 363.555...}$$

Exercise

Try all the problems in sec 1.2, 1.3, and 1.7.1 of lesson 21.

Example 5: Divide 347 by 99 (ex. 12 of lesson 21)

Ans:

```
99 | 3 : 47  00
01 |   : 03  50
   |-------------
   | 3 • 50  50
```

$$\therefore \mathbf{347 \div 99 \rightarrow 3.5050...}$$

Note: *When dividing by 99 the recurring takes place of two digits (like 50 in the above case and 91 in the following example 6)*

Example 6: Divide 21673 by 99 (ex. 14 of lesson 21)

Ans:

Divisor				
99	02	16	73	00
01		02	18	91
	02	18 •	91	91

$\therefore$ **21673 ÷ 99 → 218.9191...**

Example 7: Divide 633891 by 99(ex.15 of lesson 21)

Ans:

Divisor						
99	63	38	91	00	00	
01		63	101			
	63	[1]01 •	1	92		
				01		
	6402	•	93	93	93	

$\therefore$ **633891 ÷ 99 → 6402.9393...**

Example 8: Divide 213134 by 999 (ex.17 of lesson 21)

Ans:

Divisor				
999	213	134	000	000
001		213	347	347
	213 •	347	347	347

$\therefore$ **213134 ÷ 999 → 213.347347...**

Example 9: Divide 619990 by 9999 (ex.19 of lesson 21)

Ans:

Divisor			
9999	0061	9990	
0001		0061	
	0061	1	0051
			0001
		1	0052
0062 •	0052	0052	

$\therefore$ **619990 ÷ 9999 → 62.00520052 ...**

Exercise

Try all problems from lesson 21 for decimalising.

Example 10: Divide 206 by 7 (ex.1 of lesson 23)

Ans:

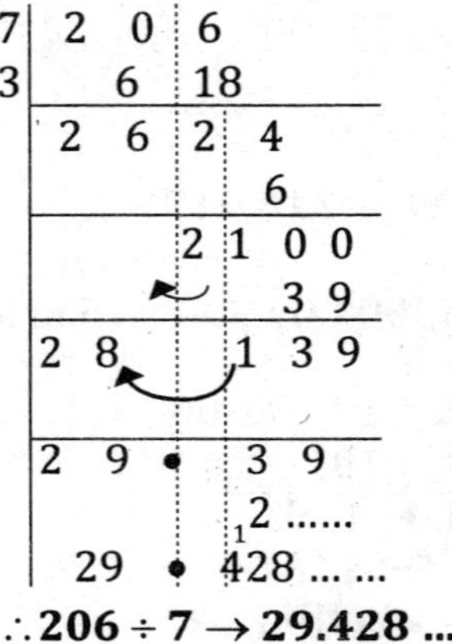

$\therefore$ 206 ÷ 7 → 29.428 ...

Example 11: Divide 390 by 8 (ex.2 of lesson 23)

Ans:

```
8 | 3  9 | 0
2 |    6 | 30
  |----------------
  | 3 ₁5 | 3 | 0
  |          | 6
  |----------------
  | 4  5 | 3 | 6  0
  |          | ₁2
  |----------------
  |  48      • 6 ₁2
  |            7  2
  |               2  8
  |            7  4  8÷8→1/0
  |               1←———————┘
  |----------------
  |  48      •  75
```

$\therefore$ 390 ÷ 8→ 48.75

Example 12: Divide 3045 by 88 (ex.3 of lesson 23)

Ans:

88	3	0	4	5		
12		3	6			
			3	6		
	3	3	1	41		
		↙		12		
				53		
				6	0	
					10	8
				6 0	$_1$0	8
					1	2
	3	4 •	602			

∴ 3045 ÷ 88 → 34.602

Example 13: Divide 41703 by 71 (ex.1 of lesson 26)

Ans:

1	4	1	7	0 •	3	0	0		
7		6	6		3	5	5	2	
		5	8	7 •	3	6	6	2	

Steps:

1. 41 ÷ 7 → q-5 & r-6
2. 67 − 1/5 → 67 − 5 = 62 ÷ 7 → q-8 & r-6
3. 60 − 1/8 → 60 − 8 = 52 ÷ 7 → q-7 & r-3
4. 33 − 1/7 → 33 − 7 = 26 ÷ 7 → q-3& r-5
5. 50 − 1/3 → 50 − 3 = 47 ÷ 6 → q-6 & r-5
6. 50 − 1/6 → 50 − 6 = 44 ÷ 7 → q-6 & r-2

∴ 41703 ÷ 71 → 587.366 ...

Example 14: Divide 34567 by 39 (ex.3 of lesson 26)

Ans:

$$\begin{array}{r|ccccccccc} \bar{1} & 3 & 4 & 5 & 6 & \vdots & 7 & & & \\ 4 & & & 2 & 1 & \vdots & 0 & 1 & 1 & 1 \quad 1 \\ \hline & & 8 & 8 & 6 & \bullet & 3 & 3 & 3 & 3 \quad 3 \end{array}$$

Steps:

1. $34 \div 4 \rightarrow$ q-8 & r-2
2. 25 – $\left|\begin{array}{c}\bar{1}\\ 8\end{array}\right| \rightarrow 25 - (-8) = 33 \div 4 \rightarrow$ q-8 & r-1
3. 16 – $\left|\begin{array}{c}\bar{1}\\ 8\end{array}\right| \rightarrow 16 - (-8) = 24 \div 4 \rightarrow$ q-6 & r-0
4. 07 – $\left|\begin{array}{c}\bar{1}\\ 6\end{array}\right| \rightarrow 07 - (-6) = 13 \div 4 \rightarrow$ q-3 & r-1
5. 10 – $\left|\begin{array}{c}\bar{1}\\ 3\end{array}\right| \rightarrow 10 - (-3) = 13 \div 4 \rightarrow$ q-3 & r-1

$\therefore 34567 \div 39 \rightarrow 886.33333$ ...

Example 15: Divide 7039 by 813 (ex.1 of this lesson 27)

Ans:

$$\begin{array}{r|ccccccc} 13 & 7 & 0 & \bullet & 3 & 9 & & \\ 8 & & & \vdots & 6 & 7 & 1 & \bar{6} \cdot \bar{5} \\ \hline & & 8 & \bullet & 6 & 6 & 1 & 9 \quad 4 \end{array} = 8.65806$$

Steps:

1. $70 \div 8 \rightarrow$ q-8 & r-6
2. 63 – $\left|\begin{array}{c}1\\ 8\end{array}\right| \rightarrow 63 - 8 = 55 \div 8 \rightarrow$ q-6 & r-7
3. 79 – $\left|\begin{array}{c}13\\ 86\end{array}\right| \rightarrow 79 - 30 = 49 \div 8 \rightarrow$ q-6 & r-1
4. 10 – $\left|\begin{array}{c}13\\ 66\end{array}\right| \rightarrow 10 - 24 = -14 \div 8 \rightarrow$ q-(-1) & r-(-6)
5. -60 – $\left|\begin{array}{c}13\\ 61\end{array}\right| \rightarrow -60 - 17 = -77 \div 8 \rightarrow$ q-(-9) & r-(-5)
6. -50 – $\left|\begin{array}{c}13\\ 19\end{array}\right| \rightarrow -50 - (-12) = -38 \div 8 \rightarrow$ q-(-4) & r-(6)

$\therefore 7039 \div 8 \rightarrow 8.65806$

Example 16: Divide 6789 by 1089 (ex.5 of this lesson 27)

Ans:

$$
\begin{array}{r|ccccc}
\overline{11} & 6 & 7 & \bullet\, 8 & 9 & \\
11 & & & 1 & 2\;\;4 & 1\;\;6 \\
\hline
 & & 6 & \bullet\, 2 & 3 & 4\;\;1
\end{array}
$$

Steps:

1. $67 \div 11 \rightarrow$ q-6 & r-1
2. $18 - \left|\begin{array}{c}\overline{1}\\ 6\end{array}\right| \rightarrow 18 - (-6) = 24 \div 11 \rightarrow$ q-2 & r-2
3. $29 - \left|\begin{array}{c}\overline{11}\\ 62\end{array}\right| \rightarrow 29 - (-8) = 37 \div 11 \rightarrow$ q-3 & r-4
4. $40 - \left|\begin{array}{c}\overline{11}\\ 23\end{array}\right| \rightarrow 40 - (-5) = 45 \div 11 \rightarrow$ q-4 & r-1
5. $10 - \left|\begin{array}{c}\overline{11}\\ 34\end{array}\right| \rightarrow 10 - (-7) = 17 \div 11 \rightarrow$ q-1 & r-6

Exercise

1. $2250255 \div 721$ **2.** $1251413 \div 519$ **3.** $2006 \div 623$

4. $167 \div 88$ **5.** $111010 \div 725$ **6.** $23654 \div 713$

7. $253545 \div 821$ **8.** $13531 \div 629$ **9.** $7676 \div 588$

10. $47832 \div 1198$

□

29

Division (Part-IX)

Division – Miscellaneous Methods

Introduction

We have seen in ex. 5 & 6 of sec 2.2 of lesson 10, **'Multiplication'** as to how to multiply by 11 and 12 using Trachtenberg's Technique. For recollection the same is repeated here –

Dividing by 11

Before division by 11, we shall review multiplication by 11 by Trachtenberg's method.

Multiplication by 11 by Trachtenberg's Method

For multiplication by 11 – Trachtenberg has formulated a simple one line rule – **'Add the neighbour'**; and also Trachtenberg has defines neighbour – as the immediate digit right of the digit under consideration. Suppose you are to multiply 3451 by 11 –

Example 1:

1. the right most digit of the multiplicand is 1 and it has no neighbour
2. next 5 has neighbour 1 and 5+1=6
3. next 4 has neighbour 5 and 4+5=9
4. next 3 has neighbour 4 and 3+4=7
5. the assumed 0 has neighbour 3 and 0+3=3
6. ∴ **3451 × 11 = 37961**

   {4} × {2}   {8}→DR check

3451 × 11
1
3451 × 11
61
3451 × 11
961
3451 × 11
7961
03451×11
37961

From ex.1 above we get a clue to deal with division by 11. We subtract the last answer digit at each step (starting from left). See ex. below –

Example 2: Divide 12678 by 11

Ans: Steps–

1. first bring down the initial 1
2. 2 – 1 = 1
3. 6 – 1 = 5
4. 7 – 5 = 2 and
5. 8 – 2 = 6 → this is the remainder.

$$\begin{array}{r|l:l} 11 & 1\,2\,6\,7 & 8 \\ & \downarrow & \\ \hline & 1\,1\,5\,2 & 6 \end{array}$$

If you decimalise the remainder, continue this subtraction as shown below –

Steps:

1. first bring down the initial 1
2. 2 – 1 = 1
3. 6 – 1 = 5
4. 7 – 5 = 2
5. 8 – 2 = 6
6. 0 – 6 = -6
7. 0 – (-6) = 6
8. 0 – 6 =-6 and so on

$$\begin{array}{r|l:l} 11 & 1\,2\,6\,7 & 8\,0\,0\,0\,0 \\ & \downarrow & \\ \hline & 1\,1\,5\,2 & \bullet 6\,6\,6\,6 \end{array}$$

∴ **12678** ÷ 11 = **1152.5454**

Example 3: Divide 20304 by 11

Ans: Steps–

1. first bring down the initial 2
2. 0 – 2 = -2
3. 3 – (-2) = 5
4. 0 – 5 = -5
5. 4 – (-5) = 9

$$\begin{array}{r|l:l} 11 & 2\ \ 0\ \ 3\ \ 0 & 4 \\ & \downarrow & \\ \hline & 2\ \ \bar{2}\ \ 5\ \ \bar{5} & 9 \\ & \quad = 1845 & 9 \end{array}$$

∴ **20304** ÷ 11 = **Q-1845 & R-9**

Example 3 in decimalised form

Steps:

1. first bring down the initial 2
2. 0 – 2 = -2
3. 3 – (-2) = 5
4. 0 – 5 = -5
5. 4 – (-5) = 9
6. 0 – 9 = -9
7. 0 – (-9) = 9
8. 0 – 9 = -9

$$\begin{array}{r|l:l} 11 & 2\ \ 0\ \ 3\ \ 0 & 4 \\ & \downarrow & \\ \hline & 2\ \ \bar{2}\ \ 5\ \ \bar{5} & \bullet 9\ \bar{9}\ 9\ \bar{9} \end{array}$$

= 1845 • 8181

∴**20304** ÷ 11 = 1845.8181

Dividing by 12

Before division by 12 we shall review multiplication by 12 by Trachtenberg's method.

Multiplication by 12 by Trachtenberg's Method

For multiplication by 12 – the one line rule is – **'Double the digit and add the neighbour'**. Suppose 3111x12 –

Example 4:

1. from right double of 1 is 2, no neighbour, so 2. — $\frac{3111 \times 12}{2}$
2. double of 1 is 2 plus 1 is 3 — $\frac{3111 \times 12}{32}$
3. double of 1 is 2 plus 1 is 3 — $\frac{3111 \times 12}{332}$
4. double of 3 is 6 plus 1 is 7 — $\frac{3111 \times 12}{7332}$
5. double of assumed 0 is 0 plus 3 is 3 — $\frac{03111 \times 12}{37332}$
6. ∴ **3111 × 12 = 37332**
   {6} × {3} {9} → DR Check

From ex.4 above we get a clue to deal with division by 12. We subtract double the last answer digit at each step (starting from left). See ex. below –

Example 5: Divide 1234 by 12

Ans: Steps:

$$\begin{array}{r|ccc:c} 12 & 1 & 2 & 3 & 4 \\ & \downarrow & & & \\ \hline & 1 & 0 & 3 & \bar{2} \\ & & & -1 & +12 \\ \hline & & 102 & & 10 \end{array}$$

1. first bring down the initial 1
2. 2 – 1×2 = 0
3. 3 – 0×2 = 3
4. 4 – 2×3 = -2

∴ **1234 ÷ 12 = Q-102 & R-10**

Note: Remainder 10 is found as below i.e. we have to take out 1 quotient (from 103) i.e. 12 and add the same to the remainder -2 i.e. -2 + 12 = 10.

Example 4 above is decimalised as below –

Steps:

1. first bring down the initial one
2. 2 – 1×2 = 0
3. 3 – 0×2 = 3
4. 4 – 2×3 = -2

$$\begin{array}{r|ccc:cccc} 12 & 1 & 2 & 3 & 4 & & & \\ & \downarrow & & & & & & \\ \hline & 1 & 0 & 3\bullet & \bar{2} & 4 & \bar{8} & {}_{1}6 \\ & & 102 & . & 8333\ldots & & & \end{array}$$

5. $0 - 2\times-2 = 4$
6. $0 - 2\times4 = -8$
7. $0 - 2\times-8 = 16$

$\therefore$ **1243 ÷ 12 = 102.833 ...**

Exercise

9.3.1: Divide the following numbers by 11 as well as by 12 –

1. 3411	**2.** 523	**3.** 345	**4.** 543
5. 81726	**6.** 1431	**7.** 1489	**8.** 333
9. 5151	**10.** 9184		

Algebraic Division

Example 5: Divide $(2x^2 + 5x + 8)$ by $(x - 1)$

Ans:

$x - 1$	$2x^2 + 5x$	$+ 8$
1	2	7
	$2x + 7$	15

$\therefore$ **$(2x^2 + 5x + 8) \div (x - 1) \rightarrow$ Q$2x + 7$ & R15**

Procedure: $(x - 1)$ is just like number 9 i.e. $x - 1$ is 1 below x and 9 is 1 below 10. So we can adopt the same method used for dividing by 9 i.e.

9	2 5	8
	2	7
	2 7	15

In the above x– 1 is replaced by 9 and 2, 5 and 8 are coefficients and constant of the binomial equation $2x^2 + 5x + 8$. We bring the first coefficient 2 down into the answer [dividing the first by first we get $2x^2 \div x = 2x$]. Then we add this 2 to the five (the second coefficient of the given equation) and put down 7; adding this 7 to the 8 (constant in the given equation) the value 15 is the remainder.

Example 6: Divide $(2x^2 + 3x + 4)$ by $(x - 2)$

Ans:

$x - 2$	$2x^2 + 3x$	$+ 4$
2	4	14
	$2x + 7$	18

$\therefore$ **$(2x^2 + 3x + 4) \div (x - 2) \rightarrow$ Q$2x + 7$ & R18**

Here dividing by x – 2 is equivalent to dividing by 8 i.e. we double the answer digit before adding it in the next column of dividend.

Example 7: Divide $(2x^2 + 3x + 4)$ by $(x + 1)$

Ans: Here dividing by x+1 is equivalent to dividing by 11. So apply CS method. i.e. we subtract the coefficient of the answer digit against adding it in the next column of dividend.

$$\begin{array}{r|l} x+1 & 2x^2 + 3x \vdots + 4 \\ -1 & \quad\quad -2 \;\vdots\; -1 \\ \hline & \quad 2x + 1 \vdots\; 3 \end{array}$$

$\therefore$ **$(2x^2 + 5x + 8) \div (x + 1) \rightarrow$ Q $2x + 1$ & R 3**

Example 8: Divide $(3x^2 + 20x + 30)$ by $(x + 5)$

Ans:

$$\begin{array}{r|l} x+5 & 3x^2 + 20x \vdots + 30 \\ -5 & \quad\quad -15 \;\vdots\; -25 \\ \hline & \quad 3x \quad 5 \vdots\; 5 \end{array}$$

(a) First divide $3x^2$ by x to get 3x and take it to answer.

(b) The coefficient of this 3x is 3 and multiply this with the complement of x+5 (here x+5 is treated as 15 and hence its complement is -5) to get -15 and take this diagonally up below 20x.

(c) Adding coefficient of 20x i.e. 20 and -15 to get 5 and this is the second answer brought down

(d) Again multiply this 5 and -5 to get -25 and take diagonally up below 30; 30 + (-25) = 5 is remainder.

$(3x^2 + 20x + 30) \div (x + 5) \rightarrow$ Q $3x + 5$ & R 5

Exercise

1. $(2x^2 + 3x + 4) \div (x - 1)$ **2.** $2x^3 + 3x^2 - 4x + 4 \div x - 1$

3. $(2x^2 + 5x + 8) \div (x - 2)$ **4.** $(2x^2 + 5x + 8) \div (x + 1)$

5. $(x^3 - 3x + 1) \div (x + 3)$ **6.** $(3x^2 + 10x + 13) \div (x + 2)$

7. $(x^3 - 5x^2 + 7x - 1) \div (x - 3)$

□

30

Divisibility Tests (Part-I)

Preface

Maths text book for std. VII or above makes a mention about divisibility rules for numbers – 2, 3, 4, 5, 6, 8, 9, 10, and 11. One has to be thorough about these rules because students may have to answer the following type of questions in competitive examinations –

1. What is the value that must be assigned to **a** so that the number 73667**a**2 is divisible by 8?
2. What is the value of **x** and **y** if the number 84**x**3216**y** is divisible by 72?
3. Which of the following number is exactly divisible by 99?
   1. 317529 **2.** 541134 **3.** 5327044 **4.** 464319

Hints

1. If the last 3 digits of a number are divisible by 8, then the entire number is divisible by 8.

2. Split (factorize) the divisor 72 as 8 & 9. First apply the rule for 8, which is explained in Hint 1 above and find the value of y and then apply the divisibility rule for 9 [which is – the **digit sum** of a number should be divisible by 9] with the known value of y and get the value of x.

3. Split (factorize) the divisor 99 as 9 & 11. First apply the rule for 9, which is explained in Hint 2 above and then apply the rule for 11 [which is the difference of sum of alternate group of digits in the given number should be zero or a multiple of 11].

So, we can easily answer the above questions almost very fast with a clear knowledge of divisibility rule for numbers 2, 3, 4, 5, 6, 8, 9, 10, and 11. Divisibility rule or method for prime numbers like 7, 13, 17, 19, 23, etc was not known so far. But a Vedic method known as **'Osculation'** is a handy tool to establish divisibility of any number.

Divisibility rule

Introduction

As we have seen in the preface of this lesson, knowledge of divisibility will be useful in competitive examinations and a few examples and hints for their solutions were also given. However, methods for testing divisibility for prime numbers like – 7, 13, 17, 19, 23, etc. were not known so far and a Vedic method known as **'Osculation'** can be employed to know the divisibility by any number. However, before knowing about osculation, let us review the divisibility rules of the numbers which we are supposed to know from Std. VII onwards.

Divisibility Rules

The following table illustrates the rules –

Table 1

Divisible by	**When**
2	when the number is even
3	The digit sum is divisible by 3
4	The last two digits from the right are divisible by 4 [Also the formula Ultimate plus twice of pen-ultimate can be applied]
5	The number should end in 5 or 0
6	The number should be even and divisible by 3 (see above)
7 & 13	Mark groups of 3 (in the number to be tested for divisibility by 7/13) from right end. Then the difference of summation of alternate groups should be divisible by 7/13.

8	The last three digits from the right are divisible by 8
9	The digit sum is divisible by 9
11	The difference of summation of alternate groups should be divisible by 11.
12	The number should be divisible by 3 as well as by 4

With the above knowledge (table) we can now answer easily the three questions asked in preface (though we have given hints, the sums are solved once again) –

Example 1:

What is the value that must be assigned to *a* so that the number 73667*a*2 is divisible by 8?

Ans: Taking the last 3 digits from right – 7a2 – and applying the divisibility rule for 8, we find a = 5.

Example 2:

What is the value of *x* and *y* if the number 84*x*3217*y* is divisible by 72?

Ans: Factorize the divisor 72 as 8 & 9; then apply the divisibility rule for 8 i.e. 17*y* should divisible by 8. This yields *y* as 6. Now 84*x*32176 should be divisible by 9. Applying the rule for 9 we get x = 5. So the number is 84532176.

Example 3:

Which of the following number is exactly divisible by 99?

1. 317529 **2.** 541134 **3.** 5327044 **4.** 464319

Ans: First factorize 99 as 9 & 11.By applying the divisibility rule of 9 as well as 11 we get the answer as alternate (2) i.e. 541134 is divisible by 99.

We shall skip examples on divisibility by 2, 3, 5, 6, 9, and 12 – since the rule are self explanatory. Rules for divisibility by 4, 7, 8, 11, and 13 are also simple – nevertheless examples in these cases are given below –

Example 4:

Which of the following number is divisible by 4?

1. 7295094 **2.** 81075368

Ans:

1. in 7295094 – the last two digits are 94 & 94 is not divisible by 4.∴ **7295094** is **not** divisible by **4**
2. in 81075368 – the last two digits are 68 & 68 is divisible by 4. ∴ **81075968** is divisible by **4**

Example 5:

Verify whether the number 12936807 is divisibly by 7 or not?

Ans: Group of 3 digits from right is 12|936|807. Sum of alternate groups are 12 + 807 →819 and 936. Difference between 936 and 819 are 117. 117 is not divisible by 7 and hence **12936807** is **not** divisible by **7**.

Example 6:

Which of the following number is divisible by 8?

1. 16089314 **2.** 34089104

Ans:

1. 16089314 has 314 as the last 3 digits. As 314 is not divisible by 8, the number 16089314 is not divisible by 8.
2. The last 3 digits 104 of 34089104 is divisible by 8 and hence the number 34089104 is divisible by 8.

Example 7:

Show that 473407 is divisible by 11.

Ans: The sums of alternate digits i.e. sum of odd digits and even digits are 4+3+0 = 7 and 7+4+7 = 18. The difference between these two sums is 18 – 7 = 11. As 11 is divisible by 11 the number 473407 is divisible by 11.

Example 8:

Is 734679 divisible by 11?

Ans:

Sum of alternate digits → 7+4+7 = 18

→ 3+6+9 = 18

Difference → 18 – 18 = 0

∴ **734679** is **divisible** by **11**.

Example 8:

Is 97346 divisible by 11?

Ans: Sum of alternate digits →9+3+6 = 18

→7+4 = 11

Difference → 18 – 11 = 7

∴ **97346**is **not divisible** by **11**.

Example 9:

Verify whether the number 12936807 is divisible by 13.

Ans: From example 5 above the difference of sum of alternate groups of 3 digits is 117. 117 ÷ 13 = 9

∴ **12936807** is divisible by 13.

Note: For testing divisibility by 4 the formula **Ultimate + twice of pen-ultimate** can also be employed (see example 10 & 11 below) -

Example 10:

Is 14876 divisible by 4?

Ans: In 14876 – 6 is the ultimate digit and 7 is pen-ultimate digit. So 6 + 2×7 = 6+14 = 20. 20 is divisible by 4 and hence, 14876 is divisible by 4.

Example 11:

Is 3654 divisible by 4?

Ans: In 3654 → 4 + 2×5 = 14; 14 is not divisible by 4 and hence 3654 is **not** divisible by 4.

□

31

Divisibility Tests (Part-II)

Divisibility Using Osculation

Introduction

Late Puri Sankaracharya 'Jagadguru Swami Sri Bharati Krishna Tirthaji Maharaja' has explained a method to test divisibility by any number by a device known as **OSCULATOR** and the procedure to test the divisibility with an **OSCULATOR** is known as **OSCULATION**. Osculators can be positive or negative. Now let us see the methods of working out the osculators.

Positive Osculator

1. For divisors ending in 9, the positive osculator is one more than the remaining digits to the left of 9.

   E.g.

   ☑ It the divisor is 9, then considering 9 as 09 – the left 0 is increased by 1 to get the osculator as 1.

   ☑ If the divisor is 19, then one more than the left digit 1 is 2 and hence the osculator is 2

   ☑ If the divisor is 59, then one more than the left digit 5 is 6 and hence the osculator is 6

2. For divisors ending in 3, we first multiply the divisor by 3 so that they end in 9 and then apply the above rule for numbers ending in 9 and find the required osculator by one more than the one before.

   E.g.

   ☑ 13, 23, 43, 63, etc on multiplication by 3 yields 39, 69, 129, 189 respectively and their respective osculators are 3+1 = 4, 6+1 = 7, 12+1 = 13, 18+1 = 19 (by one more than the one before rule)

3. For divisors ending in 7, we first multiply the divisor by 7 so that they end in 9 and then apply the above rule for numbers ending in 9 and find the required osculator by one more than the one before.

E.g.

☑ 7, 17, 47, 67, etc on multiplying by 7 yields 49, 119, 329, 469, respectively and their respective osculators are 4+1 = 5, 11+1 = 12, 32+1 = 33, 46+1 = 47 (by one more than the one before rule)

4. For divisors ending in 1, we first multiply the divisor by 9 so that they end in 9 and then apply the above rule for numbers ending in 9 and find the required osculator by one more than the one before.

E.g.

☑ 11, 31, 61, 121, etc on multiplying by 9 yields 99, 279, 549, 1089, respectively and hence their respective osculators are 9+1 = 10, 27+1 = 28, 54+1 = 55, 108+1 = 109.

5. For divisors ending in 0, 5 and other even numbers, they are to be first divided by suitable powers of 2 or 5 until the number ends in 1, 3, 7, or 9 and then the rules above can be applied.

E.g.

☑ If the divisor is 35, divide by 5 to get 7, now apply rule 3 above to get osculator as 7×7 = 49; 4+1 = 5.

☑ If the divisor is 44, dividing by 4 we get 11 and the apply rule 4 above to get osculator as 11×9 = 99; 9+1 = 10.

☑ If the divisor is 310 – divide by 10 to get 31 and apply rule 4 above to get osculator as 28.

This is all about the positive osculator. Before we explain negative osculator, let us first see how the osculator works or how the actual method of osculation works.

Methods of Osculation

(A) Chain Method–

Example 1: Is 511 divisible by 7?

Ans: The osculator for 7 is 7x7 = 49 i.e. 4+1=5. ∴ 5 is the osculator. This osculator 5 is operated upon the dividend 511 as follows–

1. Multiply the last 1 (of 511) by osculator and add the remaining digit 51 to this product
   i.e. 51 + (1 × 5) = 56
2. At this stage we know 56 is divisible by 7 and hence we conclude that 511 is divisible by 7 and stop osculation. However we continue to understand the process of osculation –
3. At step (1) we got 56. Take the last digit 6 (of 56) and multiply by the osculator 5 and add the remaining digit to the product
   i.e. 5 + (6 × 5) = 35
4. Again we know that 35 is a multiple of 7 and we stop the osculation as 511 is divisible by 7. However,
5. From 35, 3 + (5 × 5) = 28 is divisible by 7
6. From 28, 2 + (8 × 5) = 42 is divisible by 7
7. From 42, 4 + (2 × 5) = 14 is divisible by 7
8. From 14, 1 + (4 × 5) = 21 is divisible by 7;
   any further osculation will be repetition from step (4) above. So here ends osculation. As said earlier we could have stopped osculation at any step above. However, we continued till the end (another 6 steps) to emphasize the osculation procedure.

Example 2: Is 456 divisible by 19?

Ans: The osculator for 19 is 2

1. 45 + (6 × 2) = 57 is divisible by 19
2. 5 + (7 × 2) = 19 confirmed.
   ∴ 456 is divisible by 19

Example 3: Is 661 divisible by 23?

Ans: The osculator for 23 is 23 × 3 = 69; 6 + 1 =7.

So 7 is the osculator for 23.

1. 66 + (1 × 7) = 73 is not divisible by 23
2. 7 + (3 × 7) = 28 is not divisible by 23
3. 2 + (8 × 7) = 58 is not divisible by 23
4. 5 + (8 × 7) = 61 is not divisible by 23
5. 6 + (1 × 7) = 13 Here the osculator is smaller than the divisor and hence further osculation is stopped. ∴ 661 is not divisible by 23.

Example 4: Is 1748 divisible by 23?
Ans: The osculator for 23 is 7 (see ex. 3 above)
1. 174 + (8 × 7) = 230 is divisible by 23
2. 23 + (0 × 7) = 23 is divisible by 23
   ∴ 1748 is divisible by 23.

(B) Product on Single Digit Method:

In the above section, we saw the chain method of osculation for divisibility test. Here we shall see modified version of the chain method i.e. product on single digit method. The following examples explain the method –

Example 5: Is 4025 divisible by 23?
Ans: Osculator of 23 is 7 (see ex. 3 & 4 above)
1. Osculate the last digit 5 by 7 and add to the digit at its immediate left to get 5 x 7 + 2 = 37

   4 0 2 5 → 5 × 7 = 35
   37 → 35 + 2 = 37
2. Now osculate 37 by 7 to get 3 + 7 × 7 → 52 and add previous digit to the left i.e. 0 + 52 → 52

   4 0 2 5
   52
3. Now osculate 52 by 7 to get 5 + 2 × 7 → 19 and add the previous digit to left 4 to get 23. Same as divisor and hence divisible.
   ∴ 4025 is divisible by 23

Example 6: Is 6407 divisible by 43
Ans: Osculator for 43 is 43×3 = 129; 12+1→13. So 13 is the osculator

1. 6 4 0 7 → 7 × 13 + 0 = 91
2. 6 4 91 → 9 + (1×13) + 4 = 26
3. 6 26 → 2 + (6×13) + 6 = 86
→ 8 + (6×13) = 86

∴ 6407 is divisible by 43

Example 7: Is 32451 divisible by 49?

Ans: Osculator for 49 is 4+1 = 5

1. 3 2 4 5 1 → 1 × 5 + 5 → 10
2. 3 2 4 10 → 0 × 5 + 1 → 1 + 4 → 5
3. 3 2 5 → 5 × 5 + 2 → 27
4. 3 27 → 7 × 5+2→ 37 + 3 → 40

∴ **32451** is **not** divisible by **49.**

Rules for stopping Osculation

A. Osculation may be stopped whenever it is smaller than the divisor. In ex. 3 above the divisor is 23 and at 5th stage of osculation the result was 13 and hence stopped.

B. When divisor itself or zero is reached – while osculating, osculation is stopped. In ex. 1, 2, 4, and 6 above the divisor is reached, hence stopped.

C. If we get repeated results (see ex. 4 above), osculation may be stopped concluding divisibility.

D. During osculation if any intermediate result indicates divisibility, then and there osculation can be stopped.

Osculating a number by its own osculator

If we osculate a number by its own osculator, we will end up with the same number or it's multiple or it's sub-multiple.

Example 8: 71's osculator is 71×9 → 639 → 63+1 → 64. If we osculate 71 by 64 we get 7 + 1×64 → 71. That is the number itself.

Example 9: 17's osculator is 17×7 = 119; 11+1 → 12. If we osculate 17 by 12 we get 1+7×12 → 85 which is a multiple of 17.

Example 10: 245's osculator is 245÷5 → 49; 4+1 → 5 ∴Osculator is 5. ∴245 osculated by 5 yields 24 + (5×5) → 49 (which is a sub-multiple of 245).

Exercises

Ex.1: Find the positive osculator of the following -

1. 109	**2.** 17	**3.** 23	**4.** 21
5. 43	**6.** 29	**7.** 7	**8.** 89

Ex.2: Test the following for divisibility by 7

1. 898	**2.** 84	**3.** 63	**4.** 53

Ex.3: Test for divisibility by 13

1. 52	**2.** 86	**3.** 65	**4.** 97

Ex.4: Test for divisibility by 19

1. 57	**2.** 95	**3.** 76	**4.** 114

Ex.5: Test for divisibility by 29

1. 116	**2.** 57	**3.** 87	**4.** 58

Ex.6: Test for divisibility by 17

1. 56	**2.** 102	**3.** 51	**4.** 85

Ex.7: Test the following numbers for divisibility by 19

1. 23455	**2.** 2774	**3.** 30201	**4.** 589
5. 10203	**6.** 323	**7.** 1995	**8.** 4313
9. 14003	**10.** 779	**11.** 4503	**12.** 1417

Ex.8: Test the following numbers for divisibility by the numbers shown

1. 41963 by 29	**2.** 4802 by 49	**3.** 4173 by 13
4. 2254 by 23	**5.** 10404 by 17	**6.** 1003 by 59
7. 4171 by 43	**8.** 5432 by 7	**9.** 4321 by 109

Negative Osculators

In case of divisors ending in 1 and 7, positive osculator yields a large value of osculators.

E.g.

✓ Osculator of 51 is $51 \times 9 = 459$ and $45 + 1 = 46$. So for divisor 51 the osculator is 46.

✓ Osculator for 67 is 67×7 = 469 and 46 + 1 = 47. So for divisor 67 the osculator is 47.

To osculate with 46 & 47 the mental process will be difficult and hence negative osculators are used as explained below –

Osculators are used as explained below –

1. For divisors ending in 1 like 11, 21, 41, etc drop the 1 and take the remaining digits as negative osculator.
   Thus for 21, 41, 51, 91, etc the osculators are 2, 4, 5, 9, etc. (while it's positive osculators are 19, 37, 46, 82 respectively)
2. For other divisors – multiply the divisor by suitable number so that the product ends in 1 and then dropping this 1, use the remaining digits as osculator.
   Thus for 43 the negative osculator is 43 × 7 = 301→ 30
   For 17 → 17 × 3 → 51 → 5
   For 29 → 29 × 9 → 361 → 36

How Negative Osculator Works

Example 11:

(i) If 67 is osculated by -7, then 67 → 6 – 7×7 →-43

(ii) If -43 is osculated by -5, then -4 –(-3×5)→-4 + 3x5 → 11

(iii) If -246 is osculated by -3, then -24 – (-6×3) → -6

(iv) If 437 is osculated by -9, then 437 → 43 – 7×9 → -20

Example 12: Is 4346 divisible by 41?

Ans: (a) by product on single digit method

1. 4 3 4 6 → 6×-4 → -24+4 → -20

2. 4 3 -20 → -2 – (-0×4) + 3 → 1

3. 4 1 →1×-4 + 4 → 0

Since the osculation finally ends in 0 the number 4346 is divisible by 41.

(b) by chain method:

4346 → 434 – (6×4) → 410
→ 41 – (0×4) → 41
→ 4 – (1×4) → 0 ∴ 4346 is divisible by 41

Example 13: Is 345681 divisible by 27?

Ans: (a) by product on single digit method

27×3 → 81; So Osculator is 8

1. 3	4	5	6	8	1		→1×-8 → -8 + 8 → 0
2. 3	4	5	6	0			→ 0×-8 → 0+6 → 6
3. 3	4	5	6				→ 6×-8 → -48+5 → -43
4. 3	4	-43					→ -4 – (-3×8) +4 → 24
5. 3	24						→ 2 – (4×8) + 3 →-27

-27 being a multiple of 27, ∴ the number 345681 is divisible by 27.

(b) by chain method:

345681 → 34568 – 1×8→ 34560
→ 3456 – 0×8→ 3456
→ 345 – 6×8→ 297
→ 29 – 7×8 = -27 ∴ **divisible by 27.**

Note: The above problem can be done by checking with divisibility rule of 9 as 27 can be factorized as 3x9.

2.8: Exercises

Ex.1: Obtain the negative osculator for

1. 61 **2.** 91 **3.** 101 **4.** 11
5. 27 **6.** 37 **7.** 7 **8.** 13
9. 23 **10.** 19

Ex.2: Test the numbers for divisibility by the numbers shown (using negative osculator) –

1. 3813 by 31 **2.**367164 by 7
3. 11594 by 62 **4.** 6454 by 7

Ex.3: Test the following for divisibility (using negative osculator) by the given number.

1. 9658 by 11 **2.** 2914 by 31 **3.** 17949 by 93
4. 9576 by 21 **5.** 4838 by 82 **6.** 6039 by 61
7. 2394 by 42 **8.** 20022 by 71 **9.** 45787 by 7
10. 73472 by 41 **11.** 178467 by 31 **12.** 63909 by 81
13. 7071 by 61 **14.** 1728 by 91 **15.** 14715 by 27
16. 7072 by 17

Other composite numbers

Example 14: Is 6346 divisible by 38?

Ans: We first factorize the divisor 38 as 2 × 19. So the number 6346 must be divisible by 2 as well as 19. As the number 6346 is even, it is obvious that it is divisible by 2. To check divisibility by 19, we osculate the number by 2. **i.e. 6346** → 634 + 6 × 2 → 64 + 6 × 2 → 7 + 6 × 2 → 19.

∴ **6346 is divisible by 38.**

Example 15: Is 5573 divisible by 21?

Ans: The divisor 21 is 3 × 7. The number is not divisible by 3, since its DR is 2. So the number 5573 is not divisible by 21.

Example 16: Is 1764 divisible by 28?

Ans: Since 28 → 4 × 7 [it is not factorized as 2 × 14, since 2 & 14 are not relatively prime]

The last two digits i.e. 64 is divisible by 4. For 7 the osculator is 5

So 1764 → 176 + 4 × 5 → 19 + 6 × 5 → 49.

∴ **Divisible by 7 & 28.**

Note: When testing divisibility by composite numbers. We look at the factors of divisor and start with easiest factor.

Exercise: Test the divisibility for the following numbers by the number shown

1. 305448 by 52 **2.** 3538 by 58 **3.** 334455 by 39
4. 1254 by 38 **5.** 37392 by 58 **6.** 21645 by 65
7. 5985 by 95 **8.** 1771 by 46 **9.** 767 by 95
10. 26910 by 46.

Negative osculator – alternative method

Example 17: Is 4346 divisible by 41? {ex. 12 above repeated}

Ans: Here negative osculator is 4 (as usual). Then in the dividend we begin by putting vinculum over every alternate digit of 4346, starting from the 2nd digit from the right.

∴ $\bar{4}\ \ 3\ \ \bar{4}\ \ 6$

We then osculate in the normal way (using positive osculator) except that any carry figure is considered as negative.

Hence $\bar{4}\ 3\ \bar{4}\ 6 \rightarrow 6 \times 4 + \bar{4} = 20$

$\bar{4}\ 3\ 20 \rightarrow 0 \times 4 + \bar{2} + 3 = 1$

$\bar{4} \rightarrow 1 \times 4 + \bar{4} = 0$

$\therefore$ **4346 is divisible by 41**

Example 18: Is 345681 divisible by 27? {ex. 13 above repeated}

Ans:

For 27 the negative osculator is 8.

$\bar{3}\ 4\ \bar{5}\ 6\ \bar{8}\ 1 \rightarrow 1 \times 8 + \bar{8} = 0$

$\bar{3}\ 4\ \bar{5}\ 6\ 0 \rightarrow 0 \times 8 + 6 = 6$

$3\ 4\ 5\ 6 \rightarrow 6 \times 8 + \bar{5} = 43$

$3\ 4\ 43 \rightarrow 3 \times 8 + \bar{4} + 4 = 24$

$3\ 24 \rightarrow 4 \times 8 + \bar{2} + 3 = 27$

$\therefore$ **345681 is divisible by 27**

One of the applications of Osculation

The divisibility test is needed whenever we have to decide whether a given number is prime number or not. Just to recollect – if you are to test whether a given number is a prime number – take an integer larger than the square root of that number. If the square root is say 'q' – then check the divisibility of given number by every prime number less than 'q'. If it is not divisible by any of them then the given number is prime, otherwise it is a composite number.

Example 19: Is 881 a prime number?

Ans:

The nearest square root of 881 is 30 (considering higher integer). The prime numbers below 30 are – 2, 3, 5, 7, 11, 13, 17, 19, 23, and 29. By visual inspection of 881, we know that it is not divisible by 2, 3, 5, and 11.

For 7 we osculate 881 with osculator +5

i.e. $881 \rightarrow 88 + 1 \times 5 = 93$

$93 \rightarrow 9 + 3 \times 5 = 24$

$24 \rightarrow 2 + 4 \times 5 = 22$

$22 \rightarrow 2 + 2 \times 5 = 12$

$12 \rightarrow 1 + 2 \times 5 = 11$

$11 \rightarrow 1 + 1 \times 5 = 6$ $\therefore$ **Not divisible by 7**

For 13 we osculate 881 with osculator +4

i.e. $881 \rightarrow 88 + 1 \times 4 = 92$

$92 \rightarrow 9 + 2 \times 4 = 17$ $\therefore$ **Not divisible by 13**

For 17 we osculate 881 with osculator +12

i.e. $881 \rightarrow 88 + 1 \times 12 = 100$

$100 \rightarrow 10 + 0 \times 12 = 10$ $\therefore$ **Not divisible by 17**

For 19 we osculate 881 with osculator +2

i.e. $881 \rightarrow 88 + 1 \times 2 = 90$

$90 \rightarrow 9 + 0 \times 2 = 9$ $\therefore$ **Not divisible by 19**

For 23 we osculate 881 with osculator +7

i.e. $881 \rightarrow 88 + 1 \times 7 = 95$

$95 \rightarrow 9 + 5 \times 7 = 44$

$44 \rightarrow 4 + 4 \times 7 = 32$

$32 \rightarrow 3 + 2 \times 7 = 17$ $\therefore$ **Not divisible by 23**

For 29 we osculate 881 with osculator +3

i.e. $881 \rightarrow 88 + 1 \times 3 = 91$

$91 \rightarrow 9 + 1 \times 3 = 12$ $\therefore$ **Not divisible by 29**

As 881 is not divisible by 2, 3, 5, 7, 11, 13, 17, 19, 23, and 29, so it is a prime number.

Example 20: Is 979 a prime number?

Ans:

The square root of 979 lies between 31 and 32. We take the higher integer 32. The prime numbers less than 32 are – 2, 3, 5, 7, 11, 13, 17, 19, 23, 29, and 31. On visual inspection we find that 979 is divisible by 11. And hence 979 is not a prime number.

Example 21: Is 349 a prime number?

Ans:

The square root of 349 lies between 18 and 19. We take the higher value i.e. 19 and the prime numbers below 19 are – 2, 3, 5, 7, 11, 13, 17. By visual inspection we know 349 is not divisible by 2, 3, 5, and 11.

For 7 we osculate 349 with osculator + 5

i.e. $349 \rightarrow 34 + 9 \times 5 = 79$

$79 \rightarrow 7 + 9 \times 5 = 52$

$52 \rightarrow 5 + 2 \times 5 = 15$ $\therefore$ **Not divisible by 7**

For 13 we osculate 349 with osculator + 4

i.e. $349 \rightarrow 34 + 9 \times 4 = 70$

$70 \rightarrow 7 + 0 \times 4 = 7$ $\therefore$ **Not divisible by 13**

For 17 we osculate 349 with osculator +12

i.e. $349 \rightarrow 34 + 9 \times 12 = 142$

$142 \rightarrow 14 + 2 \times 12 = 38$ $\therefore$ **Not divisible by 17**

As 349 is not divisible by 2, 3, 5, 7, 11, 13, and 17, it is a prime number.

□

32

Decimalisation of fractions

Introduction

The conventional method of converting a proper (vulgar) fraction is very cumbrous and one has to be very thorough with tables because the conversion process involves division of the numerator by the denominator. Thus there is no need to emphasize that to be efficient in division one has to be thorough with tables.

For example,if say, a vulgar fraction $\frac{63}{138}$ is to be converted into its decimal form, the following method is adopted (as this is the only method known to us) –

Ex.1:

```
138) 63.0 ( 0.456521 ... ...
     552
      780
      690
       900
       828
        720
        690
         300
         276
          240
          138
```

... ...

Readers know the procedure to decimalise further and hence, the above procedure is stopped. However, we shall soon see how to solve the above differently and faster than the conventional method. But we will first deal with **denominator ending in 9** and numerator 1.

Denominator ending in 9

For example: $\frac{1}{39}$ Here we use a simple formula '**By**onemore than the previous one.' The method and application of the formula for converting $\frac{1}{39}$ to decimal is as follows –

Here the number (the denominator) is ending in 9 and the previous number is 3; therefore, one more than the previous is 4. According to literary or grammatical usage of the term **by** in the formula, it means that the operation to follow (for converting vulgar fraction to decimal) is either multiplication or division. Hence it follows that the modus operandi could be either multiplication or division.

Ⓐ By – meaning multiplication

The first method is by means of multiplication by 4 (i.e. the number which is just one more than the previous digit 3). Invariably the product of the last digit of the denominator and the last digit of the decimal equivalent of the fraction in question must end in 9. As the last digit of the denominator in this case is 9, therefore it automatically follows that the last digit of the decimal equivalent is 1 (so that the product of the multiplicand and the multiplier concerned may end in 9).

So the right-hand-most digit of the decimal is 1 and we start continuously multiplying this 1 by 4 and proceed leftward till the operation repeats or recurring decimal is observed.

Ex.2: $\frac{1}{39}$

1. right-most-digit — 1
2. multiply 1 by 4 and put 4 as preceding digit i.e. — 41
3. multiply 4 by 4 = 16. Here 16 has two digits. So we take 6 of 16 along the left of earlier result and carry the **1** in the next stage of multiplication — $^{1}641$
4. 6 x 4 + 1 (carry in the previous step) = 25; take 5 previous to 6 and carry **2** — $^{2}5^{1}641$
5. 5 x 4 + 2 (carry) = 22; take 2, carry **2** — $^{2}2^{2}5^{1}641$
6. 2 x 4 + 2 = 10; take 0, carry **1** — $^{1}0^{2}2^{2}5^{1}641$
7. From this step the results will recur and hence,

$$\frac{1}{39} = 0.\dot{0}25641\ldots\ldots\ldots\ldots\ldots\ldots\ldots\ldots\ldots\ldots\ldots\ldots\ldots\ldots \textbf{(A)}$$

Note the dot over 0 to indicate recurring.

Now the conventional method =

Ex.3:

39) 1.0 (0.025641 ... ... **(B)**

```
  0 0
 ----
  100
   78
 ----
   220
   195
  ----
   250
   234
  ----
   160
   156
  ----
     40
     39
   ----
      1
```

Both answers (A) and (B) are same, however – needless to emphasize that the result (A) is obtained in one line and that too mentally. Both methods indicated that the digits recur after 6 steps.

Ⓑ By – meaning division

The second method is **by** means of division as against multiplication explained in para A above. The process of division should commence and proceed from left to right unlike multiplication as we know that division is the opposite of multiplication. Here also the divisor is the same 4 (i.e. one more than the previous) like the multiplier 4.

Ex.4: $\frac{1}{39}$

Method:

1. Starting from the first digit of the dividend (numerator) i.e. dividing 1 by 4 we get Q as 0 and R as 1. So we take 0 as the first quotient and reminder **1** earlier to 0 as ${}_10$ (i.e. carry to the left of first quotient ... ... $0.{}_10$
2. So the next dividend is 10 from ${}_10$ and divide 10 by 4 to get new Q as 2 and R as **2** ... ... $0.{}_10{}_22$
3. Divide the new dividend 22 by 4; Q-5, R-**2**... ... $0.{}_10{}_22{}_25$
4. Divide 25 by 4; Q-6,R-**1** ... ... $0.{}_10{}_22{}_25{}_16$
5. 16 ÷ 4; Q-4, R-**0** ... ... $0.{}_10{}_22{}_25{}_164$
6. 4 ÷ 4; Q-1, R-**0** ... ... $0.{}_10{}_22{}_25{}_1641$

$\frac{1}{39}$ = 0.025641... ... ... **(C)**

Let us see one more example for number ending in 9 i.e. $\frac{1}{29}$

Ex.5: $\frac{1}{29}$

The multiplier will be 3 i.e. one more than the previous i.e. 2+1=3. As mentioned earlier the right-most-digit is 1.

1. Right-most digit - - - - - - - - - - - - - 1
2. 1 × 3 is 3 - - - - - - - - - - - - - - - - - 3 1
3. 3 × 3 is 9 - - - - - - - - - - - - - - - - - 9 3 1
4. 9 × 3 is 27 i.e. ^{27} - - - - - - - - - - - - ^{27} 9 3 1
5. 7 × 3 + 2 is 23 i.e. ^{23} - - - - - - - - - ^{23} ^{27} 9 3 1
6. 3 × 3 + 2 is 11 i.e. ^{11} - - - - - - - - - ${}^11{}^23$ ^{27} 9 3 1
7. 1 × 3 + 1 is 4 - - - - - - - - - - - - - - 4^{11} ^{23} ^{27} 9 3 1

8. 4 × 3 is 12 i.e. $^{1}2$ ---------- $^{1}2\ 4\ ^{1}1\ ^{2}3\ ^{2}7\ 9\ 3\ 1$

9. 2 × 3 + 1 is 7 -------------- $7\ ^{1}2\ 4\ ^{1}1\ ^{2}3\ ^{2}7\ 9\ 3\ 1$

10. 7 × 3 is 21 i.e. $^{2}1$ ------------ $^{2}1\ 7\ ^{1}2\ 4\ ^{1}1\ ^{2}3\ ^{2}7\ 9\ 3\ 1$

11. 1 × 3 + 2 is 5 ------------ $5\ ^{2}1\ 7\ ^{1}2\ 4\ ^{1}1\ ^{2}3\ ^{2}7\ 9\ 3\ 1$

12. 5 × 3 is 15 i.e. $^{1}5$ ----------- $^{1}5\ 5\ ^{2}1\ 7\ ^{1}2\ 4\ ^{1}1\ ^{2}3\ ^{2}7\ 9\ 3\ 1$

13. 5 × 3 + 1 is 16 i.e. $^{1}6$ ------ $^{1}6\,^{1}5\ 5\ ^{2}1\ 7\ ^{1}2\ 4\ ^{1}1\ ^{2}3\ ^{2}7\ 9\ 3\ 1$

14. 6 × 3 + 1 is 19 i.e. $^{1}9$ --- $^{1}9\ ^{1}6\ ^{1}5\ 5\ ^{2}1\ 7\ ^{1}2\ 4\ ^{1}1\ ^{2}3\ ^{2}7\ 9\ 3\ 1$

15. 9 × 3 + 1 is 28 i.e. $^{2}8$ ------- $^{2}8$

$^{1}9\ ^{1}6\ ^{1}5\ 5\ ^{2}1\ 7\ ^{1}2\ 4\ ^{1}1\ ^{2}3\ ^{2}7\ 9\ 3\ 1$

16. 8 × 3 + 2 is 26 i.e. $^{2}6$ ------- $^{2}6\,^{2}8$

$^{1}9\,^{1}6\,^{1}5\ 5\ ^{2}1\ 7\ ^{1}2\ 4\ ^{1}1\ ^{2}3\ ^{2}7\ 9\ 3\ 1$

17. 6 × 3 + 2 is 20 i.e. $^{2}0$ ------- $^{2}0\,^{2}6\,^{2}8$

$^{1}9\ ^{1}6\ ^{1}5\ 5\ ^{2}1\ 7\ ^{1}2\ 4\ ^{1}1\ ^{2}3\ ^{2}7\ 9\ 3\ 1$

18. 0 × 3 + 2 is 2 ------------- $2\ ^{2}0\,^{2}6\,^{2}8$

$^{1}9\ ^{1}6\ ^{1}5\ 5\ ^{2}1\ 7\ ^{1}2\ 4\ ^{1}1\ ^{2}3\,^{2}7\ 9\ 3\ 1$

19. 2 × 3 is 6 ---------------- $6\ 2\ ^{2}0\,^{2}6\,^{2}8$

$^{1}9\ ^{1}6\ ^{1}5\ 5\ ^{2}1\ 7\ ^{1}2\ 4\ ^{1}1\ ^{2}3\ ^{2}7\ 9\ 3\ 1$

20. 6 × 3 is 18 i.e. $^{1}8$ ----------- $^{1}8\,6\,2\,^{2}0\,^{2}6\,^{2}8$

$^{1}9\ ^{1}6\ ^{1}5\ 5\ ^{2}1\ 7\ ^{1}2\ 4\ ^{1}1\ ^{2}3\ ^{2}7\ 9\ 3\ 1$

21. 8 × 3 + 1 is 25 i.e. $^{2}5$ ------- $^{2}5\,^{1}8\,6\,2\,^{2}0\,^{2}6\,^{2}8$

$^{1}9\ ^{1}6\ ^{1}5\ 5\ ^{2}1\ 7\ ^{1}2\ 4\ ^{1}1\ ^{2}3\ ^{2}7\ 9\ 3\ 1$

22. 5 × 3 + 2 is 17 i.e. $^{1}7$ ------- $^{1}7\,^{2}5\,^{1}8\,6\,2\,^{2}0\,^{2}6\,^{2}8$

$^{1}9\ ^{1}6\ ^{1}5\ 5\ ^{2}1\ 7\ ^{1}2\ 4\ ^{1}1\ ^{2}3\ ^{2}7\ 9\ 3\ 1$

23. 7 × 3 + 1 is 22 i.e. $^{2}2$ ------- $^{2}2\,^{1}7\,^{2}5\,^{1}8\,6\,2\,^{2}0\,^{2}6\,^{2}8$

$^{1}9\ ^{1}6\ ^{1}5\ 5\ ^{2}1\ 7\ ^{1}2\ 4\ ^{1}1\ ^{2}3\ ^{2}7\ 9\ 3\ 1$

24. 2 × 3 + 2 is 8 ------------- $8\,^{2}2\,^{1}7\,^{2}5\,^{1}8\,6\,2\,^{2}0\,^{2}6\,^{2}8$

$^{1}9\ ^{1}6\ ^{1}5\ 5\ ^{2}1\ 7\ ^{1}2\ 4\ ^{1}1\ ^{2}3\ ^{2}7\ 9\ 3\ 1$

25. 8 × 3 is 24 i.e. $^{2}4$ ----------- $^{2}4\,8\,^{2}2\,^{1}7\,^{2}5\,^{1}8\,6\,2\,^{2}0\,^{2}6\,^{2}8$

$^{1}9\ ^{1}6\ ^{1}5\ 5\ ^{2}1\ 7\ ^{1}2\ 4\ ^{1}1\ ^{2}3\ ^{2}7\ 9\ 3\ 1$

26. 4 × 3 + 2 is 14 i.e. $^{1}4$ ------- $^{1}4\,^{2}4\,8\,^{2}2\,^{1}7\,^{2}5\,^{1}8\,6\,2\,^{2}0\,^{2}6\,^{2}8$

$^{1}9\ ^{1}6\ ^{1}5\ 5\ ^{2}1\ 7\ ^{1}2\ 4\ ^{1}1\ ^{2}3\ ^{2}7\ 9\ 3\ 1$

27. 4 × 3 + 1 is 13 i.e. $^{1}3$ ------- $^{1}3\,^{1}4\,^{2}4\,8\,^{2}2\,^{1}7\,^{2}5\,^{1}8\,6\,2\,^{2}0\,^{2}6\,^{2}8$

$^{1}9\ ^{1}6\ ^{1}5\ 5\ ^{2}1\ 7\ ^{1}2\ 4\ ^{1}1\ ^{2}3\ ^{2}7\ 9\ 3\ 1$

28. 3 × 3 + 1 is 10 i.e. $^{1}0$ --- $^{1}0\ ^{1}3\ ^{1}4\,^{2}4\ \ 8\ 2\ ^{1}7\,^{2}5\,^{1}8\ \ 6\ \ 2\,^{2}0\,^{2}6\,^{2}8$

$^{1}9\ ^{1}6\ ^{1}5\ 5\ ^{2}1\ 7\ ^{1}2\ 4\ ^{1}1\ ^{2}3\ \ ^{2}7\ 9\ 3\ 1$

$\therefore \frac{1}{29}$ = **0. 0 3 4 4 8 2 7 5 8 6 2 0 6 8**
9 6 5 5 1 7 2 4 1 3 7 9 3 1

The same Decimalisation can be done by division as explained below –

Starting from dividend 1 i.e. the numerator 1, with the same divisor i.e. 3 we get,

Ex.6: $\frac{1}{29}$

1. 1 ÷ 3; Q-0, R-1 ... ... $0._{1}0$
2. 10 ÷ 3; Q-3, R-1 ... ... $0._{1}0\ _{1}3$
3. 13 ÷ 3; Q-4, R-1 ... ... $0._{1}0\ _{1}3\ _{1}4$
4. 14 ÷ 3; Q-4, R-2 ... ... $0._{1}0\ _{1}3\ _{1}4\ _{2}4$

and so on.

The first 4 steps tally in ditto with the last 4 steps of **Ex.5** above, except that we have written the carry over as superscript in **Ex.5**, while it is shown as subscript in **Ex.6** above. The Ex.6 can be extended up to step 28 and we will get the same result i.e. $\therefore \frac{1}{29}$ = **0. 0 3 4 4 8 2 7 5 8 6 2 0 6 8 9 6 5 5 1 7 2 4 1 3 7 9 3 1**

Numerator Other than 1

We have seen above, wherein the denominator was ending in 9, but the numerator was 1. We shall now extend our knowledge – in the sense that the denominator would still be ending in 9, but the numerator other than 1.

Hereinafter we shall restrict our answer to 5 to 6 places of decimal as the effectiveness of the method is proved. We shall decimalise $\frac{14}{29}$. The formula **'By** one more than the previous' holdswell here also, but the **'By'** here will be used **meaning division.** So the divisor here is one more than 2 i.e. 3

Ex.7: $\frac{14}{29}$ is –

1. 14 ÷ 3; Q-4, R-2 ... ... $0._{2}4$
2. 24 ÷ 3; Q-8,R-0 ... ... $0._{2}4\ 8$
3. 8 ÷ 3; Q-2, R-2 ... ... $0._{2}4\ 8\ _{2}2$
4. 22 ÷ 3; Q-7,R-1 ... ... $0._{2}4\ 8\ _{2}2\ _{1}7$
5. 17 ÷ 3; Q-5,R-2 ... ... $0._{2}4\ 8\ _{2}2\ _{1}7\ _{2}5$
6. 25 ÷ 3; Q-8,R-1... ... ... $0._{2}4\ 8\ _{2}2\ _{1}7\ _{2}5\ _{1}8$

and so on

$$\therefore \frac{14}{29} = \mathbf{0.4\,8\,2\,7\,6}$$

Similarly –

Ex.8: $\frac{57}{69}$ ... ... divisor here is 6+1=7

1. 57 ÷ 7; Q-8,R-1 ... ... $0._{1}8$
2 18 ÷ 7; Q-2, R-4 ... ... $0._{1}8\,_{4}2$
3 42 ÷ 7; Q-6, R-0 ... ... $0._{1}8\,_{4}2\,6$
4 6 ÷ 7; Q-0, R-6 ... ... $0._{1}8\,_{4}2\,6\,_{6}0$
5 60 ÷ 7; Q-8, R-4 ... ... $0._{1}8\,_{4}2\,6\,_{6}0\,_{4}8$
6 48 ÷ 7; Q-6, R-6 ... ... $0._{1}8\,_{4}2\,6\,_{6}0\,_{4}8\,_{6}6$

and so on

$$\therefore \frac{57}{69} = \mathbf{0.\,8\,2\,6\,0\,9}$$

One more example -

Ex.9: $\frac{83}{139}$ ... ... divisor here is 13+1=14

1. 83 ÷ 14; Q-5, R-13 ... ... $0._{13}5$
2. 135 ÷ 14; Q-9, R-9 ... ... $0._{13}5\,_{9}9$
3. 99 ÷ 14; Q-7, R-1 ... ... $0._{13}5\,_{9}9\,_{1}7$
4. 17 ÷ 14; Q-1, R-3 ... ... $0._{13}5\,_{9}9\,_{1}7\,_{3}1$
5. 31 ÷ 14; Q-2, R-3 ... ... $0._{13}5\,_{9}9\,_{1}7\,_{3}1\,_{3}2$
6. 32 ÷ 14; Q-2, R-4 ... ... $0._{13}5\,_{9}9\,_{1}7\,_{3}1\,_{3}2\,_{4}2$

and so on

$$\therefore \frac{83}{139} = \mathbf{0.\,5\,9\,7\,1\,2}$$

The present conventional method known to us is tedious and cumbrous (as table of 139 is involved in actual division) as detailed below –

$\frac{83}{139}$ = 139) 83.0 (0. 5 9 7 1 2 2 … …

695
1350
1251
990
973
170
139
310
278
320
278
… …

Denominator ending in 8

Here the denominator ends in 8 – like 38,138, etc. To start with, we shall deal with numerator as 1. The methodology is – after we have divided the dividend (the numerator) by the divisor (which is again the same one more than the previous, we get the first quotient and remainder (and the remainder is written as subscript to the left of quotient – as we have already been doing), **at every subsequent division the new dividend is found by adding one time (because 9 – 8 = 1) the just calculated quotient.**

This will be clear from the example below –

Ex.10: $\frac{1}{38}$

Here the divisor will be 4 (which is one more than 3) and dividing the numerator 1 by 4 we get –

1. 1 ÷ 4; Q-0,R-1 … … … … … … … … … … … … $0.\,_{1}0$
2. New dividend is 10 and with this add the just found quotient in step (1) above
   10 + 0 = 10 ÷ 4; Q-2, R-2 … … … … … … … $0.\,_{1}0\,_{2}2$
3. Now the dividend is 22 and add 2 the Quotient found in step (2) above
   22 + 2 = 24 ÷ 4; Q-6, R-0 … … … … … $0.\,_{1}0\,_{2}2\,_{0}6$

4. 06 + 6 = 12 ÷ 4; Q-3, R-0 … … … … … $0.{}_{1}0\,{}_{2}2\,{}_{0}6\,{}_{0}3$
5. 03 + 3 = 6 ÷ 4; Q-1, R-2 … … … … … … … $0.{}_{1}0\,{}_{2}2\,{}_{0}6\,{}_{0}3\,{}_{2}1$
6. 21 + 1 = 22 ÷ 4; Q-5, R-2 … … … … … $0.{}_{1}0\,{}_{2}2\,{}_{0}6\,{}_{0}3\,{}_{2}1\,{}_{2}5$

and so on

$$\therefore \frac{1}{38} = \mathbf{0.02632}$$

Similarly –

Ex.11: $\frac{1}{138}$ … … … … … … here the divisor is 14 (13 + 1)

1. 1 ÷ 14; Q-0, R-1 … … … … … … … … $0.{}_{1}0$
2. 10 + 0 = 10 ÷ 14; Q-0, R-10 … … … … $0.{}_{1}0\,{}_{10}0$
3. 100 + 0 = 100 ÷ 14; Q-7, R-2 … … … $0.{}_{1}0\,{}_{10}0\,{}_{2}7$
4. 27 + 7 = 34 ÷ 14; Q-2, R-6 … … … … …$0.{}_{1}0\,{}_{10}0\,{}_{2}7\,{}_{6}2$
5. 62 + 2 = 64 ÷ 14; Q-4, R-8 … … … … …$0.{}_{1}0\,{}_{10}0\,{}_{2}7\,{}_{6}2\,{}_{8}4$
6. 84 + 4 = 88 ÷ 14; Q-6, R-4 … … … … …$0.{}_{1}0\,{}_{10}0\,{}_{2}7\,{}_{6}2\,{}_{8}4\,{}_{4}6$

and so on.

$$\therefore \frac{1}{138} = \mathbf{0.00725}$$

Numerator other than 1

Now we shall consider numerator other than 1. To start with we shall solve **Ex.1** above (solved conventionally in the introduction paragraph) –

Ex.12: $\frac{1}{138}$ … … … … … … … … here also the divisor is the same 14 (13+1) and divide the numerator 63 [in fact 6.3, if we take divisor as 14 instead of 138 i.e. $\frac{63}{138} = \frac{6.3}{14}$

1. 63 ÷ 14; Q-4,R-7 … … … … … … … … $0.{}_{7}4$
2. 74 + 4 = 78 ÷ 14; Q-5, R-8 … … … … …$0.{}_{7}4\,{}_{8}5$

3. 85 + 5 = 90 ÷ 14; Q-6, R-6 ... ...$0.{}_{7}4\,{}_{8}5\,{}_{6}6$
4. 66 + 6 = 72 ÷ 14; Q-5, R-2 ... ...$0.{}_{7}4\,{}_{8}5\,{}_{6}6\,{}_{2}5$
5. 25 + 5 = 30 ÷ 14; Q-2, R-2 ... ...$0.{}_{7}4\,{}_{8}5\,{}_{6}6\,{}_{2}5\,{}_{2}2$
6. 22 + 2 = 24 ÷ 14; Q-1, R-10 ... ... $0.{}_{7}4\,{}_{8}5\,{}_{6}6\,{}_{2}5\,{}_{2}2\,{}_{10}1$

and so on

$\therefore \frac{63}{138} = \mathbf{0.4\,5\,6\,5\,2}$

One more example –

Ex.13: $\frac{33}{188}$ Here also the divisor is one more than 18 i.e. 19

1. 33 ÷ 19; Q-1, R-14 ... ... $0.{}_{14}1$
2. 141 + 1 = 142 ÷ 19; Q-7, R-9 ... ... $0.{}_{14}1\,{}_{9}7$
3. 97 + 7 = 104 ÷ 19; Q-5, R-9 ... ... $0.{}_{14}1\,{}_{9}7\,{}_{9}5$
4. 95 + 5 = 100 ÷ 19; Q-5, R-5 ... ... $0.{}_{14}1\,{}_{9}7\,{}_{9}5\,{}_{5}5$
5. 55 + 5 = 60 ÷ 19; Q-3, R-3 ... ...$0.{}_{14}1\,{}_{9}7\,{}_{9}5\,{}_{5}5\,{}_{3}3$
6. 33 + 3 = 36 ÷ 19; Q-1, R-14 ... ... $0.{}_{14}1\,{}_{9}7\,{}_{9}5\,{}_{5}5\,{}_{3}3\,{}_{14}1$

and so on

$\therefore \frac{33}{188} = \mathbf{0.1\,7\,5\,5\,3}$

Denominator ending in 7

As usual we shall start with numerator 1.

Ex.14: $\frac{1}{47}$ Herealsothe divisor is one more than the previous i.e. 4+1=5. In case of denominator ending in 8 we add one time the quotient at every step after the first division. **Here we shall add two times (because 9 – 7=2) the quotient at every step, after the first division.**

1. 1 ÷ 5; Q-0, R-1 ... ... $0.{}_{1}0$
2. 10 + 0 × **2** = 10 ÷ 5; Q-2, R-0 ... ...$0.{}_{1}0\,{}_{0}2$
3. 2 + 2 × **2** = 6 ÷ 5; Q-1, R-1 ... ... $0.{}_{1}0\,{}_{0}2\,{}_{1}1$
4. 11 + 1 × **2** = 13 ÷ 5; Q-2, R-3... ... ...$0.{}_{1}0\,{}_{0}2\,{}_{1}1\,{}_{3}2$
5. 32 + 2 × **2** = 36 ÷ 5; Q-7, R-1... ... ... $0.{}_{1}0\,{}_{0}2\,{}_{1}1\,{}_{3}2\,{}_{1}7$
6. 17 + 7 × **2** = 31 ÷ 5; Q-6, R-1... ... ... $0.{}_{1}0\,{}_{0}2\,{}_{1}1\,{}_{3}2\,{}_{1}7\,{}_{1}6$

and so on

$$\therefore \frac{1}{47} = \mathbf{0.0\,2\,1\,2\,8}$$

Similarly –

Numerator other than 1

Ex.15: $\frac{71}{137}$ the divisor is 14

1. 71÷ 14; Q-5, R-1 ... ... $0.{}_{1}5$
2. 15 + 5 × **2** =25÷ 14; Q-1, R-11 ... ... $0.{}_{1}5{}_{11}1$
3. 111 + 1 × **2** = 113÷ 14; Q-8, R-1 ... ... $0.{}_{1}5{}_{11}1{}_{1}8$
4. 18 + 8 × **2** = 34 ÷ 14; Q-2, R-6 ... ... $0.{}_{1}5{}_{11}1{}_{1}8{}_{6}2$
5. 62 + 2 × **2** = 68 ÷ 14; Q-4, R-12 ... ... $0.{}_{1}5{}_{11}1{}_{1}8{}_{6}2{}_{12}4$
6. 124 + 4 × **2** = 132 ÷ 14; Q-8, R-12 ... ...$0.{}_{1}5{}_{11}1{}_{1}8{}_{6}2{}_{12}4{}_{12}8$

and so on

$$\therefore \frac{71}{137} = \mathbf{0.5\,1\,8\,2\,5}$$

Denominator ending in 6

Ex.16: $\frac{73}{136}$ **Here we shall add three times (because 9 – 6 = 3) the quotient at every step, after the first division.**

1. 73 ÷ 14; Q-5, R-3 ... ... $0.{}_{3}5$
2. 35 + 5 × **3** = 50 ÷ 14; Q-3, R-8... ... $0.{}_{3}5{}_{8}3$
3. 83 + 3 × **3** = 92 ÷ 14; Q-6, R-8 ... ... $0.{}_{3}5{}_{8}3{}_{8}6$
4. 86 + 6 × **3** = 104 ÷ 14; Q-7, R-6 ... ... $0.{}_{3}5{}_{8}3{}_{8}6{}_{6}7$
5. 67 + 7 × **3** = 88 ÷ 14; Q-6, R-4 ... ... $0.{}_{3}5{}_{8}3{}_{8}6{}_{6}7{}_{4}6$
6. 46 + 6 × **3** = 64 ÷ 14; Q-4, R-8 ... ... $0.{}_{3}5{}_{8}3{}_{8}6{}_{6}7{}_{4}6{}_{8}4$

and so on

$$\therefore \frac{73}{136} = \mathbf{0.5\,3\,6\,7\,6}$$

Denominator ending in 1

Ex.17: $\frac{73}{121}$ First reduce both numerator and the denominator by 1. $\frac{73-1}{121-1}=\frac{72}{120}=\frac{7.2}{12.0}$ The divisor will be 12 and after first quotient subsequent quotients are found as 9 – just calculated quotient.

1. 72 ÷ 12; Q-6, R-0 ... ... $0.{}_{0}6$
2. 9-6 = 3, 03 ÷ 12; Q-0, R-3 ... ... $0.{}_{0}6\ {}_{3}0$
3. 9-0 = 9, 39 ÷ 12; Q-3, R-3 ... ... $0.{}_{0}6\ {}_{3}0\ {}_{3}3$
4. 9-3 = 6, 36 ÷ 12; Q-3, R-0 ... ... $0.{}_{0}6\ {}_{3}0\ {}_{3}3\ {}_{0}3$
5. 9-3 = 6, 06 ÷ 12; Q-0,R-6 ... ... $0.{}_{0}6\ {}_{3}0\ {}_{3}3\ {}_{0}3\ {}_{6}0$
6. 9-0 = 9, 69 ÷ 12; Q-5, R-9 ... ... $0.{}_{0}6\ {}_{3}0\ {}_{3}3\ {}_{0}3\ {}_{6}0\ {}_{9}5$

and so on

$\therefore \frac{73}{121}$ **= 0.6 0 3 3 1**

□

Epilogue

How to use this book

Normally this section i.e. *how to use this book* should be at the beginning of a book. But the author has deliberately put this at the end for the following reasons –

1. The author wants the layman to read this book at least once from beginning to end.
2. Having read once then there wouldn't be any need to have a choice as what to read or what not to read as you may have to read this book repeatedly.

However

If you are a teacher use as much of all the lessons as possible and prepare your students to the best of your ability. Don't bother about syllabus or official course content. Because when the students use these methods while appearing in competitive examination, they will bless you. (Do not think how youngsters, who are supposed be seek blessings, can bless teachers. I definitely think *'Long live that teacher who taught me this!'* **So also your students can THINK in a similar way**)

If you are a parent and if you teach your ward on these lines, your ward will have you on high esteem and they will be happy that you are in alignment with their teachers perfectly or you are more advanced than their teacher (Please don't forget to read **page 11 to 16** of this book). This feeling in a student's mind is essential because it makes a lot of difference when student feels – *How smart my parents are!!*

If you are a student (above Class VIII) you would feel highly blessed with this knowledge when you are appearing for number of competitive examination.

Please also note that Lessons 4 to 6, 10, 17 & 18 may be skimmed through for dining table knowledge or may even be skipped for a leisure reading.

General Appeal

If any of the readers know any new method in Arithmetic or any shortcut please mail the same to baalaraman@gmail.com

If you are impressed with the methods, then enjoy trigonometry by Vedic methods and hence refer the book **'Triple'**.

Acknowledgements

Here also, like the epilogue, I think I am breaking a convention. But in no public function VOTE Of Thanks is proposed right at the beginning. Similarly after accomplishing a huge task, I start remembering the various persons and sources who helped me in completing the task. My late mother Jayalakshmi, who was not only a great source of inspiration, but also taught me what is hard work and how one should work unwearied till the goal is achieved (I have seen her solving cross-words – and getting prizes – solving Sudoku at the age of 92). I am ever thankful to my non-demanding highly co-operative wife who stood behind me (fortunately not in a real-physical sense) throughout these 14 years.

Regarding references I am owe the credit to many sources since I have been working on this from 1984. Still the major source is 'Vedic Mathematics' – by HH Jagadguru Swāmī Śrī Bhāratī Krisna Tirthajī Mahārāja. Otherwise, you would find at least 50 books on Vedic Mathematics. As every teacher and parent should know Vedic Mathematics, but very prudent friends of mine have challenged my audacity to write a book on Vedic Mathematics (since I know neither Veda or for that matter I know Sanskrit), To be honest I have not quoted any of the Sanskrit Sootras with which HH Puri Sankarāchārya has wonderfully narrated the entire Vedic Mathematics. With my humble Pranams to HH Jagadguru Swāmī Śrī Bhāratī Krisna Tirthajī Mahārāja, I acknowledge him as main source of reference and inspiration.

Appendix – 'A'

An easy way to prepare Times Table*

If the students know upto table 9, it is more than enough and once they are thorough with tables 1 to 9, then table for any number can be generated easily. See examples 1, 2, and 3 below for table 14, 17, and 23 respectively –

Ex: 1 Table for 14

	1	4	14
1	1	4	14
2	2	8	28
3	3	← $_1$2	42
4	4	← $_1$6	56
5	5	← $_2$0	70
6	6	← $_2$4	84
7	7	← $_2$8	98
8	8	← $_3$2	112
9	9	← $_3$6	126
10	10	← $_4$0	140

Ex: 2 Table for 17

	1	7	17
1	1	7	17
2	2	← $_1$4	34
3	3	← $_2$1	51
4	4	← $_2$8	68
5	5	← $_3$5	85
6	6	← $_4$2	102
7	7	← $_4$9	119
8	8	← $_5$6	136
9	9	← $_6$3	153
10	10	← $_7$0	170

Ex: 3 Table for 23

	2	3	23
1	2	3	23
2	4	6	46
3	6	9	69
4	8	← $_1$2	92
5	10	← $_1$5	115
6	12	← $_1$8	138
7	14	← $_2$1	161
8	16	← $_2$4	184
9	18	← $_2$7	207
10	20	← $_3$0	230

Parents and teachers can easily understand the above tables. Nevertheless, the first column indicates the **'times'** the number is multiplied; the second column is the **'times tens'**; the third column is the **'times units'**; the last column is the simple addition of col. 2 and col. 3 (taking into due consideration of the subscripted carryovers in column 3 – shown by ←). In this way any multiplication can be done easily. See examples 4, 5, and 6 below –

Example: 4

	1	4	4	144
6	6	←$_2$4	$_2$4	864

Example: 5

	1	3	7	137
8	8	$_2$4	←$_5$6	1096

Example: 6

	1	6	9	169
4	4	$_2$4	←$_3$6	676

*****Times Table**-This term is used in British schools and we in India say **Multiplication Tables.**

□

Appendix – 'B'

An easy way to prepare Table of Prime Numbers

It is always advantageous (particularly students who appear for competitive exams) to remember prime numbers at least upto 50. The easiest way to remember prime numbers is to prepare 'Sieve of Eratosthenes*' one or two times, you will automatically remember the prime numbers.

[*Eratosthenes is a Greek mathematician, astronomer, and geographer who devised a map of the world, estimated the circumference of the earth and the distance to the moon and the sun, and constructed a method for finding prime numbers.]

Table – 1

1	②	3	4	5	6	7	8	9	10
11	12	13	14	15	16	17	18	19	20
21	22	23	24	25	26	27	28	29	30
31	32	33	34	35	36	37	38	39	40
41	42	43	44	45	46	47	48	49	50

Number 1 is neither prime nor composite, so the first prime number is 2 (students must remember that 2 is the first prime number and is the only prime number which is even). Now cancel all the numbers that are divisible by the first prime number i.e. 2 (that is all even numbers get cancelled from the above table – 1). After cancellation of even numbers the table will be as shown in Table – 2

Table – 2

1	②	③	-	5	-	7	-	9	-
11	-	13	-	15	-	17	-	19	-
21	-	23	-	25	-	27	-	29	-
31	-	33	-	35	-	37	-	39	-
41	-	43	-	45	-	47	-	49	-

The next retained number after 2 is 3 and this is the next prime number. Now cancel all the numbers which are multiples of 3 from table – 2 above. After cancellation table – 3 below will emerge.

Table – 3

1	②	③	-	⑤	-	7	-	-	-
11	-	13	-	-	-	17	-	19	-
-	-	23	-	25	-	-	-	29	-
31	-	-	-	35	-	37	-	-	-
41	-	43	-	-	-	47	-	49	-

The next retained number after 2 & 3 is 5 and this is the next prime number. Now cancel all multiples of 5 from table – 3 and we get table – 4 below

Table – 4

1	②	③	-	⑤	-	⑦	-	-	-
11	-	13	-	-	-	17	-	19	-
-	-	23	-	-	-	-	-	29	-
31	-	-	-	-	-	37	-	-	-
41	-	43	-	-	-	47	-	-	-

In this way by constant sieving the final prime numbers between 1 to 50 – are 2, 3, 5, 7, 11, 13, 17, 19, 23, 29, 31, 37, 41, 43 and 47.

□

Appendix – 'C'

Tables With Fingers

Table of '9'

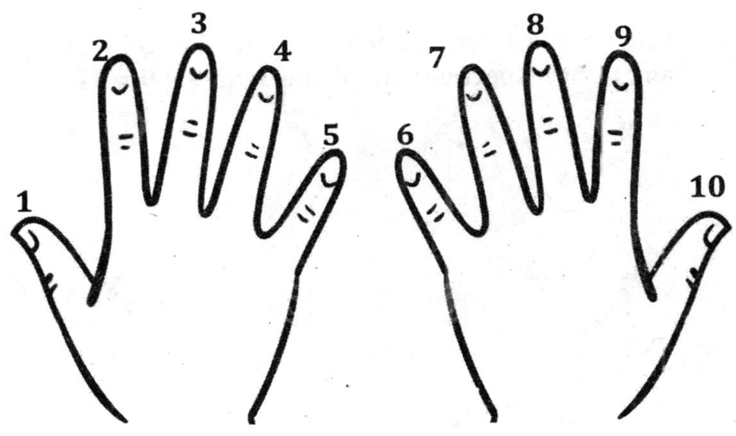

Fig : 1

9 × 1→ Fold the finger marked **1** and then count the unfolded fingers on the left and right of the folded fingers. On the left **0** and on the right **9. So 9 × 1 = 09.**

9 × 2→ Fold the finger marked **2** and unfolded fingers on the left and right respectively are **1** and **8. So 9 × 2 = 18.**

9 × 3→ Fold the finger marked **3** and unfolded fingers on the left and right respectively are **2** and **7. So 9 × 3 = 27.**

9 × 4→ Fold the finger marked **4** and unfolded fingers on the left and right respectively are **3** and **6. So 9 × 4 = 36.**

9 × 5→ Fold the finger marked **5** and unfolded fingers on the left and right respectively are **4** and **5. So 9 × 5 = 45.**

9 × 6→ Fold the finger marked **6** and unfolded fingers on the left and right respectively are **5** and **4. So 9 × 6 = 54.**

9 × 7→ Fold the finger marked **7** and unfolded fingers on the left and right respectively are **6** and **3. So 9 × 7 = 63.**

9 × 8→ Fold the finger marked 8 and unfolded fingers on the left and right respectively are **7** and **2. So 9 × 8 = 72.**

9 × 9→ Fold the finger marked **9** and unfolded fingers on the left and right respectively are **8** and **1. So 9 × 9 = 81.**

□

Appendix – 'D'

Tables With Fingers

Table of 6, 7, 8 and 9

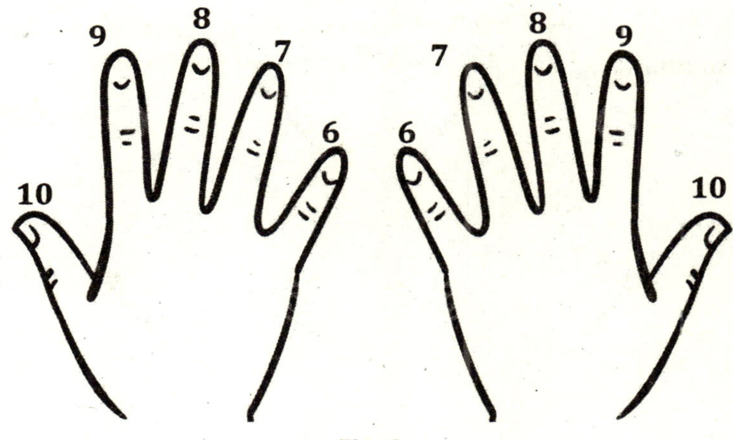

Fig : 2

[6 × 6; 6 × 7; 6 × 8; 7 × 9; 7 × 7; 7 × 8; 7 × 9; 8 × 7; 8 × 8; 8 × 9]

First mark the fingers 6, 7, 8, 9 from little fingers towards left on the left hand and 6, 7, 8, 9 from little fingers towards right on the right hand as shown in Fig: 2.

To find **6 × 6** → Fold fingers marked 6 on both hands. Assign 10 to each folded fingers. The remaining unfolded fingers are 4 in left as well as right hand. Multiply

$4 \times 4 = 16$; and add the values of folded fingers i.e. $10 + 10 = 20$; and $16 + 20 = 36$; So $6 \times 6 = 36$.

To find **6 × 7** → Fold fingers marked 6 on one hand and 6 and 7 on the other hand. Assign 10 to each folded fingers i.e. $3 \times 10 = 30$; the remaining folded fingers are 4 in one hand 3 in the other. Multiply $4 \times 3 = 12$; and $30 + 12 = 42$; So $6 \times 7 = 42$.

To find **7 × 8** → Fold fingers marked 6 and 7 on one hand; and fold fingers marked 6, 7 and 8 on the other hand. Assign 10 to each folded fingers i.e. $5 \times 10 = 50$; unfolded fingers are 3 in one hand and 2 in another hand. Multiply $2 \times 3 = 6$; and $50 + 6 = 56$; So $7 \times 8 = 56$

And so on... ... ...

□□□